DATE DUE

APR 1 4 2011	
APR 1 0 2012	
NOV 1 5 2012	
NOV 2 7 2013	WITHDRAWN
NOV 2 2 2014	
APR 2 9 2016	
NOV 2 8 2016	

BRODART, CO.   Cat. No. 23-221

Importing Democracy

Importing Democracy

Ideas from Around the World to Reform and Revitalize American Politics and Government

RAYMOND A. SMITH

New Trends and Ideas in American Politics
Raymond A. Smith, Series Editor

 PRAEGER

AN IMPRINT OF ABC-CLIO, LLC
Santa Barbara, California • Denver, Colorado • Oxford, England

Library of Congress Cataloging-in-Publication Data

Smith, Raymond A.
  Importing democracy : ideas from around the world to reform and revitalize American politics and government / Raymond A. Smith.
      p. cm. — (New trends and ideas in American politics)
  Includes bibliographical references and index.
  ISBN 978–0–313–36337–5 (hard copy : alk. paper) — ISBN 978–0–313–36338–2 (ebook)
1. Democratization—United States. 2. United States—Politics and government. I. Title.
JK1726.S65   2010
320.973—dc22   2010004065

ISBN: 978–0–313–36337–5
EISBN: 978–0–313–36338–2

14 13 12 11 10   1 2 3 4 5

This book is also available on the World Wide Web as an eBook.
Visit www.abc-clio.com for details.

Praeger
An Imprint of ABC-CLIO, LLC

ABC-CLIO, LLC
130 Cremona Drive, P.O. Box 1911
Santa Barbara, California 93116-1911

This book is printed on acid-free paper ∞

Manufactured in the United States of America

Contents

Acknowledgments

This book in some ways builds on and extends a line of argument that I began in my 2007 book *The American Anomaly: U.S. Politics and Government in Comparative Perspective*. This earlier work, however, was designed to be a supplemental textbook for use in American and comparative politics courses and as such was much more descriptive than prescriptive. Some of the potential reforms discussed at chapter length here are mentioned in that earlier volume but only as passing references because the confines of a textbook format did not allow for a great deal of speculation or create much room for advocacy of particular reforms. This volume, by its nature, calls for both.

I would like to acknowledge the excellent work of three undergraduates at Columbia University who were research assistants on this project: Brian Corman, Christine McHone, and Román Rodriguez. In addition, I am grateful for editorial and administrative support of various kinds provided by several other students: Ganiatu Afolabi, Kaley Bell, Jose Gonzalez, Ashley Lherisson, Carolina Rivas, and Gia Wakil. I would also like to thank my former graduate student and now colleague Brandon L. H. Aultman, MA, a political science instructor at Baruch College, City University of New York. In addition to offering suggestions and insights to the manuscript as a whole, he contributed so significantly to two chapters (Chapters 16 and 18) and to the glossary that he is acknowledged as the coauthor of these parts of the book. I am also grateful for the help and encouragement offered by friends and colleagues, including Kim Johnson, Shareen Hertel, Laura Nathanson, Karen Plafker, Martin Good, Susan Roberts, and Vickie and Bernie Candon as well as Anthony Chiffolo and Robert Hutchinson of Praeger. In addition, I would like to acknowledge the support of the chairs or heads of the political science departments in which I have taught, particularly Robert Shapiro, Kenneth Sherrill, Richard Pious, Kimberley Marten, Shinasi Rama, Bassam Abed, and Veena Thedani. And, as always, I would like to thank the many students who have studied American politics and government with me over the past decade. I have learned an enormous amount from their ideas and questions, their insights, and their enthusiasm.

Introduction

There is much to be proud of in the history of American democracy. Breaking free of a colonial power, the United States forged itself into what has been called the "first new nation." Rejecting hereditary monarchy and nobility, the founders took the idea of popular sovereignty out of the realm of abstract theory and made it a political reality. It began with a scope of voting rights that was unprecedented at the time and that has steadily, if at times slowly, expanded over the past two centuries. In the space of the single summer of 1787, the framers created the world's first effective written constitution, which established true separation of powers, invented federalism, and enshrined the supremacy of law over inherited privilege. Through civil war, domestic upheaval, depression, the Cold War, and terrorist attacks, the essentials of this democratic system have been maintained intact.

From its earliest days, the United States saw itself as an exemplar of democratic virtue, a "shining city upon a hill" that could serve as an example to others. Nearly all the newly independent nations of the Americas adopted the basic principles and structures of American democracy, and the idea of enshrining democratic ideals in a written constitution with a bill of rights has become nearly universal. In the twentieth century, as the United States rose to global prominence and eventually to superpower status, the country strove more and more explicitly to "export democracy," whether to the shattered countries of postwar Europe, to Asian outposts such as Japan and Korea, to the former Soviet bloc, or, most recently, to the Middle East.

Although the results have varied widely—due in no small part to the role played by the United States—there are thriving democracies to be found in every corner of the globe. Of course, each of these democracies has developed certain features that are unique, modified to fit their particular historical, institutional, economic, geographic, cultural, demographic, and other realities. Such an evolution has required an openness to change, a willingness to scrutinize the status quo, an ability to identify and correct weaknesses, and a commitment to cultivate new political processes and institutions—even if they were not part of their country's own traditions.

Had other democratic countries been unable or unwilling to make such changes, kings would still issue commands from their thrones, hereditary noblemen would exploit an enserfed peasantry, military generals would dictate policy down the barrel of guns, and individual women and men would find themselves poorly represented and largely unprotected from the arbitrary power of the state. Here are a few specific examples of major political changes in Europe from the past 60 years:

- Finding that its 1946 constitution, focused on the power of the National Assembly, was leading to chaos and gridlock, France discarded it in favor of an unprecedented semipresidential system in 1958.

- Noting that little of value was added by its upper chamber of Parliament, New Zealand abolished it in 1951, then set aside extra seats in the lower house especially for its indigenous Maori peoples.

- In order to bridge differences between linguistic communities and political parties, in 1959 Switzerland created a stable "magic formula" for the allocation of seats among its unique seven-member executive.

- Seeking to secure greater autonomy and civil liberties, Canada promulgated a new Charter of Rights and Freedoms in 1982 and once and for all "patriated" its constitution by moving final authority from London to Ottawa.

- Facing centrifugal forces along its major linguistic divide, Belgium in 1993 adopted the world's most layered system of federalism, establishing complementary federal, communal, regional, provincial, and local levels of government.

- In the decade after the election of a Labour government in 1997, the United Kingdom underwent dramatic constitutional changes, including devolving considerable power to regional and local assemblies, removing most hereditary nobles from their seats in the House of Lords, and establishing a separate Supreme Court.

As these examples demonstrate, there are many lessons to be learned in the vibrant spectrum of democratic practices from around the world. Yet the United States too rarely takes advantage of this wealth of hard-won experience and perspective; while Americans have long been eager to go about "exporting democracy," they have proven much less willing to consider "importing democracy."

Rather, much of America's self-image has been shaped by the concept of "exceptionalism," the idea that for historical, ideological, geographic, social, and other reasons, the United States has taken a unique and path-blazing road that has little to gain from examining the older, less democratic, and more corrupt route taken by other countries. Insulated by oceans, possessing vast resources on a continental scale, never subject to military conquest, and ever dynamic and growing because of westward expansion and immigration, the United States has traditionally experienced an extraordinary degree of self-sufficiency, isolation, and even introversion. And when it has interacted with the rest of the world, it has often been from a position of strength and, not infrequently, with an attitude of condescension.

Of course, there have been significant epochs of political change and reform throughout American history, from the founding to the Civil War and its aftermath to the Progressive era, the New Deal period, and the years of the Civil Rights Movement. During many of these eras, the United States benefited from the example of those from outside its borders. European thinkers of the Enlightenment, such as Jean-Jacques Rousseau and John Locke, inspired the Declaration of Independence. The French Revolution and its "Declaration of Rights of Man and of the Citizen" emboldened those who insisted on adding the Bill of Rights to the U.S. Constitution. The early successes of British abolitionists spurred the efforts of the American antislavery movement, while the New Deal drew on notions of the modern welfare state that first took shape in Europe. And where would the civil rights movement have been without its foundational Gandhian principles?

Nonetheless, it is difficult to think of major American *political institutions or processes* that have been brought into the U.S. system from outside its borders since the time of the founding. (The widespread adoption in the 1880s of the "Australian ballot"—the practice of casting votes in secret—is one of the few exceptions that readily comes to mind.) It is true that in looking for new ideas to reform and renew its democracy at the national level, Americans have benefited from the existence of the 50 states, famously termed "the laboratories of democracy" by Justice Louis Brandeis, whose smaller-scale experiences could be used as trial runs for national-level implementation. But the example provided by these states has been limited in spectrum precisely because they are also American and thus shaped by American constitutional norms, political culture, historical experiences, and institutional practices. The much vaster spectrum of democratic ideas from around the world has rarely been explored, much less adopted.

Many books have been written about the need in the contemporary United States for constitutional, electoral, institutional and other types of thoroughgoing reform, and the arguments presented in a number of these have directly influenced the writing of this volume. Political scientist James Sundquist, perhaps best known for his groundbreaking work on patterns of partisan realignment, provides a cogent overview of the deficits of American constitutional patterns in *Constitutional Reform and Effective Government*.[1] Political commentator Daniel Lazare has clearly and consistently argued against excessive reverence for the existing order, particularly in *The Frozen Republic: How the Constitution Is Paralyzing Democracy*.[2] Legal scholar Sanford Levinson attempts to build the groundwork for a new Constitutional Convention in *Our Undemocratic Constitution: Where the Constitution Goes Wrong (and How We the People Can Correct It)*,[3] while political scientist and media pundit Larry Sabato's *A More Perfect Constitution: Why the Constitution Must Be Revised: Ideas to Inspire a New Generation*[4] seeks to return to core values of the constitutional order that have been compromised or gone unfulfilled.

Each of these books is full of rigorous analysis, provocative new ideas, and concrete suggestions. Yet, aside from passing allusions to generic parliamentary models, each confines itself largely to the U.S. experience. This volume seeks to add a new voice in this debate by reaching beyond the nation's borders to promote novel thinking, fresh perspectives, and bold innovations. The changes addressed in each chapter here could, collectively, transform the American political scene. Admittedly, most of these reforms are not very likely to be adopted outright or in full; they would require extensive change of a type that the United States has only intermittently embraced in its history. However, the chapters that follow constitute a sustained thought experiment that can shed light on persistent deficits in American democracy, explore successful practices from abroad, and point the way both toward a comprehensive reform agenda and toward potential incremental solutions.

IMPORTING DEMOCRACY

The idea of "importing democracy" would not necessarily be a goal worthy of pursuit as an end in itself. But to the extent that alongside its strengths American democracy exhibits many glaring flaws, gaps, shortcomings, and oversights that other democratic systems do not, the United States could stand much to gain by learning from the experiences of the entire family of democracies. While each democratic country has various distinctive traits and idiosyncrasies, a large and growing political science literature suggests that all of them share a "family resemblance," encompassing four major characteristics:

- Democracies offer meaningful input by all citizens on a regular basis into the workings of government.
- Democracies balance the promotion of majority rule with the protection of minority rights.
- Democracies produce governments that are strong enough to be effective but limited enough not to be tyrannical.
- Democracies advance both individual liberty and social equality among their citizens.

Perhaps self-evidently, most democracies do not achieve all these aims all the time. In fact, some of them are in tension, such as the first imperative to expand popular participation, the second to respect minority rights, the third to create strong effective governance and the fourth to protect personal liberty. But different combinations are possible, and both better and worse balances exist.

The goal of *Importing Democracy* is clearly stated in its subtitle, namely, to find "ideas from around the world to reform and revitalize American politics and government." Each chapter highlights one major type of change or reform that could potentially improve American democracy in terms of one or more of its four key characteristics. Multiple examples are used in most chapters, but each chapter is anchored with a brief case study of a country whose experience reflects the potential change in a particularly clear, successful, or illuminating manner. Each case study highlights the experience of a different country, drawn from regions around the world.

As might be expected, the examples are most often drawn from countries that have the longest, most successful, and most stable history of democracy. Thus, most case studies are drawn from

continental western Europe or from parts of the British Commonwealth, such as the United Kingdom, Canada, Australia, and New
Zealand. However, a number of examples are also drawn from less
well established democracies in Latin America, Asia, or Africa if a *particular feature* within a political system helps move that country in a
more democratic direction even if there remained significant problems with the system as a whole. The large majority of the case studies
are drawn from the list of the 121 countries defined as being "electoral
democracies" in 2008 by the nongovernmental organization Freedom
House (http://www.freedomhouse.org) and scored either a 1 or 2 on
their composite 7-point freedom scale (with 7 being the "least free").
Many of the case study countries employ a parliamentary system of
government rather than one based on separation of powers. For readers who are less familiar with the basic differences between the systems, Appendix 2 of this volume includes several charts laying out
their major characteristics as well as some relative strengths and
weaknesses.

Taken collectively, the changes and reforms laid out in the chapters
in this volume would lead to government institutions and political
processes that could greatly improve the United States. However, the
country that emerges would still be highly recognizable to Americans.
It would be built on the Constitution of 1789 and include a separation-
of-powers government with a president, a bicameral Congress, and an
independent judiciary. It would feature free, fair, and regular elections
with universal suffrage, robust political parties and interest groups,
and flourishing civil liberties and civil rights. But it would also be a
different political system, one that achieves more democratic goals
more often and more effectively.

The proposed reforms are organized into three separate sections
covering, respectively, parties and elections, the presidency and
Congress, and the courts and the Constitution. Within each section
and throughout the book as a whole, the reforms are roughly organized in a sequence that would make most sense in terms of political
implementation. Thus, for instance, the use of proportional representation in elections precedes the establishment of a multiparty democracy both logically and in terms of the sequence of the book. Both
such changes would, in turn, lay the groundwork for alterations in
the relative balance of power between Congress and the presidency
as well as between the House of Representatives and the Senate.

As will be seen, it turns out that, in a few cases, some features that
are found in other democracies that might at first seem desirable turn

out to be problematic; such cases are in fact worthwhile reminders of some of the existing strengths of American democracy. In a few other cases, features of other democracies would simply be too difficult to enact outright in an American context. Nonetheless, these features can still shed light on American practices and suggest smaller, more incremental reforms that might still be enacted.

Likewise, there are some areas of American democracy that are already effective enough that they probably would not significantly benefit from importing ideas from other countries, and these are thus excluded from this volume. Perhaps the best example here is American federalism, which already effectively promotes participation and advances government effectiveness while also, thanks to federal oversight, mostly avoiding tyrannizing or marginalizing individuals or groups of citizens. Similarly, in terms of civil liberties, the protections afforded U.S. citizens are among the most expansive in the world and thus are not major concerns for a reform agenda. Finally, it should be restated that the focus of this book is on political institutions and processes rather than questions of public policy itself. Of course, since public policy is the direct output of institutions and processes, it would be profoundly impacted by some of the reforms outlined in this book. But specific areas of public policy, such as housing or public health or criminal justice or immigration standards, are beyond the scope of this book and are mentioned only for illustrative purposes.

Finally, to measure the relative value and importance of each proposed reform, each chapter concludes with brief synopsis of three key variables: the *desirability*, *practicability*, and *plausibility* of each proposed change. The assessment of the desirability, practicability, and plausibility of each reform is, of necessity, speculative and based on deductive reasoning rather than inductive data sets:

- The variable *desirability* considers how well any given reform, on balance, advances the four ideal characteristics of democracy noted previously.

- *Practicability* refers to the difficulty of achieving a goal given the existing constraints of American politics. Particularly relevant here are two dimensions: (1) whether it would require a major constitutional change or could be enacted through ordinary process of legislation or regulations and (2) whether there are multiple actors throughout the political system with the ability to block a change.

- The related but still distinct variable of *plausibility* assesses how likely existing political actors are to actually implement the reform. Once again, two dimensions are particularly salient: (1) whether political actors might be prone to adopt the change, in whole or part, mostly of their own accord and (2) how possible it would be to build public awareness of the issue and to generate sustained public pressure for the change.

Each of these three variables for each reform is ranked on a score from 1 to 5, with a score of 5 indicating that a particular reform would be highly desirable, practicable, and/or plausible and a score of 1 indicating that it would be highly undesirable, impracticable, or implausible. Scores of 2, 3, or 4, of course, reflect a more mixed conclusion. The final section of the book discusses the scores in greater detail and provides rank-ordered overview lists for each criterion as well as a composite list. The scores also suggest the broad outlines of an overall "agenda for reform" in the United States that would logically flow from the discussions in this volume.

PART ONE

REFORMING AND REVITALIZING PARTIES AND ELECTIONS

Adopt Proportional Representation

Move toward a Multiparty System

Establish Runoff Elections for Executive Offices

Abolish the Electoral College

Simplify and Shorten the Electoral Process

Advance Minorities and Women in Elected Office

Introduce Compulsory Voting

Institute a System of National Referenda

CHAPTER 1

Adopt Proportional Representation

Highlighting Ideas from Italy

An appropriate place to begin this discussion of "importing democracy" is by challenging a notion about elections that for many Americans seems so intuitive and obvious as to be axiomatic: that an election can have one and only one winner. Elections in the U.S. two-party system tend to be combative affairs. Primary elections are the opening skirmishes, with challenges flying fast and furious in all directions. In the end, only one person will have secured his or her party's nomination to face off against the other party. Then, in the general election, the two candidates, in an almost gladiatorial setting, clash most purely in the one-on-one debates generally held in October of the election year. Third-party candidates are rarely to be found and are even more rarely invited to join in debates during the general election.

Come Election Day, one—and only one—victor will emerge because one—and only one—seat has been contested in any given individual race. Most notably, every two years, there are 435 separate races for the U.S. House of Representatives in 435 congressional districts (a few of which cover entire states). Thus, there are 435 different victors who take 435 separate seats in the House. Likewise, every senator, every governor, and every president (albeit via the Electoral College) is chosen in this way. The losing side, whether it won 1 percent of the vote or 49.9 percent of the vote, is totally and completely excluded from the access to power. The tens of thousands, hundreds of thousands, or even millions of voters who supported the losing candidate will have minimal representation through that political office for the duration of that term, which can be as long as six years for U.S. senators.

True, some politicians, once in office, may, from time to time, still look out for the interests even of those who did not vote for them—such as trying to bring home "pork" in the form of federal funds or other projects. This may be because such politicians have a genuine sense of duty to serve all the citizens of the jurisdiction they serve or more likely because they are seeking to win over new voters for the next election. At a minimum, they want to keep even those who may never support them from actively organizing against them, perhaps by recruiting or fund-raising for future opponents. But this is at best a thin, weak form of representation for the losing side and one that is unlikely to carry much weight on controversial or partisan issues. For the most part, the age-old rule of combat still applies: to the victor belong the spoils, in this case all the power that comes with holding public office.

But does it have to be this way? What intrinsic property of democracy demands that as little as 50.1 percent of the people should win everything in an election and that as many as 49.9 percent should lose everything? There is none. Most Americans may be surprised to learn not only that there is no reason that there can be only one winner in an election but also that such winner-take-all electoral systems are rare among the family of democracies. In Europe, for instance, only Great Britain relies on such an electoral approach. In the Americas, only Canada, the United States, and a few other former British colonies apply this system.

The alternative? Under a system of *proportional representation*, parties that earn the support of a bloc of 8, 15, or 30 percent of the vote would be awarded 8, 15, or 30 percent of the legislative seats that are to be filled by the election. The most common practice is for each party to create a list, ranked in order of preference, for the candidates whom they wish to see in office. Then they would send the top 8, 15, or 30 percent of their party list to the legislature. (In practice, the translation of "votes into seats" rarely works out perfectly, but there are formulas that create results that are proportional.) How is it possible for more than one candidate to win at the same time—to divide up what would seem to be indivisible according to U.S. notions of elections? The modern state of Italy presents an illuminating example.

CASE STUDY: PROPORTIONAL REPRESENTATION IN ITALY

Among the parliamentary democracies of western Europe, few embrace proportional representation (PR) as completely as does Italy, in which the support of even a small percentage of the population can result in seats in the national Parliament. All Italians cast their ballots directly for political parties for both houses of Parliament in the same single nationwide election. So broad is the electoral franchise that Italy—long a country of emigration to North and South America—even sets aside seats for registered citizens living abroad. Its electoral rules also set one of the world's lowest thresholds for entry into Parliament, requiring parties to garner as little as 1 percent of the national vote. In light of sharp tensions between people from different regions and ideological orientations in Italy, the use of PR is designed to ensure that no single voice— or even a few powerful voices—can monopolize the political system.

In the general election held in April 2006, a remarkable 17 parties won at least one seat in the lower house, 12 from the political left and 5 from the political right. (Yet another 14 parties were on the ballot but did not win enough votes.) The most seats were won by a coalition of left-wing parties called "The Olive Tree," with a total of 31 percent of the vote, followed by two traditionalist right-wing parties, Forza Italia with 24 percent and the National Alliance with 12 percent. However, parties representing ideological views outside the political mainstream also won spots in Parliament. Among these were two different communist parties. With 6 percent of the vote, the Communist Refoundation Party took 40 seats in Parliament, while the Party of Italian Communists won 16 spots with just over 2 percent of the vote.[1] These two communist parties, which are divided more by disagreements over tactics than by basic beliefs, represented political views that would likely be shut out of public office in a less proportionally based electoral system, leaving their adherents outside the political system.

PR also extends a voice to blocs of voters who emphasize issues that do not line neatly up on the usual left-right spectrum. The 4.5 percent of voters who prioritized greater autonomy for the wealthier northern regions garnered 26 seats, and even the 0.5 percent of voters endorsing a party representing the country's small German-speaking population took four seats. Although they won the support of only about 2 percent of the electorate, two parties that focus, respectively, on opposing corruption and on protecting the environment also each won more than a dozen seats. Still other parties contested the election and only narrowly missed winning representation, including parties emphasizing the needs of pensioners and of consumers or opponents of the euro. Yet others called for autonomy for the Lombard region and for the Venice region, while several promoted a neofascist agenda with roots in the Mussolini era.

Although the case of Italy thus provides a vivid illustration of proportional representation, the realities of Italian politics also provide some caution. In fact, the post–World War II Italian state has proven not at all adept in governance. Corruption remains endemic, drastic income inequalities between the north and the south have persisted, organized crime has been curbed but far from eliminated, and Italy has had the dubious distinction of experiencing terrorist agitation by both right-wing and left-wing homegrown radicals. More recently, media mogul and longtime Prime Minister Silvio Berlusconi has dominated Italian politics to an unhealthy degree. By no means can all this be placed on the doorstep of proportional representation; other idiosyncratic aspects of Italian history, culture, law, and society must take the lion's share of the blame.

Nonetheless, it can fairly be argued that the hyperfragmentation of the Italian political party system has contributed to instability in that system, in which parliamentary governments have on average lasted barely a year since World War II. Most commonly, rickety parliamentary coalitions have been formed with multiple small parties, inevitably leading to instability because the smaller and more homogeneous a party's electoral base, the more likely it is to have one or two truly nonnegotiable interests. For instance, an urban-based party may have a few deep-seated concerns, such as funding for housing or subsidies for mass transit. Should the government of the day, for budgetary, regulatory, or other reasons, reject or even just neglect the few key goals of the urban-based party, it could pull out of the coalition and thus trigger the collapse of the parliamentary majority. When any one of a half dozen or more such small parties come together, even the deftest government may find it impossible to please all its partners all the time for very long.

Yet such instability is not an intrinsic attribute of proportional representation. One simple rule involves the idea of a parliamentary threshold—the minimum percentage of the national vote that a party must receive in order to be awarded seats in the Parliament. In Italy, the threshold is set very low, but most parliamentary democracies raise the minimum to about 5 percent, effectively shutting out very small or specialized or purely regional parties from national-level competition (and thus leading their potential voters to support the larger party that most closely reflects their views). By the simple expediency of a threshold, much of the political instability seen in Italy—as well as Israel and other countries with low thresholds—could be overcome.

PR IN THE UNITED STATES?

Once one moves beyond the ingrained idea that every election can have one and only one winner, the idea of PR might quickly gain favor with Americans' notions of "fair play." In fact, in a capitalist economy, few have much argument with the common practice that an investor who provides 30 percent of the funds for investment in a new project should receive 30 percent of the revenue it generates. And PR is also known in the United States, even at the highest level of politics. The Republican Party chooses its presidential nominees mostly on the basis of a winner-take-all system in which the candidate who gets the largest number of votes in any given state is awarded *all* that state's delegates to the Republican National Convention, at which the nominee will be officially named. The Democratic Party, however, applies a PR system in which the number of each candidate's delegates depends on the percentage of the vote they secure in the party primaries or caucuses. This was made vividly clear in the presidential primaries of 2008, which stretched on for nearly six months with neither Barack Obama nor Hillary Rodham Clinton able to open a clear lead in delegates since even splits of 60 to 40 percent or 70 to 30 percent did not result in the award of a decisively different number of delegates. (Ultimately, Obama was able to secure the nomination only with the help of the so-called superdelegates, which are a Democratic Party concept unrelated to PR through which top elected and party officials are given a vote at the convention.)

How can PR be applied to the U.S. system of government? First, it is important to note that the current configuration of political structures in the United States is not necessarily the optimal one, and many features of that system will be challenged throughout this book. But working with the system as it now stands, it is indeed true that in the case of the two U.S. senators from each state, who are elected separately, PR does not have an immediate application. This is even truer for the case of executive offices in the United States, such as mayoralties, governorships, and the presidency. Given that these are individual and thus indivisible offices, PR could also not be directly applied. (There are, however, other types of electoral reforms, notably runoff elections, discussed in Chapter 3, that mesh with and enhance PR that could be applied to these offices.)

Nonetheless, PR could be applied directly and immediately to a significant number of other levels of government, notably the U.S. House of Representatives, at least within the 42 states whose population allows them to send more than one representative to the House. In those cases, there is no constitutional requirement or demand of democratic theory that requires them to carve themselves up into multiple congressional districts. In fact, these districts are unlikely even to be meaningful historical, geographic, cultural, or socioeconomic units. Rather, they are most likely to be districts gerrymandered by the politicians in power in any given state to maximize the representation of their party.

Thus, instead of creating separate districts, a state could simply hold a single statewide election for all its House seats using party lists. Under PR, if a particular bloc of the electorate comprised 30 percent of voters, that bloc would receive 30 percent of the representation by sending the top 30 percent of its party list to Congress. Much the same principle could be applied at the level of state senates and assemblies as well as various municipal councils. Collectively, these changes could alter the composition of every legislature in the country, with the sole exception of the U.S. Senate, where equal representation by state is entrenched in the U.S. Constitution.

Of course, in a two-party system, PR might at first seem to be much ado about nothing. The composition of many legislatures might be only slightly altered, with Democrats and Republicans continuing to dominate in much the same proportions as before. This is, of course, because minor parties in the United States are underdeveloped and noncompetitive, rarely even fielding candidates much less winning elections. But the introduction of PR would also go a long way toward transforming the two-party system in the United States. Indeed, a major finding of the literature on political parties is that two-party systems almost never flow directly from the simple electoral preferences of voters, who do not naturally organize into just two competing camps. Rather, as most famously elucidated by French political scientist Maurice Duverger, two-party systems are the *product* of single-member plurality systems.[2] Thus, countries with PR generally also have robust multiparty systems—and so too might the United States, as discussed in the next chapter.

SYNOPSIS

Desirability: 5

The use of PR would bring the United States in line with democratic practices around the world. In a stroke, it would allow views and voices that are usually suppressed to receive representation, broadening the effective political spectrum and increasing the perceive relevance of politics too many citizens—making them more likely to vote. However, there is a danger of hyperfragmenting the political system, undermining consensus, promoting instability, and injecting extreme views into the mainstream. Thus, PR should be applied with some boundaries, as discussed in the next chapter, rather than in its more pure form, as in Italy.

Practicability: 3

There are many electoral circumstances in which PR could be practically applied—be it in both houses of all state legislatures, in nearly all city councils, in the House of Representatives (at least in the 42 states whose population allows them to elect more than one representative), and, to a limited extent, in the U.S. Senate—by electing both seats at the same time. There are no major impediments, either in the Constitution or in terms of democratic theory, to applying PR principles. However, PR as such could not be applied in races for such executive offices as mayor, governor, and president where only a single seat is being contested. However, the runoff system discussed in the next chapter could be packaged together as part of a larger effort to embrace the basic principles of PR.

Plausibility: 2

PR is a concept that is not familiar in the United States and can easily be misrepresented by opponents as a form of "quota." It would take a significant educational effort to produce grassroots pressure for change. Absent pressure from the public, Democratic and Republican officeholders themselves would have little incentive to adopt PR rules, as these would require increased power sharing on their parts. Perhaps the most likely place for an impetus to begin for PR would be within disaffected or underrepresented factions of the existing parties. Given that the Democratic Party has a more diverse base and already uses PR in its presidential nominating process, it is the more likely of the two parties to advocate the introduction of PR into general elections.

CHAPTER 2

Move toward a Multiparty System

Highlighting Ideas from Germany

Just as it seems obvious and intuitive to many Americans that an election can have one and only one winner, so too does it seem self-evident that the choices in an election should be dichotomous. With only rare exceptions, voters have but two choices in general elections: vote Democrat or vote Republican. And, more remarkably, these have been the same two choices, at least in terms of name and institutional continuity, since 1860, when the Whig Party was displaced by the Republicans.

There do exist small minor parties, often—and tellingly—referred to as third parties. But their impact is minimal and marginal: in 2009, every member of the House and 98 of the 100 senators were Democrats or Republicans. Setting aside the anomalous case of Senator Joseph Lieberman, who termed himself an "independent Democrat," only Senator Bernie Sanders of Vermont could be deemed as truly outside the party system, and even he caucused with the Democrats for purposes of establishing a majority in the Senate. The same trend extends down to the state level: not a single governor and, remarkably, only one-tenth of 1 percent of state legislators were anything other than a Democrat or a Republican.

The various "third parties" in American politics thus toil in all but total obscurity. The Libertarian Party dutifully proclaims its ideological gospel of small government, preaching mostly to the converted. The Green Party advances an environmentalist agenda but, even in an era of global warming and growing concern about ecology, remains a small-time political player. Other parties that are still more obscure, from the Socialist Workers Party to the Natural Law Party, go through the motions of collecting signatures to get on ballots and nominating candidates but to no real constructive end.

Minor party candidates are generally doomed from the outset because of the problem of the so-called wasted vote. Given the reality that it is nearly impossible under current conditions for anyone other than a Democrat or a Republican to win an election, casting a ballot for a minor party candidate can be a form of protest or a cry of frustration but is rarely a way to meaningfully participate in the election of candidates for office. At worst, minor parties can engage in a potentially high-stakes game of "chicken" in which they peel off a few percent of the vote, proving just enough to tip an election to the candidate who least represents their views. Certainly, such a "spoiler" role was the main impact of the last high-profile minor party candidacy, that of Ralph Nader with the Green Party in 2000. If Nader's votes had gone to the Democrat, Al Gore, he would have prevailed over the Republican George W. Bush, who, in office, proved to be the antithesis of what the Green Party stood for on nearly every domestic and international issue. Such outcomes only reinforce the weakness of third parties.

Of course, if the monopoly of the two parties were simply the result of the genuine electoral preferences of voters, then one might simply say "so be it." For that matter, there are some countries in which voters— in free and fair elections—have chosen to maintain a single party in power. This has been the case with the African National Congress in South African since 1994 and, even more remarkably, with the Liberal Democratic Party in Japan for all but 10 months between 1955 and 2009. Such single party rule is by no means entirely unproblematic for those countries but can also be a legitimate outcome if the election results truly reflect the will of the voters.

In the United States, however, there is strong reason to believe that the persistence of the two-party system is *not* simply a reflection of the will of the voters. The United States is a complex and diverse nation, divided along lines of socioeconomic class, religion, race, ethnicity, region, and other factors. The uneasy electoral coalitions that constitute the major parties are by no means natural or automatic. The probusiness, fiscally conservative wing of the Republican Party is often rather moderate on social issues yet must share a "big tent" with members of the religious right fixated on abortion, gay rights, and the like. At the same time, the blue-collar, union-based segment of the Democratic Party often holds traditionalist social views that do not mesh well with the party's better-educated, more socially liberal component. Other combinations earlier in American history have been even more unlikely: consider that the New Deal coalition managed to encompass both African Americans in the North and vehement white segregationists in the South for nearly 40 years.

But if the broad "umbrella coalitions" that characterize the Republican and Democratic parties are in no way inevitable or natural, then why has the two-party system proven so durable? And why is an absolutist two-party structure to be found in only a handful of democracies, none of them very large or diverse, such as Jamaica, Malta, Belize, and Ghana? The answer, as noted in the previous chapter, has been provided most compellingly in "Duverger's law," which in essence argues that the single-member plurality system provides a huge impetus toward the consolidation of the spectrum of potential parties into just two. In a winner-takes-all system, the cost of losing is simply too great. Thus, any party that is serious about trying to win government office must compromise, bend, and twist itself into a vehicle that can garner the support of the 50 percent of voters needed to *ensure* victory in an election. All other values become subordinated to the need to achieve electoral majorities. Differences of opinion and diversity of perspectives, new ideas, and new approaches must all be sacrificed to the need to maintain a broad coalition. Of course, anyone who disagrees with the two major parties or feels unrepresented by them is free to "waste" his or her vote on a minor party but only at the expense of playing no constructive role in the electoral process. But what if votes for a minor party were not "wasted"? What if under a PR system, a party that, for instance, got 15 percent of the vote in an election could send 15 percent of the representatives to a legislative body?

CASE STUDY: THE MULTIPARTY SYSTEM IN GERMANY

The case study of Italy in Chapter 1 presented a vivid example of the kind of multiparty system that can be created by PR but also an example of hyperfragmentation and instability. Italy would certainly not be anyone's "poster child" for multiparty democracy. A much better example is provided by its neighbor to the north: Germany.

Cursed with a horrific political history, Germany has strong reason to fear extremes. From 1933 to 1945, it fell under the control of perhaps the worst right-wing regime the world has ever seen. The horrors perpetrated by the National Socialist—or Nazi—Party need no introduction. While the western part of the country began a period of democratic development after 1945, East Germany was until 1989 under the control of a Communist Party that was one of the most hard lined in the Soviet bloc. Even as Hungary was experimenting with market reforms and Poland was witnessing the creating of the independent Solidarity trade union, East Germans remained under constant surveillance by the Stasi secret police, and guards along the Berlin Wall retained orders to shoot to kill.

Given this legacy, the modern German state—which was reunified in 1990—has a deep and abiding interest in maintaining sound, stable government; promoting peace with its neighbors; and curbing the influence at home of both far-right and far-left ideologies. It has succeeded brilliantly, far more so than Italy, with which it shares similar characteristics, such as late coalescence into a single state, strong regional identities, and the experience of dictatorship, war, and military defeat in the 1930s and 1940s. Yet Germany has emerged as an economic powerhouse with low inflation and dynamic industries, a pacifist state with peace at home and abroad, and a model welfare state with a high standard of living and equitable distribution of wealth.

If Germany has gone, in two generations, from global pariah to global paragon, some of the credit is due to the electoral system established in the aftermath of World War II. In the prior two decades, Germany encountered two diametrically opposed problems. First was the fragmentation and weakness of the German government under the Weimar Republic, which was unable to produce stable governing coalitions leading to volatility and discontinuity in government. The second problem emerged in part in reaction to the first: a totalitarian system in which opposition parties were banned and power was concentrated in the hands of a single Führer. Postwar Germany, under a constitution promulgated under American pressure, established a PR system with a threshold of 5 percent rather than the very low 2 percent seen in Italy and some other countries. This has had the effect of diminishing the electoral appeal of extreme parties, most notably the far-right Republikaner Party and the former Communist Party of East Germany, both of which have fallen below 5 percent in elections to the Bundestag.

It should be noted that the diverse but not excessively fragmented partisan composition of the Bundestag is due not only to the 5 percent threshold but also to a clever mixing of PR and simple member plurality voting. Each German votes not once for the lower house of Parliament, the Bundestag, but twice. This "mixed-member" system is an innovation that once again may sound strange to American ears. But voting more than once in the same election poses no particular problems from the perspective of democratic theory—as long as all citizens have the same number of votes. Thus, German citizens cast one ballot for a particular candidate in an electoral district under a single-member plurality (SMP) rule; as in the United States, these elections have one and only one winner. But then a second ballot is cast for a party; seats from this portion of the election are allocated on the basis of a party lists under PR rules. Through use of the 5 percent threshold and the mixed-member electoral system, Germany benefits both from the relative diversity promoted by PR and from the relative stability offered by SMP.[1]

A MULTIPARTY SYSTEM IN THE UNITED STATES?

The discussion in this chapter—backed by a large political science literature—has demonstrated that the SMP system pushes the number of parties in a political system toward a smaller number. In actual practice, the results of SMP in the United States are even more severe than Duverger's law would require. In fact, the more common outcome of SMP is actually not a pure two-party system, as in the United States, but what has been deemed a "two-party-plus" system. In such systems, a "center-left" and a "center-right" party dominate but not to the total exclusion of other parties, as in the United States. In the phasing in of a multiparty system in the United States, we might first see something like a two-party-plus system in the near term, with perhaps a more genuinely multiparty system in the longer term.

Two-party-plus systems might best be seen in the cases of the United Kingdom and of Canada, which employ the SMP system every bit as vigorously as the United States does but which have lingering minor parties that seriously contest elections, hold legislative seats, have a nationwide platform for their ideas and opinions, and control some local, regional, or provincial governments. They can even sometimes hold the balance of power in the formation of a parliamentary majority. This results in a quite different political party configuration than in the United States for two fairly readily identifiable reasons: the presence of highly distinctive ethnic-regional minorities and the presence of socialist parties.

On the first point, many of the minor parties in the United Kingdom and Canada specifically represent ethnic minority groups that are regionally concentrated, notably the French-speaking Quebecois (one party holding 51 of 308 seats in the Canadian Parliament in 2008) and the Welsh, Scottish, and Northern Irish in the United Kingdom (five parties holding 25 of 646 seats). The United States has experienced similar tensions; for instance, the distinctive region of the American South produced two of the five most significant minor party candidates for president in the twentieth century, Strom Thurmond in 1948 and George Wallace in 1968, who ran specifically as southern segregationist "Dixiecrat" candidates. But these were short-lived phenomena, and today no region of the country is as distinctive as the South once was. Further, most ethnic and racial minorities experience some degree of geographic concentration, such as Asians on the West Coast and Latinos along the border, but not nearly to the degree of, say, the Scots, the Welsh, or the Quebecois.

Given that the United States has not developed ethnically based parties under SMP, it seems unlikely that even under PR, parties would emerge on the basis of race and ethnicity. And it would probably not be a positive development if it did. Nonwhite minorities today account for about 30 percent of the U.S. population and less than 25 percent of the electorate both because many minorities are not citizens and because those who are citizens tend to vote at lower rates than whites. Some neonativist alarmists have begun to warn that the rapid growth of the Latinos in the United States and their retention of the Spanish language has begun to threaten traditional American identity; an ethnic Latino party would only exacerbate such ideas. And after a century of pursuing the goal of racial integration, it would be a strange turn indeed if African Americans were to seek their own political party. Asian Americans and Native Americans together constitute just 4 percent of the electorate, well below the likely threshold under PR.

There is, however, another potential basis for the cultivation of minor parties and the development of a two-party-plus or even a multiparty system, one that is evident in the case of both Canada and the United Kingdom and even more so in most western European democracies: ideology. In these cases, there are parties that reflect the values of social democracy, such as the redistribution of income, the regulation of the excesses of market capitalism, the securing of a social safety net, and the provision of a wide range of public goods through government programs. A major reason that most other democracies need to have more than two parties is that their ideological spectrum covers so much more territory—from market capitalism all the way to old-style communism. Even in countries using the SMP system, like Canada and the United Kingdom, this spectrum may simply be too broad for any two parties to stretch to cover. In the United Kingdom, the socialist Labour Party is one of the two major ones, with the Liberal Democratic Party resting between it and the other major party, the Conservatives. In Canada—the politics and society of which often occupy a midway point between the United States and Europe—the socialist New Democratic Party is one of the minor parties, with the two major parties, the Liberals and the Conservatives, to its right.

By any standard, the current U.S. party system has no trouble covering the conservative end of the political spectrum. And it is no exaggeration to say, in comparative terms, that the U.S. two-party system consists of a conservative party, called the Democrats, and a very conservative party, called the Republicans. The leftward flank of the usual political spectrum found in contemporary democracies is mostly a vacuum with little or no coverage by the existing parties. The idiosyncratic politics of a few places, it is true, do sometimes occupy part of that leftward flank; consider the Berkeley City Council and the Vermont state legislature. Yet true left-wing voices on the national scene are exceedingly few, and those who may ascend to positions of power, such as House Speaker Nancy Pelosi of San Francisco, are constrained by the need to function within a political system well to their right.

Just as it is tempting to believe that the perpetuation of the two-party system is the result of electoral preferences, it is also possible to assert that the rightward positioning of the two parties is a reflection of the preferences of voters. In this case, there would be some truth in this assertion. However, U.S. political history has proven that, given strong enough public support, left-leaning change can be achieved, as in the New Deal of the 1930s and the Great Society reforms of the 1960s.

Many learned treatises have been written about why the United States has never developed a homegrown variety of socialism. One line of argumentation is that because the United States, as a new country, fought a revolution against feudal aristocracy, the class conflict and the class consciousness found in Europe (and to a lesser extent in places like Canada and Australia) never developed. Americans, in this reckoning, have been and remain reflexively centrist. A related line of reasoning emphasizes the ethos of "rugged individualism" that was implanted by the original settler experience, cultivated by the westward expansion, and renewed by waves of immigration. From this perspective, the opportunity for individual social mobility trumped and continues to trump more collectivist, group-based approaches that might lead to calls for more expansive government programs. Yet another line of thought focuses on the pathologies of racism in the United States, in which the rigidly maintained color lines erected between poor whites and poor blacks prevented the development of the kind of class solidarity seen in western Europe.

Yet history is not destiny, at least not entirely, and one not need look far for reasons to doubt the continuing viability of the "American dream." Social mobility has become far more elusive in recent decades, as income inequality has grown. And can it be a coincidence that U.S. voter turnout is among the lowest in the democratic world and that the very groups that would most benefit from a left-wing agenda—the poorer, the less educated, the younger, and minorities—are precisely those groups that vote in numbers strikingly lower than other groups? It may well be that what is often considered a demand problem may in fact be a supply problem. That is, the truncation of the political spectrum in the United States may not be so much from a lack of demand on the part of voters as because of the fact that the system has not supplied parties that present a large segment of voters with a policy agenda that seems to address their needs. PR and multiparty democracy may not be panaceas, but they may very well be a "wonder drug" already within easy reach. Just as the humble aspirin can not only soothe headaches but prevent heart attacks and stop strokes, a new electoral system and a new party system may well be just what are needed by an ailing American political system.

SYNOPSIS

Desirability: 5

The present U.S. political party structure leaves many Americans feeling marginalized, demoralized, and alienated. Forced to compete for 50 percent plus one of the electorate, the large umbrella parties are unable to offer clear, coherent platforms and alternatives to the people. Millions of younger, poorer, less educated, and ethnic minority Americans all too often find their views and voices underrepresented by the parties. Domination by the two parties also inhibits new voices and fresh ideas. A stable system of four or five parties—closer to the German example than the hyperfragmented Italian example—would be much preferable to the existing duopoly.

Practicability: 3

There already exist a wide range of minor parties in American politics; thus, it is clear that there are no major legal, constitutional, institutional, or historical barriers to a multiparty system. And, in fact, the major parties themselves already consist of several dissimilar factions. PR elections would almost automatically, within a few electoral cycles, generate a multiparty system. The institutional and ideological shells of the existing minor parties could also serve as a platform for organizing a wider range of new, more viable parties.

Plausibility: 3

Entrenched Republican Party and Democratic Party interests have little ostensible motivation to weaken their hold on power; in fact, they often use their control of the electoral process to curb the rise of potential new competitors. However, there is dissatisfaction among many voters with the two parties, and minor party/ independent candidates have occasionally risen to prominence (although not quite to the point of electoral success). The idea of a multiparty system is also more easily grasped by the American population than is the more fundamental underlying concept of PR. In fact, public approval of and demand for PR could effectively be built by noting that it would expand voter choice by offering a greater variety of parties.

CHAPTER 3

Establish Runoff Elections for Executive Offices

Highlighting Ideas from Chile

By now it should be clear that the use of PR would be likely to promote a multiparty system and that a multiparty system might have much to offer to American democracy. But what are the chances of viable new parties emerging at the national level if the greatest prize of American politics—the White House—would remain beyond their grasp? How could one or more new parties manage to emerge from obscurity if an entire branch of government, the executive (including not just the presidency but the 50 governorships and thousands of mayoralties), could not be awarded proportionally since a single office cannot by definition be subdivided? Clearly, the full logic of PR cannot be applied to the single-office executives that are found in separation-of-power systems.

By contrast, in parliamentary systems, executive power is invested in a cabinet of ministers, of which the prime minister is but the most important and powerful member. All these ministers derive their power not from an independent mandate from the voters, as would a U.S. president, governor, or mayor, but from the support of a majority in Parliament. In such systems, while there may be only one prime minister, executive power can be shared among parties (or party factions) by awarding other ministerial positions that tend to operate with considerable autonomy. Thus, for instance, the key reason that a small rural-based farmers' party might offer its support to the formation of a parliamentary coalition would be the promise that the party would appoint one of its members agriculture minister; this member would thus exercise great power in the one field that is most of interest to farmers.

When an executive office is individual and thus indivisible, power sharing becomes impossible. And when only one seat is at stake, there can be one and only one winner, and thus notions of proportionality are rendered moot. Of course, the United States does have other executive officials, such as the high-ranking secretaries who fill the presidential cabinet. But these are all handpicked by the president to carry out the decisions made by the president on the basis constitutional authority and electoral mandate. Further, most U.S. cabinet secretaries are not themselves powerful *political* figures. More often, they are former—defeated or retired—politicians or else career bureaucrats with substantive public policy expertise. Thus, the U.S. cabinet involves not the *sharing* of executive power but rather simply its delegation.

CASE STUDY: PRESIDENTIAL RUNOFF ELECTIONS IN CHILE

Fortunately, there is a world region to which the United States can turn for experience with PR principles operating within a separation-of-powers system: South America. As in the United States, every country from Mexico running south elects its legislature separately from its executive (with the exceptions of nondemocratic Cuba and a few small former British colonies in and around the Caribbean). These Latin American nations employ PR in their legislative elections and thus have a multiparty system. But they also have U.S.-style single-office executives that cannot, by definition, be allocated proportionally.

The solution in Latin America has been to apply not the letter but rather the spirit of PR by the use of two-round elections in which all parties are free to contest the election in the first round, and then the two top "vote getters" face off against one another in a runoff election. In this way, the nominees of all parties have the opportunity to meaningfully contest races for executive office in the first round, but the ultimate winner must still receive the support of a majority of voters. If one candidate receives more than 50 percent in the first round, that person is automatically elected since he or she has already demonstrated majority support. Thus, in 2006, for instance, the sitting presidents of Brazil, Luiz Inacio Lula da Silva, and of Colombia, Alvaro Uribe, both won about 60 percent of the vote in their elections and were reelected after a single round of voting.[1]

However, when no incumbent is running for reelection, the field tends to be much more open and contested. In several other countries in recent years, presidents have assumed office only after winning two rounds. The case of Chile offers a good example. Because of term limits, Richard Lagos of the Socialist Party was ineligible to return to the presidential palace. His defense minister, Michelle Bachelet, inherited much of his relative popularity and secured the nomination of the Socialist Party. Bachelet faced off against two rivals from the right plus another from the left, easily coming in first but only with 46 percent. Her rightist opponents each won about 25 percent of the vote, with the other leftist winning 5 percent. In the subsequent runoff, her leading opponent, Sebastian Pinera, picked up nearly all the right-wing votes, but Bachelet prevailed with 54 percent and was elected Chile's first woman president.[2]

Runoff elections of this type do not entirely obviate the problem of the "wasted vote." Going into the election, polls and other manifestations of electoral support may make it clear that some candidates simply are not viable, leading voters to switch to their next preferred candidate. Still, in this single Chilean election, four presidential candidates were able to attract at least 5 percent of the vote, with three attracting more than 25 percent. By comparison, no U.S. presidential election since before the Civil War has produced even this much diversity.

Runoff elections do, however, come with their own pitfalls. The 2006 presidential elections in Guatemala offer a cautionary tale in this regard. In the first round, five candidates won 7 percent or more of the vote, while another nine candidates collectively won 16 percent of the vote. In all, more than 48 percent of the voters had voted for a first-round candidate who did not appear in the second round, and the ultimate victor had won only 28 percent of the first-round vote—he had been, in other words, opposed by 72 percent. Perhaps not surprisingly, voter turnout between the first and second rounds dropped by about 20 percent in Guatemala versus 4 percent in Chile.[3]

Fortunately, there is an alternative that eliminates the need for a second round of voting, avoids the danger of a drop in voter turnout, and at the same time expands the number of voters whose preferences contribute to the final outcome. This is called the single transferable vote (STV), as distinguished from the single nontransferable vote used in the United States today. Under the STV system—also called "instant runoff" voting, each voter lists the candidates in order of preference. All the ballots are assessed, and the candidate with the fewest votes is eliminated, but those ballots are not simply discarded. Instead, the vote is transferred to the voter's next-highest choice. This process can continue for multiple rounds until a single candidate emerges with more than 50 percent support.

Although not yet widely used in practice at the national level, the STV system is employed most widely in Ireland. In parliamentary elections, STV can be fused to the use of PR. However, it is also used to fill the largely ceremonial position of president of Ireland, and in the three-way 1990 presidential election, it functioned as promised. After the first round, the candidate from the largest party, Brian Lenihan of Fianna Fáil, had the largest number of votes, but when the second-place preference of the eliminated candidate was factored in, the second-round victory went to Mary Robinson of the Labour Party, thus satisfying more voters to a greater degree.

RUNOFF VOTING IN THE UNITED STATES?

Some readers may have noted that the U.S. political system does already have, in its own way, a two-stage system in executive elections: first securing the nomination of one of the two major parties through the primary election process and then securing public office by winning the general election. And it is true that the use of primaries is a democratizing feature of the U.S. political system, one that was first promoted during the Progressive Era and then extended more completely to the presidential nominating process after the ferment of the 1960s.

By their very nature, the major parties in a two-party system must be big enough "umbrellas" to assemble electoral majorities. In such heterogeneous coalitions, there will inevitably be multiple ideological factions, some in ascendancy and others striving for power. Factions may also break along other lines, such as region, generation, and ethnicity. Particularly for statewide offices, such as governorships and U.S. Senate seats, as well as for the presidency, primaries do thus allow for fresher, newer voices and faces in American politics.

The imperative to compete for a party nomination rather than simply have it bestowed by party elders is thus a democracy-enhancing feature (although one run amok in term of time and cost, as discussed in Chapter 5). This has particularly been the case in the Democratic Party, in part because it uses a system of PR in the allocation of its delegates to the nominating convention. This prevents a clear front-runner from locking up an insurmountable lead early in the process. Thus, insurgent candidates from outside the party establishment have a relatively good chance to score a primary victory, including Jimmy Carter in 1976, Bill Clinton in 1992, and, perhaps most dramatically, Barack Obama in 2008. By contrast, essentially all Republican primary battles since 1964 have gone to a clear-cut front-runner who had previously held or run for the presidency, the closest exception being George W. Bush, the son of a former president.

The limitation here, of course, is that elections are still bounded by the two-party system with its established interests and positions. One may run for and even win the nomination of, say, the Libertarian Party or the Green Party but still have no viable shot at ever exercising power through elected office. By contrast, runoff elections, whether via two rounds or via STV, can go a long way toward promoting the viability of multiple parties even with regard to individual offices that are not amenable to PR. However, American history does offer a word of caution with regard to runoff elections. In some southern states, they have had the effect of deterring the election of ethnic or racial minority candidates by allowing the white majority of the electorate to "rally around" *any* white candidate against a candidate of color in the second round. The same problem could arise for a female candidate or for a candidate with some other "minority" characteristic, such as religion, sexual orientation, or disability. Monitoring and enforcement of voting rights would have to accompany this reform, as with all major electoral reforms.

With this significant caveat, runoff elections could be quite a viable reform, made all the more plausible by the demonstrated willingness of Americans, even under the current two-party monopoly, to at least occasionally look beyond the Democratic and the Republican candidates for executive offices. In the 1990s, for example, Maine, Connecticut, and Minnesota all elected minor party or independent governors. Even more strikingly during that decade was the enthusiasm for the third-party presidential candidacy of H. Ross Perot of the Reform Party. He won 8 percent of the vote in 1996 but an even more stunning 19 percent in 1992, the most of any third-party presidential candidate since Teddy Roosevelt attempted a return to the White House with the Bull Moose Party in 1912. Yet Perot won not a single electoral vote because he did not win a plurality in any of the states. This is just one of the many peculiarities of the bizarre, cumbersome, antiquated institution of the Electoral College, which serves little useful purpose, as discussed in the next chapter.

SYNOPSIS

Desirability: 4

If PR and a multiparty system can be considered democracy-maximizing ideals, then runoff voting falls somewhat short. Ultimately, it is still a winner-takes-all process in which minority factions remain unrepresented or underrepresented. However, given the reality that executive positions in the United States consist of individual offices, runoff elections—particularly instant runoff elections—can be a valuable adjunct to the system and allow currently "minor" parties to have a much better chance of winning some executive seats. However, the potential for civil rights abuses must also be monitored.

Practicability: 5

Given that runoff elections are already commonly practiced in parts of the United States, it is clear that there would be few impediments to implementing this idea. Runoff elections are within the capacity of the states to establish as long as they do not violate minority voting rights. In its own crude way, the Electoral College, by requiring the winner to take an absolute number of electoral votes, acts as a type of runoff. As described in the next chapter, the United States would do well to completely abolish the Electoral College; this could create a vacuum that could neatly be filled by runoff or even instant runoff voting.

Plausibility: 3

Of their own accord, most established politicians would not want to erect a barrier to their own reelection, adding a third election to the primary and general elections. However, runoff elections make up a concept that would resonate well with several important American ideals, including the value of free and open competition as well as the notion that majority rule should ultimately prevail in any given election. The existence of precedents for runoffs in the U.S. tradition could also probably help build support for runoff elections, especially in the context of the cultivation of a multiparty political system.

CHAPTER 4

Abolish the Electoral College

Highlighting Ideas from Argentina

It may be a cliché, but it nonetheless remains true that the founders of the United States were in many ways a wise and prescient group. Drawing on the political philosophy of the Enlightenment and their own brief history of self-government at the state level, the framers of the U.S. Constitution devised a number of ingenious solutions to the problems facing the young nation. Some of them have endured the test of time—federalism, for example, remains a productive approach to government that has been adopted by more than two dozen countries around the world. Some other innovations have required periodic fine-tuning, such as the sharing and balancing of power between Congress and the presidency. Some, discussed in other chapters of this book, cry out for reform, including equal representation in the Senate and the arduous amending process. In one area, the results were tragic, namely, the blind eye turned toward the institution of slavery, the effects of which have haunted the nation ever since. But no provision of the Constitution is more ill conceived, pointlessly complicated, and distorting of the democratic electoral process than the Electoral College.

The roots of the Electoral College are well known: having no experience with any executive other than a hereditary king and the colonial governors he appointed, the framers had no idea how to actually elect a national executive. Congress could choose the president, but would that compromise the separation of powers they counted on to prevent tyranny? The people could elect the president directly, but could such trust be put in ordinary citizens? And would the Constitutional Convention be able to sustain yet another round of negotiation and compromise over how to elect the executive? It had taken a great deal already to assuage the fears of the smaller states by providing equal representation in the Senate and satisfying the southern states by including a portion of the slave population for purposes of apportioning House seats (the notorious Three Fifths Compromise).

In the end, the framers chose the expedient path of simply applying the arduously negotiated formula for congressional representation as the basis for selecting the president. The legislature of each state would be able to determine a process for choosing presidential "electors," with each state having as many electors as it had members of the House and Senate combined. To prevent intrigue and collusion, all the electors would need to be citizens who held no federal office, and they would meet only once, in each respective state capital rather than as a collective body in the national capital.

The Twelfth Amendment of 1804 required electors to cast their votes for a combined ticket of president and vice president. But otherwise, the Electoral College has remained much the same to the current day, comprised today of 538 electors (reflecting 435 House members, 100 senators, and three electoral votes for Washington, D.C.). Although each state legislature could, technically, simply appoint electors, today all are allocated by means of the popular vote. In nearly all the states, whichever candidate gets the most popular votes wins *all* of that state's electoral votes, meaning that Electoral College tallies break quite lopsidedly in the direction of the winner of the national popular vote.

For more than a hundred years after 1888, the Electoral College was occasionally a topic of discussion, but, like a dead tree that was easier to leave in place than to remove, it was simply left alone—until, that is, the political "perfect storm" of 2000 that toppled the tree and nearly brought down the political house with it. When the storm passed, of course, the candidate who got the most votes nevertheless did *not* end up in the White House. Once passed through the lens of the Electoral College, a narrow half-million-popular-vote win for Vice President Al Gore was refracted into a four-electoral-vote loss in the Electoral College to George W. Bush, who pursued a very different set of public policy priorities than Gore would have.

Thus, it is no longer acceptable to simply ignore the faults of the Electoral College. In fact, the peculiarities of the 2000 election do not begin to exhaust the possible ways in which bizarre quirks and unpredictable convolutions of the Electoral College can cause potential problems in the election of the nation's highest office. Consider just these five most prominent concerns:

- Electoral votes are cast not automatically but by the actual people who are appointed by the political parties to act as "electors." While it has not historically been a major problem, in a close race just a few "faithless electors" could switch their votes and chance the outcome of an election. The law is quite unclear about the extent to which an elector can change his or her vote; in fact, one elector withheld a ballot in 2000 as a form of protest.

- The less populated states are considerably overrepresented in the Electoral College. Wyoming, with half a million people, has three electoral votes, but Texas, with 46 times Wyoming's population, has only about 10 times more electoral votes. This is because the smaller states are also overrepresented in the Senate, relative to their population, which carries over into the formula for allocating electoral votes. The problem of equal representation in the Senate is discussed in Chapter 15. Suffice it to say that many high-population areas, particularly the urban areas that are homes to many ethnic and racial minorities, are underrepresented in the Electoral College.

- An Electoral College victory requires an *absolute* majority, not simply a plurality, of the electoral votes. If no candidate wins 270 votes, the winner is chosen by the House, with each state delegation having one vote, again grossly inflating the influence of more sparsely populated states and veering the result of the election even further from the popular will. That this has happened only twice in American history, in 1800 and 1824, should provide no false comfort—particularly if other reforms discussed earlier lead toward a multiparty system.

- The practice of using a winner-take-all system of electoral vote allocation in all but two of the states can also distort the popular will. In practice, this has the effect of denying *any* electoral votes to candidates who do not win any states—a likely scenario at least when new parties first begin to contest the presidential elections in a nascent multiparty system.

- The need to win an Electoral College majority means that candidates focus disproportionately on so-called swing states, particularly the larger ones such as Florida and Ohio, which might go to either candidate. With New York all but sure to go to the Democrats and Texas to the Republicans, two of the largest states—along with many others—are nearly ignored by the campaigns. Neither side has an incentive to try to increase voter turnout or try to craft policy positions that might appeal to those states.

Some 220 years after the ratification of the Constitution, it is more than clear that the choice of a president should be invested directly in the people, scrapping the anachronistic and distorting apparatus of the Electoral College. When looking for examples from most other presidential systems, the most notable characteristic is the *absence* of any such contraption. However, a few Latin American countries did initially have electoral colleges that they, tellingly, later abolished.

CASE STUDY: ABOLITION OF THE ELECTORAL COLLEGE IN ARGENTINA

At the time of the founding, every other country in the Western Hemisphere was still under the control of European colonizers, particularly Spain and Portugal. Each of those Spanish and Portuguese colonies, as they became independent, chose to adopt a separation-of-powers system based on the U.S. model; in some cases, the language of their constitutions is drawn explicitly from that of the United States and include such key elements as a presidency, a *usually* bicameral national legislature, a supreme court, a written bill of rights, and a formal system of checks and balances. Yet, unlike the United States, most of these countries simply choose their president through direct popular vote.

Argentina, the constitution of which is exceptionally closely based on the U.S. Constitution, was the last to abolish its Electoral College, doing so only in 1994.[1] One of the more atypical South American nations, Argentina has only a small population of indigenous peoples and a large population of people of direct European descent, particularly from Italy and Spain. It has also traditionally had a relatively large and prosperous middle class, for many decades enjoying a "First World" standard of living. Yet it has never been as advanced politically, with long stretches of effective dictatorship and even direct military rule. During the famous presidency of Juan Peron, the Electoral College was briefly abolished in favor of direct elections, but after a military coup, it was reinstated, making it easier for the military to manipulate the office.

Since the collapse of the last military junta following the country's humiliating quick defeat in the 1982 war with Britain over the Falkland/Malvinas Islands, Argentina has made significant strides in terms of restoring democratic practice and constitutional norms. However, it became clear that since Argentina employs PR and thus has a multiparty system, the Electoral College could not consistently produce a winner with the required absolute majority, sending the final decision to the Argentinean Congress. Further, differences in the sizes of provinces led to malapportionment and further distorted the role of the popular vote (a problem, of course, that still plagues the United States).

In order to ensure the selection of a president with sufficient popular support to govern effectively, the Electoral College was again abolished in 1994 in favor of a two-stage runoff system as in Chile (which abolished its own Electoral College in 1973). To date, four Argentine presidents have been freely and directly chosen by the people. In a unique variation, anyone in the first round who wins 45 percent (rather than an absolute majority) or 40 percent with a 10 percent lead over the next candidate is declared the victor; partly as a result, no runoffs have actually yet occurred.

It should be acknowledged that this change has not been a panacea for the Argentine political system. Indeed, during a severe economic meltdown and currency crisis in late 2001, the sitting elected president was forced out, and in a bizarre cycle, the country had five different presidents or acting presidents in 12 dramatic days. But by 2003, the system of direct elections had allowed the Argentine people to freely choose a new, very much "outsider"—Nestor Kirchner, the governor of a remote Patagonian province—who earned enormous popularity and managed to stabilize the country. In 2008, he was succeeded by his wife, Senator Christina Fernandez de Kirchner, who won 44 percent of the vote but a 22-point lead over the next candidate that enabled her to avoid a runoff.

DIRECT ELECTION OF THE U.S. PRESIDENT?

Given the distorting effects of the Electoral College in the United States and the examples provided by Argentina and Chile of direct, two-round popular elections, there would seem to be little reason to argue further about the need for reform. However, even beyond simple tradition and inertia, the Electoral College does have its defenders. Perhaps the most potentially valid defense is that the Electoral College requires presidential candidates to build support from across the entire country. However, as revealed in the infamous "red state" and "blue state" maps of the presidential elections of 2000 and 2004, the support for the two major parties is already quite concentrated in certain geographic areas. Another defense is that the Electoral College makes candidates pay attention to more sparsely populated areas rather than just the major population centers. But, in reality, the big cities already vote very heavily Democratic, the suburbs split, and the rural areas are strongly Republican, guaranteeing that all types of locality are addressed at some point. And, in any case, U.S. population centers are widely scattered, with the nation's 10 largest cities accounting for just 5 percent of the national population. In Argentina, where fully one-third of the population lives in the Buenos Aires metropolitan region, Nestor Kirchner was nonetheless elected from a power base in the thinly populated Patagonia region. If anything, direct competition between the two parties, unmediated by the Electoral College, would likely lead to a push to increase the sadly low voter turnout in the United States. At present, each state keeps its full share of its electoral votes no matter what the actual turnout in that state.

One reason that the Electoral College has persisted for so long is that, as we have discussed, relative to population it overrepresents the small populated states by virtue of their overrepresentation in the Senate. Of course, these same small states also have disproportionate influence over the constitutional amending process. This problem is examined in some detail in Chapter 20. Suffice it to say now that if the legislatures of the many of the smaller states were unwilling or unable to look beyond their narrow individual interests, they might refused to ratify an amendment abolishing the Electoral College—and only 13 states would need to so refuse.

Fortunately, there are other remedies, and the very state legislatures that could block the constitutional reform route could also be the solution. The most distorting element of the Electoral College is actually *not* a constitutional provision but rather the winner-take-all practice established by the various state legislatures under their own authority. In theory, the basic reason for allocating electors on this basis is to make each state a richer "pot" and thus to draw more candidate attention to it—winning a state by even a narrow margin can result in big gains. In practice, however, we have seen that only the relatively few swing states benefit in this way.

Indeed, there is already some impetus and precedent for Electoral College reform at the state level. Two states, Maine and Nebraska, already use a system in which the statewide winner is allocated two electoral votes (representing, in a sense, the votes they derive from their statewide senators); then the winner in each congressional district is awarded one vote. In 2004, the idea of allocating electoral votes on a purely proportional basis made it all the way to a statewide referendum in Colorado, although it was ultimately rejected by the voters. Part of that rejection was a perception that Colorado was somehow "unilaterally disarming" in the sense that it was devaluing its electoral clout without other states doing the same thing simultaneously.[2] More compelling is a law passed by the Maryland legislature promising to allocate its electors to the winner of the popular vote regardless of the specific outcome in Maryland. Notably, this practice would take effect only once enough state legislatures made the same move—specifically, that an Electoral College majority would be guaranteed.[3]

Such creative thinking may point the way forward for reform of the Electoral College. There is no reason that the United States could not do so, and many reason that it should include the fundamental integrity of the system itself. And, while the United States is in the process of reforming the *end* of the presidential electoral process, it should consider a range of reforms for the broader electoral process itself. Several of these are the subject of the next chapter.

SYNOPSIS

Desirability: 4

For the reasons discussed here, the Electoral College is a loose cannon, one which badly misfired in 2000, as it had done in at least four other occasions, in 1800, 1824, 1876, and 1888. Even when it does not actively thwart the will of the voters, it still has the unnecessary and unproductive distorting effect of overemphasizing swing states rather than the population at large. Presidents who take office without the Electoral College would be more able to unambiguously claim the mandate of the entire nation.

Practicability: 3

It would be relatively simple to amend the Constitution to simply state that "the President shall be elected by the direct vote of the citizens of the United States." Such an amendment could probably pass the House but would have a harder time in the Senate and with the process of ratification by the states since some small states might balk. Although anything short of out-right abolition would not be optimal, it might be possible to muster support for changes other than the allocation of electoral votes, such as getting rid of "electors" and eliminating the need for an absolute majority (and thus also the danger of an election ending up being decided by the House). In all, the state-by-state approach might be the more readily feasible.

Probability: 3

If the 2000 election did not succeed in provoking action on Electoral College reform, it is not clear what it would take. If far-reaching reforms of the electoral process began in the United States, however, such as the adoption of PR principles and a multiparty system, Electoral College reform might also seem more natural. Were there more demand among the people for reform or if such changes gathered steam at the state level, Electoral College reform would also be more likely to secure a place on the political agenda in Washington, D.C.

CHAPTER 5

Simplify and Shorten the Electoral Process

Highlighting Ideas from Great Britain

Chapter 4 focused on the need to replace the Electoral College with direct popular voting for the president, an issue that in the aftermath of the 2000 election would be a demonstrably significant reform. But there are also major problems with the U.S. electoral process well before the Electoral College stage of presidential elections as well as in the many elections for other political offices. Indeed, compared to most other countries, elections in the United States are inordinately long, complicated, costly, distracting, and alienating to voters.

Ironically, it was originally a democratizing impulse that led to some of these problems. For example, the desire for a greater range of voices to be heard in the selection of candidates led, over the course of the twentieth century, to a steadily more universal use of party primaries rather than simply appointment of nominees by party leaders. And since there are only *currently* two viable major parties in general elections, primaries genuinely do have the effect of creating greater competition and diversity among candidates. Likewise, after about 1950, the proliferation of mass media, in particular television, made it possible for candidates to reach out to the people directly. This allows politicians to be far more independent and to bypass existing partisan and other power structures and thus, in theory at least, to be more focused on the needs and desires of their constituents.

Unfortunately, in practice, these two potentially democratizing factors—primary campaigns and candidate-centered elections—have contributed to a system that has become so overinflated, elongated, and complicated that it can have antidemocratic effects. Formal campaigns, especially for the presidency, can last 18 months or longer, strung out through an archipelago of different state-level primary elections and caucuses. Throughout this period of time, enormous sums of money are needed for outreach to voters, particularly television time in large media markets. The need for fund-raising is constant and relentless, including for members of Congress, governors, and big-city mayors. The elections of 2004 were collectively estimated to have cost more than $4 billion; in 2008, Barack Obama alone spent more than half a billion dollars.

The deleterious effects of this need to be in "permanent campaign mode" and to constantly raise funds have been amply documented. Suffice it here to note that when candidates—up to and including incumbent presidents—are pouring their efforts into fund-raising, their ability to do their jobs is inevitably compromised. The longer the campaign period, the more fund-raising is needed and thus the longer that public officials are distracted from their jobs, perhaps for as long as half the term to which they were elected. In some cases, the well-known toll of these pressures may prevent some qualified individuals from even attempting to run for office in the first place, sending them instead into private industry or other spheres.

At the same time, the need to raise enormous funds over long periods of time runs the strong risk of putting politicians "in the pockets" of wealthy interests. Of course, those with wealth and power are always going to have disproportionate influence in almost any government. And most politicians are smart enough—and perhaps even principled enough—to avoid quid pro quo exchanges with donors. Usually, both sides in these transactions know better than to spell out anything that could later provide a "smoking gun" to investigators in the form of a written document or a recorded statement. Much murkier, however, is the overall corrupting influence of money in politics, namely, the extent to which campaign contributions affect the overall process of agenda setting. To an extent, that is hard to quantify but is nonetheless very real; the pervasive influence of money helps determine which issues de facto are prioritized and which are marginalized or excluded from the political process. Fortunately, there is no essential reason that U.S. elections have to be so cumbersome and protracted; as in so many other ways, the U.S. case is an outlier when compared to the system in most other countries.

CASE STUDY: SHORT AND SIMPLE ELECTIONS IN GREAT BRITAIN

Although the United States derived many of its political institutions and much of its political culture from the British system, a lengthy electoral process is most definitely not one of them. In fact, by law, the United Kingdom limits the campaign season for the House of Commons to three weeks or less, sometimes triggered on very short notice. While no more than five years may elapse between parliamentary elections in the United Kingdom, the prime minister may call an election at any time prior to that. Often, elections are timed in the fourth or early fifth year of a Parliament as the mandate is winding down. However, a "snap" election can be called at any time the prime minister deems that doing so would be politically advantageous for his or her party, such as after a major policy accomplishment or when the opposition is in disarray.

The process is triggered by a formal petition to the Queen to dissolve Parliament and call a new general election. The royal proclamation is then followed by a lightning-fast schedule, with the election generally held within 17 working days unless Parliament approves a slightly longer schedule. For example, the Parliament in 2005 was dissolved on April 11, and the general election was held on May 5. With campaign seasons lasting less than a month, the British elect their Parliament—and thus indirectly their government—on a schedule that is well less than one-tenth of the protracted U.S. presidential campaign schedule.

It is true that this quick turnover is facilitated by a feature inherent in the very nature of the structure of Parliament, namely, the presence of an "Official Opposition" formed by the party with the second-most seats. The Official Opposition does not oppose the *state* itself but rather is tasked with scrutinizing the government and proposing alternatives to its programs. (Its role is nicely captured by referring to "Her Majesty's Loyal Opposition," underscoring that all members of Parliament pledge allegiance to the same sovereign and serve the same state.) The Leader of the Opposition is a well-known politician and a household name. Further, there is a "Shadow Cabinet" composed of senior officials who play a lead role in questioning and critiquing each of the ministries within the actual governing cabinet. Together, the Leader of the Opposition and the Shadow Cabinet thus form an alternative government-in-waiting, which is particularly useful in parliamentary systems in which the government of the day can be brought down at any time by a vote of no confidence. Thus, British voters can go to the polls quickly because, if they should opt for a change in the government, they know that the Leader of the Opposition will be their new prime minister and that most of the members of the Shadow Cabinet will become senior ministers in the new government.

Other factors further streamline the process. In the United Kingdom, party leaders determine who their party will put forward as candidates for each parliamentary seat. This produces a far less active role for individual candidates given that there are no primary elections and that voters are somewhat more likely in the United States to vote for a particular party than for a candidate based on his or her personal characteristics. Tellingly, whereas American candidates "run" for office, in the United Kingdom they are said to "stand" for office.

The burden of fund-raising is also dramatically reduced. Not only does a three-week election by its very nature cost much less than a longer one, but campaign financing is generously available under the guidelines of the Political Parties, Elections and Referendums Act of 2000.[1] The current limit for *total* party expenditures in elections is set at around £19 million (just over $27 million) for campaigns. Given that the Labour Party has 356 members in the House of Commons, that works out to about $76,000 for each member. The comparable figures in 2006 for the U.S. House of Representatives were just under *$752 million* total for the two parties, or an average of about $995,000 per candidate.[2]

Expenditures—and indeed the entire electoral process—are further limited by regulations regarding campaigning via the mass media, including television and radio. Prospective members of Parliament and parties are further limited by what materials can appear on the mass media. The Representation of the People Act of 1983 prohibits "personal electioneering" on public broadcasting outlets and, to that end, makes illegal false statements made by candidates or incumbents about other candidates.[3] Subsequent legislation, like the Communications Act of 2003, also enforces equal time and access for opposing candidates in an election or referendum. During general elections, they may be further prevented from speaking about their own constituencies on air, limited instead to appearing as party spokespeople on general issues and in publicized debates. As a result, candidates often adhere to an older and simpler mode of electioneering, including distributing party pamphlets, canvassing door-to-door, and mailing a limited number of campaign materials.

Finally, if elections are executed far more quickly and efficiently in Britain than in the United States, so too is the transition to power of a new government. In the most recent handoff of power, the Conservative Party ended 18 years of rule with a loss on May 1, 1997. The incumbent prime minister, John Major, handed off power to his successor Tony Blair—up to including the codes to launch nuclear missiles—the very next day.

SHORTEN THE U.S. ELECTORAL PROCESS?

The intrinsic structural and institutional differences between the United States and the United Kingdom mean that elections in the United States could never be as streamlined as their British counterparts. In particular, the United States does not have an established Leader of the Opposition or Shadow Cabinet who is well known to the public and ready to take over government at a moment's notice. Such a feature could not be feasibly introduced in to the U.S. system, nor would it necessarily be desirable, as it tends to limit power to a small circle of parliamentary insiders. Indeed, relative unknowns such as Jimmy Carter, Bill Clinton, or Barack Obama would not have been able to "take Washington by storm" under the British system, nor could political outsiders such as Dwight Eisenhower have moved directly to the top position. Similarly, it would be overkill to go back to a system in which political party leaders outright appointed their nominees rather than having them chosen by the party rank and file through primary elections. Particularly in presidential elections, elimination of the primary phase would obviously reduce the time and expense of elections but at the cost of a more closed system in which party leaders inordinately control the nomination process.

Still, the British example points out that it is eminently feasible for U.S. elections to be much simpler and more streamlined. A principal reform would be to drastically condense the time frame. In 2008, presidential primaries took place on 22 separate days stretched out over the six months between January 3 and June 3. This grueling marathon creates extraordinary demands for continuous fund-raising, particularly considering the need for further massive expenditures in the general election in the fall. The primaries are also exhausting and distracting to the candidates, a particular issue when they already have demanding jobs, such as being a sitting governor, senator, vice president, or president. And it is unclear how much these protracted

primaries really add to voters' knowledge of candidates, their management styles, or their positions on issues. Instead, the media seem to
fixate on the "horse-race" issue, with some candidates ostensibly gain-
ing and others losing momentum based on primaries in just a few
small states, such as Iowa and New Hampshire. A further complication comes from the labyrinthine rules for the caucuses and primaries
that allocate delegates for the party nominating conventions. This is
particularly acute in the Democratic Party, which uses a PR system
and also empowers senior party politicians as superdelegates, a process
that led to a confusing outcome in 2008 when Hillary Rodham Clinton
won more overall support by voters but Barack Obama secured more
delegates and, ultimately, the party nomination.

Yet many of these issues could be resolved by a single, simple
expedient: holding all the presidential primaries on a single day much
closer to Election Day. For example, for offices other than the
presidency, the State of New York holds its primary elections in
mid-September, limiting the general election to eight weeks—which
is still three times the length of national elections in Britain. One valid
objection to a condensed time frame would be that it could "stack the
deck" in favor of more established candidates and make it more difficult
for insurgents or lesser-known figures to make their case. However, it
would apply only to the primary election itself, not to the period of
campaigning that precedes it. Many politicians test the waters and
position themselves, more or less formally, for years before an actual
run. In fact, it has been said, only half jokingly, that the United States
always has 151 presidents-in-waiting—the vice president plus 100 senators and 50 governors. Nothing would prevent declared or potential
candidates from beginning their campaigns as early as they wished;
in fact, the First Amendment would clearly block any attempts to limit
the free speech or expression of candidates as is done in the United
Kingdom.

If the U.S. parties emulated the idea of late primaries, such as the
practice in New York, the parties could produce their candidates on a
single day in September and then within two weeks hold the national
conventions that they now hold usually in August. Rather than continue
the fiction that the candidates are actually nominated at these conventions, the nominees could be determined directly by the nationwide
vote. The conventions, though, could continue their role of framing
the party's positions and promoting its nominee for president as well
as nominees for lower offices. The vice-presidential nominee could
still be introduced at that time (though abolition of the vice presidency

is recommended in Chapter 10). In a new innovation, the nominating conventions could also profitably be used for the presidential nominee to name an entire slate of cabinet officers (as discussed further in Chapter 12), giving voters the ability to make a more fully informed choice about the entire presidential team.

The rest of the election would then play out as it currently does, with focused campaigning and debates through the fall leading up to Election Day. However, there is no need for the lengthy interregnum between Election Day in early November and Inauguration Day on January 20. During this awkward 10-week period, the country has both a president and a president-elect, yet the former continues to have all the constitutional powers of the office—even in cases when incumbent presidents have been rejected by the voters, as was the case with Gerald Ford in 1976, Jimmy Carter in 1980, and George H. W. Bush in 1992. Yet the American people clearly deserve to be governed by the person they have chosen to be president—and only by that person—for all but the shortest possible time span (a theme that is further explored in Chapters 10 and 11).

It is true that in parliamentary systems, the existence of a Leader of the Opposition and a Shadow Cabinet as a government-in-waiting facilitates a quick change to new leadership. But even in other countries with powerful, directly elected presidents, the transition to new leadership can be much shorter, such as six weeks in Argentina in 2008 and a mere 10 days in France in 2007. In 1933, the Twentieth Amendment to the U.S. Constitution nearly halved the time between the election and inauguration of a new president; another such amendment could make it even shorter, perhaps as little as two weeks. Other changes proposed in this book, such as abolition of the Electoral College and preelection nomination of the cabinet, would also have the salutary effect of eliminating most of the arguments for a protracted waiting period.

A shortened electoral time frame would also naturally go a long way toward reducing the inordinate costs of elections. A detailed discussion of campaign finance reform would require moving into the realm of public policy reform, which is beyond the scope of this volume. Suffice it to say, however, that a veritable arsenal of approaches to campaign finance reform can be assembled from the examples of U.S. states and municipalities as well as other countries. These range from generous matching funds to free media airtime and print ad placements to spending caps and beyond. What has been missing is not the ideas but the political will.

Under the Constitution, the conduct of elections is mostly a power reserved to the states rather than provided to the federal government. This has led to an exceptionally decentralized, even chaotic system with some 3,000 government entities throughout the nation having responsibility for elections using different policies and procedures and with uneven safeguards against fraud and abuse. However, Congress has at times also found a proactive role for itself in electoral regulation, particularly in the area of voting rights enforcement since the civil rights era. Should it wish to do so, Congress could also be far more proactive in reforming the electoral process in general and issue campaign finance reform; as long as its members remain under the influence of such campaign donations, however, the road to reform will remain steep indeed.

SYNOPSIS

Desirability: 5

Fair, competitive, and periodic elections are the lifeblood of a democracy. When convoluted rules, protracted time frames, and the flow of cash distort the ability of the people to elect the representatives of their choice, reform is urgently required. Although the U.S. electoral process will never achieve the brevity offered by a parliamentary system, the example of Great Britain clearly illustrates that elections can be held in a drastically condensed time frame, with attendant benefits in terms of reduced cost, increased voter engagement, and minimized influence by special interest groups.

Practicability: 5

Because streamlining and simplifying the electoral process raises few constitutional issues and can be approached from multiple angles in an incremental fashion, this is perhaps the single most practicable of all the reforms proposed in this book. Through ordinary legislation on the state and national levels, along with simplifying reforms passed by the political parties, the electoral process in the United States could be drastically improved.

Plausibility: 3

Many politicians are, perhaps inevitably, reluctant to carry out reforms that might increase the odds of potential challengers; after all, the existing system has rewarded them with elected office, and they now have the advantages of incumbency. At the same time, they—more than anyone—realize how exhausting and distracting the process of campaigning can be, and many also have aspirations to higher office. With the right combination of public pressure and practical solutions, government officials may well be willing to support sensible moves to simplify and streamline the system.

CHAPTER 6

Advance Minorities and Women in Elected Office

Highlighting Ideas from Belgium

Thoroughgoing reforms of the electoral process identified so far in this book would, on their own, go far in promoting a far broader political system, greater opportunities for candidates with a range of backgrounds, and ultimately more diversity of officeholders in terms of race, ethnicity, and gender. PR elections would empower a greater array of political parties, with different social bases and political priorities. Runoff elections and the abolition of the Electoral College would reinforce the establishment of PR for executive offices up to and including the presidency. And a shortened, more streamlined approach to political campaigning would reduce the barriers to entry into the political process for candidates of all types.

Yet, the experience from countries in which many of these reforms have been implemented reveals that these steps alone do not guarantee that women and minorities will hold elective offices in numbers fully commensurate with their percentage of the general population. In fact, it seems clear that extra, proactive steps need to be taken in order to overcome the inertial forces that have limited the number of election winners and officeholders among women as well as ethnic, racial, and other types of minorities.

The arguments for why it is preferable to have greater diversity among officeholders can be organized into three major if somewhat overlapping clusters: individual, societal, and substantive. Individual arguments stress that in a democracy, all citizens deserve the right to engage fully and equally in all forms of political participation—the highest form of which is the actual wielding of political power in elected or appointed government office. Societal arguments maintain that in a polity that is de facto multiracial, multiethnic, and multicultural, political institutions cannot truly serve the assorted interests of the population unless officeholders also do so since only members of a group—based on their own experience—can fully understand, support, reflect, and respond to the needs and desires of the group. Substantive arguments continue this line of reasoning to argue that the actual practice of politics and the articulation and prioritization of policy goals can be improved by the addition of previously underrepresented groups who add new perspectives, draw on different experiences, help to reorder priorities, and bring new supporters into the system.

The U.S. Constitution comprehends some of these arguments in ways both obvious and subtle. Obvious manifestations would be the prohibition of titles of nobility in article I—to prevent the entrench-ment of a hereditary elite—and the banning of "religious tests" for office in article VI. On other issues of contemporary concern, however, the Constitution and the Bill of Rights are silent. While it appears that women as "persons" were meant to be guaranteed civil liberties such as freedom of speech and trial by jury, there is no mention of whether women could vote or hold office, and it would take until 1916 before the first woman took a seat in Congress and until 1920 before the right to vote was clearly established by the Nineteenth Amendment. To this day, the Constitution makes no reference whatsoever to sex or gender other than the Nineteenth Amendment. An Equal Rights Amendment, stating that "[e]quality of rights under the law shall not be denied or abridged by the United States or by any State on account of sex," was proposed by a two-thirds vote of both houses of Congress. But with 35 states ratifying it by the deadline of March 1979, it fell just short of the three-fourths (38) of the states required. Parallel court rulings have interpreted the Fourteenth Amendment's guarantees of equal protec-tion to de facto include equality between women and men, but these offer protection that is much less clear-cut, reliable, and comprehensive than would a textual change to the Constitution.

The lot of ethnic and racial minorities in the constitutional scheme was murkier still in part because "race" and "ethnicity" are less objec-tively established categorical concepts than "gender" (notwithstanding much recent scholarship that gender is actually a far less obviously binary concept than once thought). In the Constitution, slavery was gingerly treated as an accepted reality rather than explicitly approved or prohibited, and in some places people of color were able to vote and exercise other rights. Equal protection and voting rights were in theory extended to African Americans and at least by analogy to other ethnic and racial minorities with the Fourteenth Amendment of 1868 and the Fifteenth Amendment of 1870. But, of course, these were frequently and egregiously violated until a century later with the Civil Rights Act of 1964 and the Voting Rights Act of 1965, despite which various forms of discrimination and disenfranchisement persist to the present.

Examining the current percentage of holders of high office in the United States in terms of race and ethnicity is decidedly a dilemma of "glass half empty, glass half full." The most obvious manifestation of the half-full glass comes from the election of Barack Obama as president, a development wholly inconceivable a generation before. Although Obama is biracial and the son of an African immigrant rather than the proverbial "descendant of slaves," he would have been fully subject to the Jim Crow laws of segregation, and his parents' "mixed-race" marriage in 1961 would have been illegal under the anti-miscegenation laws existing in many states. Along the same lines, in recent years, the United States has also seen increasing numbers of ethnic and racial minorities in high-level government offices, including key positions such as secretary of state (twice since 2000) and attorney general (twice since 2004). Nearly half of the 22 secretaries and other officials afforded cabinet rank at the outset of the Obama administration were ethnic or racial minorities, including four African Americans, three Asian Americans and two Latinos (as well as a total of seven women, three of whom were women of color).

Yet Obama's election also immediately highlighted the half-empty glass of the U.S. Senate, whose African American membership dropped back to zero out of 100 seats on his resignation to assume the presidency. The subsequent appointment of an African American, Roland Burris, to fill the vacant seat brought that figure back to a meager 1 percent even though about 12 percent of the U.S. population is black. Strikingly, Burris was still only the fourth African American U.S. senator since the end of Reconstruction in 1877 (although, oddly enough, the third to fill the same Senate seat from Illinois). The parallel figure among the 50 U.S. governors was just two African Americans (4%). One of these, David Paterson of New York, ascended to the office from the lieutenant governorship, leaving Deval Patrick of Massachusetts as just the second elected black governor since Reconstruction. Latinos were about at 14 percent of the population (although only 9% of the electorate because of lower rates of citizenship), but there were just two Latino U.S. senators (2%) and one U.S. governor (2%). Additionally, Asians and Pacific Islander Americans (API), at roughly 6 percent of the population (and 3% of the electorate), fared about the same as Latinos with two API senators (both from the majority nonwhite state of Hawaii) and one governor. Native Americans, representing 1 percent of the population, could claim not a single senator or governor.

Thus, while ethnic and racial minorities do, in contrast to the past, hold a few major offices, in a country that is a bit under 70 percent white, 95 percent of U.S. senators and 96 percent of U.S. governors were white in 2009. In brief, then, ethnic and racial minorities clearly continue to face formidable obstacles to winning office at the state-wide level. Lower offices, with smaller constituencies that are more likely to have large concentrations of minorities than any state could muster, are somewhat more amenable to minorities. With roughly 30 percent of the U.S. population being nonwhite, we might expect to find about 130 nonwhite House members, but the actual figure was barely half that, 69, or 16.5 percent, encompassing 41 (11%) black, 23 (5%) Latino, 5 (1%) Asian American, and 1 (0.4%) Native American. The figures at the state and city levels vary more, with some minorities making major gains in offices, such as big-city mayoralties and state legislatures, but the overall pattern remains one of significant underrepresentation.

This pattern of underrepresentation at the national level is all the more pronounced in the case of women, who actually represent some-what more than half the population and of the electorate. The glass-half-empty, glass-half-full analogy again works here. Phrased one way, it could be claimed that women's representation in the U.S. Senate rose 850 percent over the period 1993–2009, a tremendous rate of growth but one that depends on the reality that, until 1993, there had never been more than two female senators at any one time. The period since 1993 has also seen three female secretaries of state and one attorney general, all positions that had never before been held by women, as well as the first female Speaker of the House in Nancy Pelosi and the first truly competitive female presidential candidate in Hillary Rodham Clinton. Still, in 2009, women represented roughly about one in six high-level elected officials, including 17 (17%) female senators, 8 (16%) governors, and 74 (17%) members of the House. By this measure, women are even more underrepresented than ethnic and racial minorities in high elected office. Women of color, at about 16 percent of the population, are at a further disadvantage, with no senators or governors and just 21 (5%) of the House, including 12 black, 7 Latina, and 2 Asian American congresswomen. In the entire sweep of U.S. history, only one woman of color—former one-term Senator Carol Moseley Braun of Illinois, an African American—has ever been elected to the U.S. Senate, and none have held a state governorship (although the Commonwealth of Puerto Rico has had an elected female governor).

Underrepresentation of ethnic and racial minorities and of women is, of course, found throughout the world, and no country has found a way to completely or perfectly balance its representative institutions. PR systems help foster at least some degree of office holding by even disfavored or disadvantaged minorities; for instance, the Arab Israeli parties hold 7 of 120 seats in that country's Knesset, and a party representing the marginalized Roma people (Gypsies) is part of the governing coalition in Bulgaria. Some other countries have gone further; in New Zealand, several parliamentary seats are set aside to ensure a voice for the indigenous Maori peoples, while India reserves seats for the "scheduled castes," better known in the West as "Untouchables." Perhaps no democratic nation, however, has gone further to reorganize its entire political structure to ensure broad representation and self-determination than the small but deeply divided state of Belgium, which has emerged as a paradigmatic example of what political scientists have termed "consociational democracies."

CASE STUDY: REPRESENTATION IN BELGIUM

PR and multiparty systems, along with the parliamentary power-sharing coalitions that are the natural outcome of such systems, can go a long way toward ensuring wide-ranging power sharing. But a few deeply divided states have taken the further steps to ensure extraordinarily wide-ranging participation, representation, decentralization, and self-determination. Perhaps the most successful of these consociational democracies has been Switzerland (discussed further in Chapter 8) with its exceptional decentralization of power, its frequent use of the public referendum, and its unique seven-member collective executive. But another small western European state, Belgium, has likewise gone to unparalleled lengths to try to heal the tensions between its major ethnic and linguistic groups while also not neglecting the gender divide by proactively promoting the election of women to higher office.

Belgium has the misfortune to be situated at one of the major historical, cultural, and linguistic divides in western Europe. Those in the southern region of Wallonia speak French and identify with Gallic and Mediterranean European cultures and societies, while the more numerous residents of the northern region of Flanders speak the Flemish variant of the Dutch language linked to Germanic and Scandinavian civilization—a fundamental and defining division that has caused generations of tensions and conflict. Traditionally, the French speakers formed the political and economic elite, subjugating and alienating the Flemish. In World War II, significant numbers in Flanders collaborated with the German occupiers, further exacerbating the split in the postwar era.

With rising industrial strength and demographic numbers, the Flemish reasserted themselves in the 1960s, going so far as to refuse to speak French and to propose self-determination and even secession. By the 1990s, the viability of Belgium as a single state seemed in grave doubt, but faced with such centrifugal forces, the Belgians turned to consensus rather than conflict by constructing the world's most layered—and complex—system of federalism, with no fewer than six separate layers of overlapping, shared, and dispersed authority.[1]

The two lowest layers would be familiar to any student of federalism: local governments, called communes, which were organized within 10 historically based provinces. Like local and provincial governments everywhere, these two levels concern themselves largely with day-to-day issues such as social services, police services, sanitation, and roadways. However, the Belgians have added three additional layers that are not arranged in the usual hierarchical arrangement but rather described as parallel levels of authority each with its own distinctive "competencies." The federal government largely manages the organs of the state itself, such as the military, the diplomatic corps, and the national treasury. Three regional governments—in Flanders, Wallonia, and the Brussels capital region—take responsibility for territorial concerns, such as energy, agriculture, and transportation. Then, in a complete innovation, the country created three language-based community governments—for French speakers, Flemish speakers, and a tiny group of German speakers in the east—to deal with cultural affairs, language policy, education, and family policy. To top matters off, Belgium is a founding member and enthusiastic participant in the European Union, even hosting its capital, thus adding an increasingly important sixth supranational level of authority.

The complexity of this six-tiered system is dizzying, but this diffusion of power, representation, and self-determination appears to have worked. Faced with comparable ethnic divisions, other European countries have found themselves in far worse circumstances, such as the protracted sectarian conflict of Northern Ireland or the ruthless centralization of power and suppression of minorities of Franco-era

Spain or the outright genocidal "ethnic cleansing" of the former Yugoslavia. But Belgium has persisted as a peaceful and prosperous—if at times tense and polarized—democracy. If a political division does yet come to pass, it will almost certainly be peaceful and orderly.

In the meantime, the spirit of consociational democracy has also extended to another major social division, gender, which cuts across all ethnic and linguistic groupings and thus cannot be addressed using geographic schemes. Fortunately, another mechanism is available to Belgium since it, like most parliamentary countries with PR systems, uses party lists to allocate legislative seats. Thus, if an electoral district has a population that allows it to send 10 members to Parliament, each party contesting the election would create a rank-ordered listing of candidates; if that party were to win 20 percent of the vote, the top two names on its list would win a seat. Along with a number of other European parliamentary democracies, Belgium has taken advantage of this system to require men and women to be equally represented on these party lists—including in the two top slots. Today, the proportion of women in the Belgian lower house of Parliament is 35 percent—placing it among the top 10 in the world, with twice as many women legislators than in the United States.

As with most of the prosperous countries of western Europe, Belgium is rapidly becoming a far more diverse county because of mass immigration. The unique status of Brussels as the capital of the European Union and a global hub has contributed to this diversity, but most of the change has come through an influx of people from Muslim countries, such as Morocco and Turkey, who originally arrived as temporary guest workers but who have stayed on and had Belgian-born children. The politics of immigration have not been as heated in Belgium as in some other countries, including the famously tolerant Netherlands next door, but frictions persist, and few Muslims have yet won elected offices. Time will tell whether its consociational arrangements will allow Belgium to continue to be better positioned than some of its neighbors to manage the challenge of increasing diversity.

ENHANCED REPRESENTATION
IN THE UNITED STATES?

The Belgian case study highlights two principal strategies for remedying patterns of underrepresentation: the creation of new jurisdictional structures and the mandating of quotas for public offices.

The lessons to be drawn for the United States are, however, ambiguous at best. To some extent, the United States already employs some of these strategies, and it is not easy to envision how further constitutionally and legally based changes could be enacted.

Federalism, of course, has long been a key feature of American democracy—indeed, the concept itself was basically invented by the founders at the Constitutional Convention of 1787. And federalism does already provide a great deal of self-governance to individual states, and this may be particularly important for geographically atypical states such as Hawaii and Alaska as well as socially distinctive states such as New Mexico and Florida. Robust devolution of home rule to counties and municipalities also further enhances the ability of some distinctive populations to govern themselves, whether in great metropolises, small border communities, rural villages, or suburban townships.

The Belgian example goes much further, however, and its "community-level" governments would suggest an additional layer of representation overlapping and/or parallel to such geographically based jurisdictions. With regard to race and ethnicity, the obvious categories would be those of the so-called ethnoracial pentagon, or the five officially recognized ethnic and racial groupings in the United States: African American (black), Asian and Pacific Islander, Hispanic/Latino, Native American, and European American (white). These categories have been used since the mid-1960s for the purpose of the enforcing civil rights laws relating to areas such as voting rights and antidiscrimination statutes as well as social goals, such as school integration and affirmative action. Hypothetically, each of these groups could be endowed with control over a variety of types of cultural and social policy, as are the three linguistic communities in Belgium.

Something rather like this, in fact, already exists for one part of the ethnoracial pentagon in the form of Native American tribal sovereignty. Within the boundaries of American Indian reservations, Native Americans elect their own tribal governments with responsibility for a broad range of policies and programs, including family law, land use and zoning, law enforcement, court systems, and social services. Although little noted by people who are not Native Americans and not always fully respected by federal and state governments, tribal governments provide Native Americans with crucial tools to govern their own communities and cultivate their languages and cultures. However, Native American sovereignty is a unique product of historical development rather than a circumstance that is replicable for other groups. Further, Native American sovereignty also thrives in practice because large numbers of Native Americans continue to live on or near tribal lands, creating heavy demographic concentrations—one that, given the endemic poverty of many of these regions, is not always to their benefit.

The prospect of attempting to construct a comparable level of communal authority for other ethnic and racial groupings raises numerous theoretical and practical objections, but three of the most important may suffice to rule out this as a viable reform. First, many subgroups within existing panethnic categories are as different as they are similar. In particular, the Asian and Pacific Islander category includes ethnic groups as diverse as Japanese and Hmong, Filipino and Pakistani, and Chinese and Sri Lankan. Comparable, if somewhat less pronounced, differences exists as well for blacks, whites, and Hispanics. Native Americans likewise do not form a single national community but rather are organized into approximately 560 completely separate tribal groupings. Thus, promoting community-level self-governance for ethnic and racial groupings would require either subordinating these dramatic differences or creating hundreds or thousands of separate microjurisdictions, all to dubious or even counterproductive ends.

Second, formally recognizing ethnic and racial communities would run counter to more than half a century of societal progress in desegregation and integration. Even if such reforms were impelled by progressive goals, they could easily end up reverting to older patterns of ethnic and racial separatism. Indeed, one of the thornier critiques of programs such as affirmative action has been that they may end up reinforcing the very group identities and boundaries the grip of which they seek to weaken. And if ethnic and racial groupings are to be given special rights of self-determination, could these long be denied to whites, whose numbers and affluence would merely reinforce their position as a hegemonic group?

Finally, the challenge of determining group membership would probably be insuperable. Native American tribes have long-standing policies for determining the "blood quantum," or percentage of ancestry, needed for tribal membership. Traditionally in the United States, the white establishment perpetuated the "one-drop" rule in which one drop of minority (in particular African) ancestry rendered a person nonwhite. Other regimes—notably odious ones such as Nazi Germany and apartheid-era South Africa—have used pseudoscientific methods to assign racial categories. In an increasingly mixed and diverse society, the only viable approach would be to allow individual self-determination. But what of those who preferred to belong to no category or to more than one category or whose families and communities were of such mixed racial and ethnic composition that they could not imagine themselves part of any one group?

What, then, of the second strategy for promoting minority representation: the mandating of quotas for underrepresented groups such as women or ethnic and racial minorities? First, the word "quota," used in the international context, has toxic associations in the United States because of the ongoing debate over affirmative action. So-called rigid quotas, in which a set number of seats in a university class or in a workplace are reserved solely for women or minorities regardless of their qualifications, were ruled unconstitutional in the United States in the *Bakke* case of 1978. More recently, courts have, barely, continued to allow "set-asides" in which race, ethnicity, or gender can be factored into decisions in educational admissions or hiring, particularly when they promote the nebulous concept of "diversity." It is conceivable that the concept of set-asides could be extended to public office holding, although it is far from clear that contemporary courts would be amenable to such a dramatic expansion of the role of affirmative action in the political sphere at the same time that they are narrowing its role in education and employment; this would most likely require a constitutional amendment.

Were the United States to adopt a PR electoral system, as discussed in Chapter 1, it would be possible to use party lists to mandate parity for male and female candidates as well as to promote minority candidates. Such a reform has actually been discussed in Canada, one of the few other established democracies to use the single-member plurality system. The introduction of PR would also promote the emergence of new parties, some of which might have an explicit gender or ethnoracial identity. Even more important, the growth of new parties would occur mainly on the left of the political spectrum, which is underrepresented by the current two-party system and which also disproportionately includes women and minorities.

Before the adoption of PR, however, it is hard to construct a legally enforceable path to ensuring higher levels of representation. Since voters choose party nominations via primary election as well as officeholders via general elections, the only way to guarantee particular gender or ethnic/racial outcomes would be to somehow limit the choices of voters or to override their decisions—certainly two outcomes that would curtail rather than promote democracy.

It seems clear, then, that the promotion of women and minorities in elected office in the United States will need to come more from voluntary steps originating within society rather than resulting from legally enforced mandates. A number of such initiatives already exist to increase the number of women and minorities at every stage of the "pipeline," the term often used to describe the process by which people enter and then advance through the ranks of political office holding. One major example of such a strategy is provided by The White House Project (http://www.thewhitehouseproject.org), which focuses on promoting women as engaged citizens and holders of public office up to and including the White House. Through seminars, conferences, training, mentoring, and related activities, the organization advances a spectrum of activities, including simple voter registration, participation in campaigns and political party activities, seeking nominations and running in general elections, and advancing from local to state to federal office holding.

The parties can also, on a voluntary basis, do much to promote the participation of women and minorities, as revealed by a closer examination of the pattern of growth in the number of women in the U.S. Senate. Between the 102nd Congress (1991–93) and the 111th Congress (2009–11), the number of female U.S. senators increased from 2 to 17 for an average increase of 1.7 seats per Congress. At this rate, it would not be until the 132nd Congress convenes in 2053 that women senators would reflect the female percentage of the electorate (54%). However, adding a partisan dimension to this analysis is revealing. In 1992, there was one woman Democratic senator and one woman Republican senator, but by 2009 there were 13 female Democrats and 4 female Republicans in the Senate, meaning that the Democrats have added women as senators more than *three times faster* than the Republicans. (The figures in the Senate are even more pronounced regarding ethnic and racial minorities: of the six senators of color [all male], five [84%] were Democrats.) On some levels, it comes as no surprise that women and minorities are disproportionately Democrats given the strong preference of nearly all minority groups (Cuban Americans excepted) for that party, along with the lesser but still important skew of women toward the Democratic Party. However, the advances made by women in the Democratic Party have also been due to a far greater commitment both ideologically and institutionally by the Democratic Party to advance all members of its electoral base.

At the same time, demographic trends are also on the side of enhanced participation by women and minorities. The nonwhite percentage of the population has dropped from more than 80 percent in 1980 to under 70 percent in 2010, and the gap in income and education between minorities and whites—and even more markedly between women and men—has narrowed considerably during that same time period. Women and minorities today represent more than two-thirds of all voters and are also an increasingly important presence in the professional ranks, such as law and business, from which political officeholders are often drawn. The U.S. party system proved adept for many generations at electing white men to office when they wielded the most social authority and economic clout. That same flexibility and adaptiveness can also be applied to an increasingly multicultural America.

SYNOPSIS

Desirability: 4

A basic tenet of democracy is that every adult citizen should have the opportunity to participate in governing. To the extent that an electoral process systematically blocks certain individuals from holding office or marginalizes certain groups from equal competition, proactive reforms are needed. Fortunately, there has been notable progress in the diversification of officeholders in the United States from the former near monopoly of white Protestant men. Yet women and minorities remain badly underrepresented on many fronts, particularly in powerful statewide offices, such as governorships and Senate seats.

Practicability: 2

The promotion of women and minority candidates is an idea much easier said than done in part because attempts to promote particular candidates quickly run into conflict with the equally important principle that voters should be free to choose whomever they wish as their representatives. The remedies presented in the case study on Belgium are not ones that could be plausibly adapted to the United States, at least not unless and until a system of proportional representation were enacted in the United States. Although sweeping, comprehensive reforms would not be very practicable, much could be done on the societal front and within the political parties to make greater efforts to support candidacies that might otherwise falter.

Plausibility: 3

Taken together, women and minorities already represent a significant majority of the U.S. population and electorate as well as a steadily, if slowly, increasing percentage of officeholders, political activists, and others with clout in American society. As diversity grows within the halls of power, there is likely to be a reinforcing effect in which further opportunities are enhanced for women and for ethnic and racial minorities. Concentrated efforts, however, will be needed to accelerate the pace of change to more accurately reflect the reality of the twenty-first-century U.S. population.

CHAPTER 7

Introduce Compulsory Voting

Highlighting Ideas from Brazil

Broad, engaged political participation—an essential feature of any flourishing democracy—can be thought of as having both "supply" and "demand" dimensions, with supply referring to the choices offered by the system and demand to the intensity with which the population participates in the system. The reforms outlined in the previous five chapters could go a long way toward enhancing the supply of choices offered by the political system. PR and runoff elections would allow the electoral choices of a larger portion of the population to be translated into political office holding. A multiparty system would broaden the range of voters who are able to find parties that reflect their own views. A shortened, streamlined political process, without an Electoral College in presidential elections, could prevent alienation from the system and curb the excessive influence of "monied" interests.

All these reforms, taken collectively, could go far in terms of promoting voter turnout. Indeed, in countries that employ many of these electoral features, voters show up at the polls in strikingly higher numbers. Most established democracies routinely see 80 percent or more of their eligible voters cast a ballot. For example, in a study of 29 national elections held around the year 2000, 19 had voter turnout rates above 70 percent. With 51.2 percent turnout in 2000, the United States ranked twenty-eighth, ahead only of Switzerland. Not coincidentally, the countries in positions 26 and 27, Canada and the United Kingdom, are the other major countries that do not use PR and/or a runoff system and that, as a result, do not have robust multiparty systems.[1]

It is noteworthy that voter turnout in the United States, relative to 2000, increased about 9 percentage points in 2004 and 12 percentage points in 2008. Indeed, 2008 saw the highest turnout since 1968, mostly because voters saw that the stakes were high and because the system appeared to deliver a real, substantive choice between candidates and parties as well as a historic first in Barack Obama. But it remains to be seen if this higher level of engagement can be sustained or whether it will remain subject to the ups and downs of the political process.

In order to consolidate this increase, there are a number of fairly easy institutional steps that could be readily adapted from practice in other countries. Government agencies could bear more of the burden of registering new voters and reregistering those who move to new addresses instead of leaving this mostly to the individual. Election Day could be a holiday or else moved to a weekend to make it easier to get to the voting booth. Polls could be kept open longer, either with extended evening hours or even through an entire 24-hour period. With due regard for concerns about fraud, mail-in and even Internet-based voting could be promoted.

Americans are also particularly susceptible to "voter fatigue" since, because of the combination of federalism and the separation of powers, elections in the United States are far more frequent than in most other countries. To take but one extreme example, residents of New York City were asked to go to the polls 23 times in the decade between 2000 and 2009, more than twice a year on average. In addition to national primaries and general elections in 2000, 2004, and 2008 (eight times, including special presidential primaries in 2004 and 2008), there were gubernatorial primary and congressional elections in 2002, 2006, and 2010 (six times) and New York City local primary and general elections in 2001, 2003, 2005, and 2009 (nine times, including a Democratic primary runoff in 2001).[2] A further burden is added by the sheer complexity of these ballots, with collectively more than 100 candidates running for more than a dozen different offices at various legislative, executive, and judicial offices along with complicated state and local ballot questions.

While there are steps that can be taken to shorten and simplify the electoral process, it may be that even the panoply of reforms outlined would not be enough to raise voter turnout rates to the norms seen in other democracies. Some of these countries do, however, have another rather controversial arrow in their quiver: compulsory voting.

CASE STUDY: COMPULSORY VOTING IN BRAZIL

While provisions for compulsory voting can be found in various countries around the world, the greatest regional concentration by far is in Latin America. In fact, every Central and South American country besides Colombia, Nicaragua, and Venezuela has some provision for compulsory voting, although these provisions vary greatly. Some, such as El Salvador and Costa Rica, simply have a basic statement of principle in their constitutions stating that voting is a right and a responsibility of citizenship but do not have specific laws mandating electoral participation. Others have laws, but these either provide no penalty, as in Costa Rica; go unenforced, as in Honduras; or provide only a minimal penalty, such as a fine of 220 pesos (less than $10.00) in Uruguay. One outlier in terms of both legislation and enforcement has been Brazil, which, alongside Australia and Belgium, has the world's strictest and most strictly enforced compulsory voting rules.[3]

Although the vast majority of countries do *not* have compulsory voting rules, where they do exist they are often introduced at the same time that a more democratic constitution is promulgated or when there is a major expansion of the right to vote, attempting to shore up democratic principles with democratic practices. At other times, when parties with strong popular support from the poorer segments of society win control of government, they attempt to cement their power by ensuring continued high rates of turnout. More cynically, authoritarian governments have sometimes introduced, maintained, or enforced such compulsory voting laws as a way to give the impression of broad popular support while rigging the election itself. In the case of Brazil, the provision was first introduced in the 1930s alongside women's suffrage, in part to ensure that women would indeed participate. However, the democratic potential of the compulsory voting statutes remained dormant for most of the next half century because of long stretches of dictatorship.

With the reestablishment of a more stable democracy in the 1980s, however, the case reemerged for a mandate for broad citizen participation. The arguments in favor of compulsory voting are fairly straightforward and usually framed in terms of the negative effects of low voter turnout. By mandating electoral participation, regimes are able to maximize their democratic legitimacy and also to ensure a base of support among the entire body of eligible voters. At least in theory, such mass voting cancels out some of the advantages of interest-group organization and big-money interests as well as the inertia of incumbents.

Compulsory voting is also intended to foster civic pride and engagement and to encourage participation in other forms of political activity.

In Brazil, all literate citizens between the ages of 18 and 70 are required to vote, with 16- and 17-year-olds, those over 70, and the illiterate also having the optional right to vote. Those who can demonstrate that they were ill or out of the country can win an exemption, but this takes at least as much work as voting itself, thus reducing the number of shirkers. Brazil uses electronic touch screens for all elections, and although it has a complex multiparty system, voting is facilitated by the use of video clips alongside written instructions and numbers with photos for candidates so that even those unable to read can participate. The government goes to exceptional lengths to make voting booths widely accessible, even in the most remote areas of the Amazonian jungle, and Election Day is a national holiday marked by festivities throughout the country.

Voters in Brazil receive a *título eleitoral*, a card proving that they had cast a ballot in the previous election. Those unable to produce their card or a waiver are ineligible to take professional exams, are unable to secure loans or conduct some other banking transactions, cannot win government jobs or run for office, are excluded from state-run educational institutions, are denied exemptions for military service, and/or are refused issuance of government documents, including passports. First-time offenders may in practice only receive a small fine, equivalent to a portion of the minimum wage, but penalties escalate over time.[4]

The results, at least in terms of voter turnout, are strong but not absolute, with turnout rates hovering around 80 percent. However, given that about 30 percent of eligible voters are illiterate and thus exempt from the voting requirement, the statistics are somewhat more impressive, but Brazil remains only in the middle of the pack of democracies in terms of turnout. In practice, the actual level of enforcement appears to be hit or miss, pointing in part to limits in the bureaucratic capacities of the Brazilian state and in part to other priorities for law enforcement in one of the world's most violent countries. Compulsory voting laws clearly can help increase overall turnout but are not a panacea for full participation.

COMPULSORY VOTING IN THE UNITED STATES?

If one major goal of a democracy is to involve as many citizens as frequently and as meaningfully as possible, then compulsory voting would appear to be a proactive step that government could take to promote citizen engagement. Of course, one clear lesson of the wave of democratization over the past half century has been that voting does not in itself create democratic conditions in a simple or straight-forward manner.

Even authoritarian regimes can demand that their citizens cast a bal-lot, but the results can hardly be considered democratic if there is no real choice among candidates or parties, if the final outcome is rigged, or if elected offices hold no real power. Even the highly undemocratic Soviet Union used to stage such so-called acclamatory elections as sup-posed evidence of the support of the population for the Communist Party. In the run-up to the U.S. invasion of Iraq in 2003, the Iraqi government declared that they had held an election with 100 percent of the vote going to President Saddam Hussein—evidence either that Saddam had become completely delusional or that he had no regard for the intelligence of the rest of the world or perhaps both.[5]

While such concerns do not particularly apply to the United States, other objections to compulsory voting do arise. The most fundamen-tal is constitutional: that the First Amendment's freedom of "speech" prevents the government from forcing citizens to express a political view by means of voting. This objection in itself does not withstand much scrutiny since it is clear that government may coerce *actions* of all types, such as payment of taxes, participation in jury duty, and sup-port for national defense via military conscription. As long as an indi-vidual would have the option to cast a blank or "spoiled" ballot, no political opinion has been expressed. For those relatively few whose genuine political or religious views would be violated by even this level of participation, a conscientious objector status could be allowed that would be time consuming and complex enough to dissuade all but the most ardently committed nonvoters.

A related ideological dimension, however, raises deeper concerns. A powerful strand of the American political tradition is that of "negative liberty," or the "right to be left alone." In the other examples used in this chapter, government coercion may be justified by the reality that without payment of tax revenues, the government could not create a budget for essential activities. Likewise, without a sufficient number of jurors, article III of the U.S. Constitution, and the Fifth, Sixth, and Seventh amendments, separate and collective guarantees of a quick and public trial by one's peers could not be ensured. And, at times, national defense needs have gone beyond the ability of an all-volunteer army to deliver. Conversely, low voter turnout does not impact the ability of an election to deliver a winner; in theory, any election by two candidates can be decided by the participation of just three voters.

The focus of this debate, then, must be on whether coercing all or nearly all eligible voters (perhaps exempting the elderly or infirm) would somehow decisively improve the quality of democracy itself. In this regard, there are compelling arguments on both sides. Proponents of compulsory voting argue that regular participation in the voting process fosters civic education and engagement and that elections involving a greater proportion of the electorate produce governments that have greater legitimacy. Likewise, more voters will subsequently have a greater sense of "ownership" in the government, promoting further engagement in other forms of political life. Compulsory voting might also reduce the demands placed on parties and candidates to conduct get-out-the-vote activities, enabling them to spend less money while concentrating more on policy-related campaigning.

On the other hand, opponents of compulsory voting may point, indelicately, to the computer-science maxim GIGO: garbage in, garbage out. They would contend that simply compelling mass participation in no way promotes high-quality outcomes and would in fact bring citizens into the political process who are poorly informed, uninterested, and even resentful. These new voters may cast meaningless ballots or be swayed by shallow demagogic appeals. At worst, a sudden influx of first-time voters could destabilize the political system, at least in the short run.

Compulsory voting is unquestionably a viable approach to enhancing democratic participation but may be better left as a last resort rather than the front line of offense in the United States. Surely, enhanced civic education in schools and improved communications about the electoral process could on their own go a long way toward demystifying the voting process and promoting participation. If compulsion were to be used, it would perhaps be most justifiable for the first one or two elections after a citizen reaches the age of 18. Since voting is, in part, an acquired habit, early compulsion might achieve increases in participation across the life span. An alternative to compulsion could be incentivization, such as a tax rebate or a voucher for some government service, such as a passport fee. (The suggestion that all voters be entered into a nationwide lottery, however, is likely taking things too far.) Other, simpler reforms to ease the burden of registration, to make Election Day a holiday, and to allow mail and Internet balloting would also carry far fewer potential complications than compulsory voting.

But most of all, as noted at the outset of this chapter, it would be much better for voters to *want* to vote rather than to be forced to vote. A shorter, more streamlined process with PR, runoff elections, and multiple parties might well, on its own, naturally raise voter turnout rate in the United States to levels more commonly found in the established democracies.

SYNOPSIS

Desirability: 1

The goal of compulsory voting—increased and sustained democratic participation—is a highly worthy one. But the mechanism of compulsory voting would treat the symptoms rather than the causes of low voter turnout. Under ideal circumstances, compulsory voting might help increase and enhance civic engagement, but there are better ways to engage voters short of compulsion. Government coercion of unwilling and uninformed voters puts the cart before the horse, and while it would undoubtedly increase the quantity of participation, its effect on quality is uncertain at best.

Practicability: 5

Laws making voting compulsory could be passed fairly easily by ordinary legislative means in state lawmaking bodies and in Congress. If carefully crafted, such laws should pass constitutional muster with regard to First Amendment issues, such as by allowing blank or spoiled ballots for those who do not wish to express a view or through opt-out provisions for true conscientious objectors comparable to those that require students to attend school but not to pledge allegiance to the flag while there.

Plausibility: 3

If existing officeholders designed and enacted compulsory voting laws that they believed would help entrench them in power, then such laws would not have the desired effect or could in fact backfire. Of course, if those in power saw compulsory voting as likely to diminish their standing or force them to address issues they would prefer not to, they would be less likely to support it of their own accord. As for popular support, given that many individuals actively seek to avoid other forms of government-mandated activity, such as paying taxes, serving on juries, and being drafted into the military, adding a new category of compulsory voting would seem unlikely to generate much support.

CHAPTER 8

Institute a System of National Referenda

Highlighting Ideas from Switzerland

To many, the purest form of democracy would seem to be "direct democracy," in which all eligible voters—ideally reflecting universal suffrage among adult citizens—have the opportunity to vote on all major issues of public policy. The world's first great democracy, Athens during the age of Pericles in the fifth century BCE, operated as such, while direct democracy via the "New England town meeting" is within the living memory of some Americans.

The seeming logic and simplicity of direct democracy, however, quickly runs afoul of two complicating factors. First, as population size increases, it becomes exponentially harder to coordinate the actions of citizen assemblies, and the risk of the "mob mentality" quickly arises. Even in ancient Athens, the highly restricted electoral franchise of which never exceeded 30,000 male citizens, direct democracy proved unwieldy and demanding, involving assemblies of as many as 6,000 people and meetings as often as 40 times in a single year, requiring vast amounts of citizens' time.

Yet Athens at least had the benefit of being a premodern, scientifically primitive society. The complexity of societies tends to increase dramatically over time because of such processes as scientific modernization, social dehomogenization, economic differentiation, and mass concentration in urban areas, and thus the degree of technical expertise and specialization needed to produce laws becomes impossible to secure at the level of the mass public. Even in the most sparsely populated areas of New England, town meetings have long since become mostly public forums for discussion rather than official decision making, sometimes with once-a-year votes on some budgetary matters.

These two primary factors—increasing population and the need for specialization—have made it inevitable that the principal form of democratic organization would inevitably involve the election of government officials to act on behalf of the public. Such representative democracy is, in fact, essentially the only form of democratic governance above the level of small associations and activist groups. Of course, under representative democracy, the people do not lose their political voice; not only does there continue to be periodic elections, but the will of the public can be channeled through interest groups, public opinion, and protest politics as well. Still, some critics yearn today for the seeming purity of direct democracy, looking back fondly to historical precedents or sometimes to the country in which direct democracy most fully persists: Switzerland.

CASE STUDY: NATIONAL REFERENDA IN SWITZERLAND

Among the democracies of the world, perhaps none is more anomalous than Switzerland. It is by far the world's oldest democracy, founded in 1291, and, almost uniquely in Europe, it has never been never subject to rule by a monarchy or aristocracy. Rather, the great natural boundaries of the Alps insulated the small valley towns and cantons (provinces) of Switzerland not only from outside expansionist powers but also, to an extent, from one another. This localization has been further enhanced by the presence of three different major linguistic communities speaking dialects of German, French, and, to a lesser degree, Italian and by a roughly even split between Protestants and Catholics.

Located geographically in the very heart of Europe yet in some ways quite apart from it, Switzerland has remained scrupulously neutral, rejecting membership in both NATO and the European Union and joining the United Nations only in 2002. Its political institutions are also distinctive, most notably in a unique seven-person collective executive chosen by the legislature. Further, the seven seats are allocated through a voluntary "magic formula" that incorporates all the major ideological and ethnic groupings, with a low-key ceremonial presidency rotating among the seven members each year.

Swiss governance is also extraordinarily decentralized. Although technically a "federation" because the central government in Berne does retain final authority over such issue areas as foreign policy, defense, and monetary policy, most other authority resides with the 26 cantons. In this sense, Switzerland has retained many of the characteristics of a loosely knit "confederation" rather than a "federation" with a more robust central government, as in the United States. Indeed, the country was formally the called the Helvetic Confederation until 1848, and its Internet suffix remains ".ch," the initials for the French "Confédération hélvetique."

Yet perhaps the most distinctive political dimension of Swiss government is its frequent and extensive use of the referendum as a mechanism of direct democracy at both the national and the cantonal level. Most commonly, referenda are placed before the people by the government or may be initiated by a set number of citizens or cantons, covering nearly any issue. In 2008, for instance, a xenophobic measure was proposed by a right-wing party to allow local communities rather than the government to secretly determine whether to permit the naturalization of immigrants in their communities. The proposal was soundly defeated by the voters, but had it not been defeated, the government would have been bound to respect the results and cede this authority to the citizenry.

Citizens can also petition to reverse a law passed by the government; if this is successful, it becomes legally binding. Later in 2008, the Swiss voted to approve the government's liberalization of narcotics law but reversed the creation of a statute of limitations in crimes involving child pornography. Likewise, proposed amendments to the federal constitution must also be placed before the people, subject to a "double majority" of approval by more than 50 percent of the national population and more than half of the 26 cantons. In another controversial referendum in 2010, voters enacted a constitutional amendment ban the construction of minarets on mosques—symbols of the uneasy relationship between native Swiss and more recent Muslim immigrants. Finally, major international agreements require approval by the citizenry. It was through this mechanism that the Swiss finally joined the United Nations but also rejected participation in the European Union. Far more than in any other nation in the world, the Swiss citizenry retains direct and extensive power over government decision making.[1]

Most other democracies make use of the referendum under much more limited circumstances than Switzerland. For example, all constitutional amendments passed by the Parliament in Ireland and Japan require support by a simple majority of voters, while Australia employs the double majority system of voters and states. From time to time, governments in New Zealand and Italy turn to the voters for guidance on major decisions, with, for example, New Zealanders voting for a smaller legislature and Italians legalizing divorce and abortion.

Treaties of particular importance are also often placed before the voters; the decision to join the European Union was the occasion for majorities in Denmark and Sweden to say yes but Norway and Iceland to say no. Referenda may also be used in unique circumstances. Costa Rica rejected membership in a Central American Free Trade Agreement in 2007, while in Chile a referendum was used to make the epochal decision to end rule by the military in 1988. Yet of all the democracies in the world, there is one glaringly prominent exception: the United States has *never* held a national referendum and, indeed, lacks any mechanism for doing so.

NATIONAL REFERENDA IN THE UNITED STATES?

On initial examination, few potential reforms seem as clearly and genuinely democratic as the use of referenda. And in many U.S. states and cities, referenda are familiar in one form or another; referenda may be placed on ballots by government officials for public approval or rejection, or, through the collection of signatures, they may be put forward by citizens or groups themselves, a process usually differentiated by the term "citizen initiatives." Such referenda or initiatives may either seek to enact a regular piece of legislation or take the more far-reaching step of amending a state constitution or a city charter. (The related concept of the "recall" is perhaps better termed a type of "reverse election" in which an official is voted *out* of office before the end of a term.) Despite their intuitive appeal, referenda in practice often yield unpredictable and unfortunate results for a variety of reasons. In the United States, many of these problems can be clearly seen in California, the state with the widest and most high-profile use of referenda.

One problem is that referenda or initiatives do not simply "spring up" from nowhere; rather, they must garner sufficient interest and support to be placed on the ballot. Then there must be funds available to wage wide-scale publicity campaigns, seeking support for one side or the other via television, radio, direct mail, and other costly media. Thus, even when the voters speak directly, the political agenda is still being set by relatively well-organized and well-funded interest groups.

By law, referenda must be brief, must deal with only a single topic, and must yield a simple yes-or-no answer. Such brevity and straight-forwardness is necessary to ensure that the voters have an acceptably clear view of the issue. But it ensures that a referendum can, at best, be only a very blunt instrument of policymaking. By contrast, in the legislative process, it is possible for bills to be elaborate in scope and detail, to address interconnected issues, and to allow for amendments and compromise. Perhaps the foremost example would be the infamous "taxpayer revolt" of 1978 in California via Proposition 13, which capped property taxes statewide. Driven by the simple short-term economic incentive of lower tax bills, home owners overwhelmingly supported it. But Proposition 13 has haunted the state ever since, undermining the efficiency of the housing market and denying the state and localities a sufficient tax base and resulting in a compensatory hike in sales taxes. All of this had a regressive effect both economically and socially, with better-off property owners sheltering their assets but the poorer being deprived of access to adequate educational and other basic services.

Another issue is that under representative democracy, the various layers of representation and the system of checks and balances within government help ensure that minority interests are not entirely subject to the "tyranny of the majority." As such, legislative outcomes are relatively likely to embody a broad social and political consensus. On the other hand, referenda translate majority preferences in the rawest of forms into statute law or, more important, into constitutional law itself via the amendment process. It is thus not surprising that unpopular minority groups are often targeted. Among these have been undocumented immigrants (cut off from all services except emergency rooms by California's Proposition 187 in 1994), ethnic and racial minorities (who were denied affirmative action in employment by Proposition 209 in 1996), criminals (the "three-strikes rule" allowing lifetime incarceration for a third felony in Proposition 184 in 1994), and gay men and lesbians (whose right to marry was revoked via constitutional amendment by 2008's Proposition 8 in 2008).[2]

Of course, not all referenda result in harsh or socially retrogressive outcomes; in the 1990s, California voters also approved the medical use of marijuana, an increase in the minimum wage, and educational improvements. And those referenda that enact ordinary law are subject to review by the judiciary (which struck down, for example, Proposition 187). But, on the whole, the bias toward more socially and economically advantaged groups and against the disadvantaged is stark. Escalating the use of referenda to a national scale runs the risk of drastically magnifying the underlying problems into new areas, such as fundamental federal guarantees of civil liberties and civil rights, the conduct of foreign and military policy, and the national budget and deficit.

There are a few possible approaches to the problem of referenda. Some countries have created a special type of "advisory" or "consultative" referendum in which the results are not binding but simply meant to clarify the will of the people. These have been used, for example, in New Zealand, where the government periodically places broad issues before the population. The wording of the referenda is not detailed enough for those referenda to be considered laws in themselves, and in any case the concept of parliamentary supremacy in New Zealand means that the voters cannot compel the Parliament to act in a particular way. Of course, the results of nonbinding referenda would still be compelling and hard for politicians to ignore. But the battle may go to whichever side is better able to wage the propaganda war, and in the end it is not very clear how the result is different from a public opinion poll. If anything, a well-designed public opinion poll might actually be preferable to a nonbinding referendum because pollsters can reach into parts of the citizenry who might not turn out to vote but who nonetheless have a meaningful opinion on the issue at hand. Others have proposed randomly convening relatively small bodies of private citizens to deliberate, not unlike juries, over whether and in what form referenda might be proposed. (This concept of deliberative democracies is discussed further in Chapter 21 regarding the possibility of a constitutional convention.)

One final argument to address would be the idea that the best response to the problems of referenda would be "more referenda," including greater ease of access to the process for a broader range of people, just as civil libertarians argue that the best response to harmful speech is "more speech"—by which bad attitudes might be flushed out and confronted. But the use of referenda runs the risk of further complicating the process of voting and thus of driving up rates of voter nonturnout. Were ease of access to increase significantly and the number of referenda to rise, American voters might find it even more onerous to go to the polls; it is by no means a coincidence that the *only* established democracy whose voter turnout is consistently and significantly below that of the United States is Switzerland, the bastion of the referendum.

SYNOPSIS

Desirability: 1

More than perhaps any other potential reform discussed in this volume, national referenda represent a case in which an idea that is intuitively democratic turns out to be less so on closer scrutiny. There are compelling reasons that direct democracy is not practiced in any part of the world and that national referenda are used sparingly in most countries other than Switzerland. The potential for manipulation and demagoguery and the danger of the tyranny of the majority make the pitfalls of national referenda outweigh the benefits. However, there are potentially valid uses of nationwide votes for other purposes, such as to confirm a congressional removal of the president (see Chapter 9) and to ratify constitutional amendments (see Chapter 20).

Practicability: 2

Procedurally, Congress would be able to establish a process for nonbinding, advisory referenda by means of ordinary law; these could then be placed on ballots during ordinary elections. However, it is unclear how meaningful or useful such referenda would be, and a complex and far-reaching constitutional amendment would be required for national referenda to become an alternative path for the making of laws or, for that matter, overturning laws already passed by Congress.

Plausibility: 2

The many strong precedents set by the use of referenda in the states would make it relatively easy to adapt this concept to the national level. The crucial difference is that our national government has different domains of activity, including foreign and military policy, that are particularly unamenable to referenda. Since the adoption of referenda at the national level would directly undermine the authority of Congress, this idea is exceedingly unlikely to gain much traction absent a major public clamor, which does not appear particularly likely.

PART TWO

REFORMING AND REVITALIZING THE PRESIDENCY AND CONGRESS

Allow "Removal for Cause" of the President

Abolish the Vice Presidency

Hold Special Presidential Elections

Add Elected Officers to the Executive

Rein in the President's Legislative and Judicial Powers

Synchronize the Terms of Congress and the President

Weaken the Senate

Depoliticize the Creation of Congressional Districts

CHAPTER 9

Allow "Removal for Cause" of the President

Highlighting Ideas from Canada

Given that the first part of this book spent so much time talking about reforming how a president is selected, it may seem odd that the first topic of business in this part on the executive is how to undo the results of an election. However, both topics underscore the central significance and enormous power of the presidency. Just as it is crucial that a president be elected as democratically as possible, it is crucial that the nation not be saddled with an ineffective president for an excessive period of time. Indeed, American democracy would be much better off if the United States could replace its president for failures of policy or performance.

The immediate counterargument, of course, is that Congress *already* has the power to remove a president by a simple majority vote to impeach in the House and then a two-thirds majority vote following a trial to convict in the Senate. However, the U.S. Constitution explicitly states that a president can be impeached and removed only for "bribery, treason, or other high crimes and misdemeanors." Proposals at the Constitutional Convention to include "maladministration" as a reason for impeachment were quickly rejected in part because it was thought that Congress already might be too powerful relative to the fledgling office of president.[1]

As is well known, the narrow grounds permissible for impeachment did not in practice stop the Republican leadership of Congress from carrying out an impeachment process in 1998 and 1999. The impeachment was rooted in President Bill Clinton's sexual dalliance with a young White House intern and subsequent attempts to cover up the scandal. Even here, though, the official "cause" for impeachment was that

Clinton had committed perjury while under oath and then tried to obstruct justice. In reality, impeachment proceedings were wholly inappropriate in these circumstances given that no abuse of presidential power had occurred, and in the end Clinton was acquitted by the Senate. Still, the business of the country was sidetracked for a solid year.

The Clinton impeachment was, ultimately, a relative sideshow compared to the epic political opera of Richard Nixon's potential impeachment. From the break-in at the Watergate Hotel in June 1972 through Nixon's final boarding of a helicopter on the White House lawn in August 1974, the country was faced with a "long national nightmare" in the words of his successor, Gerald Ford. The scandal also nearly precipitated a constitutional crisis, most notably when Congress subpoenaed tapes that Nixon had made of conversations in the White House and the president refused, with the Supreme Court stepping in to break the deadlock. Democracy has broken down in some Latin American countries over lesser constitutional conflicts.

Over the course of nearly two years, multiple sources had also reported that Nixon was drinking heavily and behaving erratically. White House Chief of Staff Alexander Haig is said to have virtually been running the country as a "regent" of sorts. Years after the fact, James Schlesinger, who was the secretary of defense, revealed that he had issued a constitutionally questionable internal order that nuclear weapons could not be launched on the president's command without Schlesinger's approval. He even had an emergency plan for the army to remove Nixon from power should he be impeached but refuse to leave the White House.[2]

The Nixon example is the worst of the bunch, but numerous others come to mind. It became clear by the middle of his single term that Jimmy Carter was not up to the task of the world's most important job, but he remained ineffectually twisting in the wind at the Oval Office. President George W. Bush was all but fired by the American people, through their low poll numbers and overwhelming election of Democrats to Congress in the 2006 midterm elections, but remained in office his full eight years until January 20, 2009. Despite such rejection and although evidence of potential crimes abounded, the new Democratic majority in Congress refused to seriously address the question of impeachment, partly out of political calculation but also because of the arduousness of the process.

There is, it should be noted, another, much newer constitutional mechanism for removing the powers, although not the title, of a president. The Twenty-Fifth Amendment of 1967 allows the vice president to assume all executive authority in the new office of "acting president" in cases in which the president is "unable to discharge the powers and duties of his office." In practice, this provision has been briefly used only three times, when Ronald Reagan and George W. Bush were undergoing scheduled medical procedures. In these cases, the president transferred power on his own initiative and then reclaimed it within a few hours on recovery from anesthesia. More problematic under the Twenty-Fifth Amendment would be cases in which the president is unable to authorize the transfer of power, such as after a debilitating stroke or an assassination attempt. This provision requires the vice president to initiate the transfer, subject to a confirmatory vote by a majority of the officers of the cabinet. In part because this has the feel of a "palace coup," the one occasion on which the Twenty-Fifth Amendment unambiguously should have been invoked—the 1981 shooting that gravely wounded Ronald Reagan—it was not.

The Twenty-Fifth Amendment is potentially a very useful mechanism for replacing an ill or injured president but still not one that can effectively tackle the problem of a president who is incompetent or whose leadership is failing for other reasons. As usual, practices in other countries can shed light on the situation in the United States, in this case simply by looking northward.

CASE STUDY: REPLACING THE EXECUTIVE IN CANADA

When compared to American presidents, prime ministers have relatively little job security. In fact, there are three principal methods by which a prime minister—who has no fixed term office—can be replaced on short notice by a simple majority vote of just one house of the legislature. In Canada, two of these methods were exercised in the mid-2000s. The third method, one that is very rarely used in parliamentary democracies and never in Canadian history, also nearly occurred in 2008.

A prime minister, by definition, holds office only because he or she is the head of the majority party or a coalition of parties in the Parliament. (For a fuller explanation of the difference and similarities between a separation-of-powers and a parliamentary system, see Appendix 2 in this volume.) Should the leader of the party step aside—whether freely or under pressure from members of his or her party—the new party leader can become prime minister without a new election. Such a transition can take place at any time and for any number of reasons, whether they are personal, such as illness or scandal, or political, such as policy disagreements or electoral considerations.

In 2003, when Canadian Prime Minister Jean Chretien was essentially forced to step aside, he managed to do so more or less on his own timetable. Chretien had been prime minister for 10 years and leader of his Liberal Party for an additional three, a long period of time for any chief executive. A native French speaker, Chretien had deftly brokered the severe tensions between his home province of Quebec and the nine other Canadian provinces. He was also popular for effectively managing the nation's debt with the help of Finance Minister Paul Martin, who himself harbored aspirations for the prime ministership. After years in power, however, the Chretien government lost focus, energy, and most of all credibility in light of a scandal in which the Liberals diverted government funds to their own campaign coffers.

Aware that he could be deposed at any time, Chretien moved to set his own timetable, ceding the party leadership and thus the prime ministership to Martin in 2003. In Westminster-style parliaments, such a switch of leadership is not common, yet it is far from unheard of. A similar scenario played out in 2007 in Great Britain, where Tony Blair, aware that patience had been growing thin ever since he first committed British troops to Iraq, stepped aside in favor of his long-standing rival Gordon Brown. In fact, no less a figure than Margaret Thatcher was also forced out in this way in 1990, much more precipitously when she resigned after just a few days of pressure and under threat of almost certain removal by her Conservative Party. In all three cases, no new election was required for a new prime minister to be appointed.

The second major way for a prime minister to be removed is through a vote that signals that he or she has lost the support of a majority in the Parliament as a whole. Such was the case barely a year into the Paul Martin prime ministership in Canada. Martin inherited a thin parliamentary majority from Chretien, one that dropped below an outright majority after elections were held in 2004. For a time, the three other parties in the Parliament continued to allow Martin to lead a so-called minority government, an arrangement in which the largest party is allowed to govern but must negotiate all major issues on a case-by-case basis with the opposition. However, as more details about the campaign-financing scandal came to light (even though Martin was not personally implicated), Canadian legislators exercised the ultimate weapon of a parliamentary system for keeping the executive in line. They held a "vote of no confidence," in which more than 50 percent of Parliament withdrew their support from the Martin government, triggering an immediate new election.

The Liberals lost that election, and the next government was formed by Stephen Harper, leader of the Conservative Party. With only 124 of 308 seats, Harper lacked an outright majority but was also allowed to continue to cautiously lead a minority government. Hoping to earn a majority, Harper called a new election late in 2008 and made gains but still fell slightly short, and within a month the opposition grew unhappy with the Harper government's response to the then-unfolding global financial crisis. They then attempted the third—and quite rare—method for replacing a prime minister, namely, electing the Leader of the Opposition to form a new government *without* new elections. However, Harper countered with parliamentary maneuvers that ended up delaying the process long enough for the opposition pact to collapse, partly because public opinion seemed to be on his side.

"REMOVAL FOR CAUSE" OF THE U.S. PRESIDENT?

Transposed into the American system, the Canadian example does raise certain concerns. One obvious concern involves the theory of the separation of powers—that Congress should not have the power to bring down the president, who does not answer to Congress and who has an independent electoral mandate from the people, even in cases of maladministration. However, this argument does not bear scrutiny well. To begin, Congress and the presidency are by no means as hermetically sealed off from one another as a strict conception of "separation" might suggest, even with regard to filling the presidential office. For instance, the law of presidential succession is determined by Congress and actually places two congressional leaders—the Speaker of the House and the president pro tempore of the Senate—in the line of presidential succession right after the vice president. Similarly, in cases in which no one candidate has a majority in the Electoral College, the House selects the president and the Senate the vice president. When the vice presidency is vacant, Congress must confirm the president's choice to fill the position. Additionally, Congress already has the basic power of impeachment and removal and the ability to essentially define the term "high crimes and misdemeanors" as it sees fit. The problem, thus, is not a theoretical one regarding separation of powers—it is clearly not a problem for Congress to play a major role in determining who serves as president.

A rather different role involves the unique character of the presidential role, and, in particular, the president is not only a *head of government* as is a prime minister but also a *head of state*—the symbolic leader of the nation, both part of politics but in some ways above it as well. In the Canadian case, this would be akin to also removing not only a prime minister but also simultaneously the monarch, a possibility far more fraught with questions of national identity. Consider the parallel case of Australia, where there has long been strong popular sentiment to become a republic but where the voters have not yet been able to "pull the trigger." In the most recent Australian referendum, in 1999, the monarchy survived, although some do think it may not outlast the current sovereign, Elizabeth II. In Canada, however, there is little sentiment for abolition of the monarchy, which in fact is a feature that helps differentiate that country from the United States.

The conflation and excessive identification of the state itself with the person who happens to be the head of state can itself be a problem, as seen most notably in Latin America and Africa; this question is addressed further in Chapter 12. Suffice it to say here that the U.S. presidency resonates in American history, politics, and popular culture much more than any prime minister would. Even Winston Churchill is recalled more for his larger-than-life personality during World War II than for his high political office, which the British people snatched away from him in the election of 1945 before the war had even officially ended in the Pacific.

While, if more than a prime minister, the president is still far from a monarch deserving of untouchable tenure in office. Why should the fixed four-year term of the presidency be more sacrosanct than the actual substance of democracy, with failed presidents allowed to linger for years, accomplishing nothing constructive and in all likelihood doing even more harm? Certainly, simple issues of stability would make it unwise to have a president who could be *too* easily removed from office. Not all policies yield immediate dividends, and it would be counterproductive for a president to be hustled out of office if a military engagement led to a short-term setback or a key economic indicator failed to improve as quickly as might be desired. But could there be a happy medium, one that makes the U.S. president as vulnerable to being fired as any other American but not without a reasonable process and a fair hearing? How might a system be devised to replace a president more easily but not too easily and for a broader range of causes, as in Canada and other parliamentary systems?

Narrowly speaking, the textual change to the Constitution itself might be very minimal indeed: adding the word "maladministration" to article I might suffice, although the amending process would need to make clear the exact definition of the term. The process for carrying out the change, however, opens another crucial question: how can the president's valid electoral mandate not be reversed for purely partisan gain, and how can Congress be deterred from abusing such an important power? The key would seem to be either to create some costs that might give Congress pause or to create some new check on the Congress's ability to act unilaterally. Three possibilities are suggested by the experience of other democracies.

The first would be to directly adopt the Westminster parliamentary convention that a vote of no confidence triggers a new election not only for the executive but for legislature as well. In this way, a congressional majority that believed it was moving against a president on weak grounds or against strong popular opinion would be forced to think twice—today's congressional majority might not survive the quick new election. Yet the Clinton impeachment provides clear evidence that Congress can be petty and foolish, as do a panoply of other anecdotes. (The embarrassing 2003 renaming of "French fries" as "freedom fries" in the congressional cafeteria after France refused to invade Iraq comes to mind.) In 1998–99, the Republican leadership pressed on even though public opinion strongly opposed impeachment, the Republicans lost seats in the 1998 midterm elections, and their leader, Newt Gingrich, was forced to resign from the speakership and even his seat in the House (Gingrich's history of alleged extramarital liaisons did not help the matter).

A second possibility would be the system used in Germany called the "constructive vote of no confidence," in which the German chancellor can be removed by a simple majority vote of the Bundestag but only if they can agree on a replacement. Although this term is not used in Canada, this bears a similarity to what was proposed in 2008 by the opposition parties in Canada. Such an approach sets a high bar in that a majority of the Bundestag must agree on a new chancellor before bringing down the existing one. In the U.S. system, however, in which the president has an independent mandate from the people, it would be antidemocratic to sweep out a popularly elected president only to replace him or her with one appointed by Congress. Such an approach also genuinely would undermine the president's latitude for independent action under separation of powers and perhaps set the stage for a "de facto coup" in which a president is removed on spurious grounds by a power-seeking member of Congress from the opposing party. Certainly, Gingrich might have tried such a maneuver against Clinton when the Republicans took control of Congress in 1995, undoubtedly proposing himself as the new president. Yet Clinton went on a year later, in 1996, to handily defeat his congressionally based Republican rival, Senate Majority Leader Bob Dole. A variation on this theme, proposed by law scholar Sanford Levinson, among others, would be for only those members of Congress who belong to the president's party to select a replacement.[3] This would address the issue of a sudden change in party control but still not the question of the president's independent popular mandate. (In addition, this would work less well in the type of multiparty system proposed in Chapter 2.)

It would seem, then, that Congress itself should be checked in this process. One method would be to require supermajorities, such as three-fifths, two-thirds, or even three-quarters, in *both* houses. This would require a high level of bipartisan support for replacing the president but might also have the effect of making removal too difficult—much harder even than impeachment, even if the acceptable grounds were expanded to include "maladministration."

Another possibility would be to turn to the judiciary as a check on Congress. However, given that impeachment would be a political rather than a legal proceeding, this would not be in keeping with the role of the Supreme Court. Indeed, it could hasten the arrival of a constitutional crisis since it would compromise the ability of the courts to act as neutral arbitrators between Congress and the president, as they did during the Watergate scandal of 1974. Further, because federal judges are appointed rather than elected, they lack the democratic credentials required to overturn the results of a valid election.

Fortunately, there are two other sources of sovereign legitimacy recognized under the Constitution: the states and the people themselves. Either of these could be called on to confirm a simple majority vote of both houses of Congress to ask whether the president should be removed. A vote by 26 state legislatures or directly by a simple majority of the voters in a confirmatory vote could check Congress but also legitimize their judgment if the president really does deserve removal from office. There is also no strong reason that the sequencing could not be reversed. For example, a petition by some proportion of the states should be enough to trigger a presidential removal vote in Congress; in fact, such a move can already initiate a constitutional convention. A direct popular nationwide vote is certainly also plausible, although this could run afoul of some of the problems discussed in Chapter 8 with regard to national referenda. A few states allow a popular initiative to recall their governor, and the voters of the California did just that to the unpopular and ineffective Gray Davis in 2003. Similarly, the voters of Venezuela had the opportunity to remove president Hugo Chavez through a recall election in 2004, although they declined to do so.

And if—by whichever route—an unpopular, ineffectual, or corrupt president were to be removed from office, what should happen next? The obvious answer would be to follow the traditional route of succession by the vice president or beyond that down the existing line of presidential succession. However, for reasons to be explored more fully in the next chapter, the vice presidency itself is a deeply flawed institution. Further, succession to the presidency, except in a brief caretaker capacity, by anyone other than a person clearly elected to be president runs counter to the spirit of democracy. Rather, should the presidency be vacated—by some new removal procedure or for such traditional reasons as impeachment, death, or resignation—the best next step would be to hold a special election for a new four-year term, the topic of Chapter 11.

SYNOPSIS

Desirability: 5

The presidency is far too important to allow a clearly failed chief executive to remain in office. An ineffectual president, such as Jimmy Carter by 1979, or a manifestly incompetent one, such as George W. Bush by 2005, at best allows the country to drift and at worst can lead it in dangerously wrong directions. The inability of the U.S. system to effectively replace a failed executive is one of its greatest institutional vulnerabilities. Although the actual procedure for replacing a failed executive would need to be carefully devised, the basic principle would greatly promote governance that is both democratically accountable and effective.

Practicability: 4

This reform would require a constitutional amendment of varying degrees of complexity, ranging from the addition of a single word ("maladministration") into article I of the Constitution to much more elaborate mechanisms. However, this need be no more elaborate than the Twenty-Fifth Amendment of 1967, which clarified the role of the vice president and created the position of acting president and was ratified by 47 states within two years of its passage in Congress. Of course, the term "maladministration" would have to be clearly defined in the debates surrounding enactment of the amendment.

Plausibility: 3

The president plays no formal role in the constitutional amending process and thus would be unable to block such a change officially, although, of course, the president always remains politically influential. Further, there is a strong precedent in terms of amending the Constitution to adjust the term, selection, and office of the presidency; indeed, of the eight constitutional amendments enacted since 1932, this has been the subject of half of them (the Twentieth, Twenty-Second, Twenty-Third, and Twenty-Fifth). Members of Congress would have no strong disincentive to oppose this change were the public to call for it. However, the "sacred" status of the four-year term would need to be addressed, perhaps in the context of eliminating the vice presidency and holding special presidential elections.

CHAPTER 10

Abolish the Vice Presidency

Highlighting Ideas from Mexico

Of the 43 individuals who have held the American presidency, nearly one-quarter did not complete the term to which they were elected. Four died in office of natural causes (William Henry Harrison, Zachary Taylor, Warren Harding, and Franklin Delano Roosevelt), four were assassinated (Abraham Lincoln, James Garfield, William McKinley, and John F. Kennedy), and one resigned (Richard Nixon). In each case, the vice president immediately assumed office, and thus, for a total of 24 years, more than one-tenth of American history since 1789, the United States has had a president whom no one had elected to that specific office. Only half of those vice presidents who succeeded to office were subsequently chosen by the people to fill the office in their own right, with not a single one being reelected to a second full term.

It is undeniable that some vice presidents have acquitted themselves well in the top job. Theodore Roosevelt's larger-than-life presidency comes to mind first, although Harry Truman's impressive management of the Cold War and Lyndon Johnson's advancement of civil rights and social welfare programs also merit praise. Yet, but for chance, the country could also have been saddled with such probable disasters as President Henry Wallace in the 1940s, President Spiro Agnew in the 1970s, or President Dick Cheney in the 2000s. And, indeed, in the nineteenth century, that was more or less the way vice-presidential succession played out—in the person of such hapless presidents as John Tyler, Millard Fillmore, Chester A. Arthur, and, worst of all, Andrew Johnson, who was expelled from his own political party, impeached by the House, and saved from removal in the Senate by a single vote.

The point is that vice-presidential succession is a shot the dark. So too, it could be argued, is the presidency itself, considering the failed terms of Herbert Hoover, Jimmy Carter, and George W. Bush. However, these presidents were at least democratically elected by the people, although, as the previous chapter argues, it would have been preferable for each of those presidencies to have been cut short. Vice presidents are also in some sense approved by the people but not really as the term "elected" is commonly used to describe the mechanism of approval. Yes, their names do appear on the ballot, and, yes, people could in theory vote against a ticket based on the vice-presidential nominee. But, in reality, the modern vice presidency is an appointed position, chosen by the presidential nominee at the quadrennial party conventions, and most people vote for the presidential candidate regardless of the vice-presidential nominee. In this sense, vice presidents are closer to being like a cabinet secretary than a president—except that they cannot be fired, and they stand a reasonably good chance, nearly one in four historically, of succeeding to the presidency. (By contrast, no sitting cabinet secretary has been elected president since Commerce Secretary Herbert Hoover in 1928.) Further, several vice presidents have used the momentum gained in the number-two spot to later win their party's presidential nominations, including Richard Nixon, Hubert Humphrey, Walter Mondale, George H. W. Bush, and Al Gore, and successfully so in the case of Nixon and Bush.

During the campaign, great lip service is inevitably paid to choosing the "best possible person" for the vice-presidential slot, someone who can "take over on day 1." But there is abundant evidence that vice-presidential nominees are usually chosen for other considerations: were John Edwards in 2004 and Sarah Palin in 2008, with their thin résumés, really the second-most-qualified people in their parties to lead the nation? Rather, other motivations often come into play. Vice-presidential selection may be done to unify the party, as when Ronald Reagan of the conservative wing of the Republican Party chose George H. W. Bush of the moderate wing or when the Washington outsider from Georgia, Jimmy Carter, chose a northern, inside-the-Beltway veteran in Walter Mondale. Or the vice-presidential choice may be intended to pick up an important state, such as when John F. Kennedy chose Lyndon Johnson partly in the correct belief that he could help carry Texas.

The selection may also be made for more idiosyncratic personal reasons. George H. W. Bush's selection of the little-known Dan Quayle is perhaps best understood in light of his desire not to once again be overshadowed by an authority figure, as he had by his own father, a senator, and by political patrons such as Ronald Reagan and Richard Nixon. Ironically, one case in which a presidential nominee did look beyond electoral considerations to the ability of the vice president to help govern, the case of Dick Cheney, proved to be disastrous. Although the ultimate evaluation of the relationship between Bush and Cheney must be left to the historians, there is already considerable reason to believe that Cheney played a leading role in many of Bush's greatest foreign policy and military debacles.

The role of the vice presidency is also famously murky. Vice presidents have virtually no constitutional authority of their own within the executive. At most, they have an established "right to be advised" to prepare for the possibility of sudden succession. No one wants to see a repeat of the case in which Harry Truman assumed the presidency amidst World War II without even knowing about the existence of nuclear weapons. It is for this reason that, for example, the vice president is a statutory member of the National Security Council and receives regular intelligence updates. However, the only shred of constitutional authority that vice presidents might be said to have is in the mostly ceremonial role of presiding over the Senate and breaking the occasional tie vote.

Although vice presidents lack actual *power*, many of them have not lacked *influence* in the executive. This may seem innocuous enough: there are many people with influence in the government, and vice presidents are usually experienced members of the president's party. Further, for most of American history, vice presidents played a peripheral role; it was not until the Carter administration that the vice president even got an office within the White House. Those who were admitted into the inner sanctum, such as Lyndon Johnson during some deliberations regarding the Cuban missile crisis, were allowed in only temporarily and at the explicit invitation of the president.

More recent developments, however, have made the vice presidency much more troubling, invoking images of intrigue in a royal court. With their unique constitutional status and their increasingly "insider" position, shrewd vice presidents can become manipulative "powers behind the throne," as in the case of Cheney. Given the possibility that they could become presidents at any time, vice presidents more than ever before have come to resemble "crown princes." Particularly if a president is sick or dying or in danger of removal from office or if they are running for election in their own right, vice presidents are well positioned to become an alternative power center within the executive. Al Gore was in many ways a "shadow president" from the impeachment of Bill Clinton in 1998 until his own narrow and contested Electoral College loss in 2000. In such a position, a more unscrupulous politician than Gore or one with significant policy differences with the presidency might well have become a rival.

The major problem with a still ambiguous but greatly strengthened vice presidency is that vice presidents are de facto unelected but also largely unaccountable. The president cannot fire them, Congress cannot conduct oversight of them because of the shield of executive privilege, and the courts are highly unlikely to intervene into the inner workings of the executive. What was long a benign if perhaps pointless office now threatens to become an antidemocratic one; indeed, it did become so under Cheney.

How might a country with a president operate without a vice presidency? There are surprisingly few examples of this since most presidential systems retain a vice president and sometimes more than one, but one example is provided immediately south of the U.S. border.

CASE STUDY: THE ABOLITION OF THE MEXICAN VICE PRESIDENCY

For most of its history, Mexico has been no model of democracy. From independence from Spain in the 1800s, through the revolution against the landed elites in the early 1900s, down to the 72-year monopoly of the Revolutionary Institutional Party (PRI) in power between 1928 and 2000, the normal procedures of democracy have not been found in abundance. In this sense, Mexico may not be an obvious choice as a model of democratic processes. However, a strong case can be made that the powerful Mexican presidency has been the country's principal source of constructive government action and that the abolition of the Mexican vice presidency served to strengthen the presidency itself.

Among the countries of Latin America, Mexico stands out for its stability. Since the Mexican Revolution, the country has seen periodic upheavals, such as the student riots of 1968 and the Zapatista uprising of 1994, but none of these posted a fundamental challenge to control of the Mexican state. By contrast, over the past half century, many Latin American nations, such as Chile, Argentina, and Brazil, fell under the sway of dictators, while others, including Colombia, Guatemala, and El Salvador, have suffered debilitating civil wars. But the Mexican regime has remained rock solid, and the focal points of this stability have been the presidents of Mexico.

Mexican presidents have powers so potent and centralized that some have termed them "elected dictators." But neither part of that term was ever quite accurate. Mexican presidents were only nominally elected since, until 2000, the PRI relied on pressure, enticement, coercion, genuine popularity, and, when necessary, electoral fraud to ensure that only its candidate could win. Further, each successive PRI presidential candidate was chosen by the incumbent president just before the next election, further ensuring continuity. At the same time, Mexican presidents were much more servants than masters of their party in contrast to, for example, Fidel Castro, who personally dominated the Community Party of Cuba and remained president for half a century. Rather, Mexican presidents are subject to an iron-clad single six-year term of office and are then barred from reelection for life, with several choosing after their terms even to go into exile abroad rather than remain in Mexico.

Almost uniquely in the Western Hemisphere, the Mexican executive has not had a vice president for more than 150 years, a institutional decision with deep roots in earlier eras of instability. The period following formal independence from Spain in 1821 was marked by constant battles between liberal and conservative forces, with the country rapidly cycling through some 50 successive presidential administrations in the space of three decades. Many of these changes reflected the shifting power between the liberal and conservative factions, but at times presidents were also overthrown through the collusion of their own vice presidents.

One of the most chaotic periods took place when the famous general Antonio López de Santa Anna was elected president but was constitutionally ineligible to simultaneously act at the nation's chief executive officer and its highest military officer. Repeatedly over the course of years, he would act as president, then step aside to act as a field general at times of conflict on the northern border, leaving his vice president, Valentín Gómez Farías, to govern from Mexico City. This awkward arrangement worked for a while until Gómez Farías began to govern with increasing independence from Santa Anna—and also in a way that increasingly threatened the interests of the Catholic Church and the middle class. Faced with a revolt that threatened to bring him down as well, Santa Anna hastily pushed through a constitutional change abolishing the vice presidency, thus depriving the unpopular Gómez Farías of a power base. Except for a brief time after the Mexican Revolution in the early twentieth century, Mexico has remained without a vice president and, notably, without as many coups or as much instability.[1]

The Mexican example demonstrates that a political system with separation of powers can function perfectly well without a vice president.
A less promising part of the Mexican case, however, is the murky procedure for replacing a president, which allows Congress to appoint an
interim or substitute president for over a year. Since this eventuality
has not arisen since the 1930s, it is unclear how the Mexican system
would deal with a vacancy in the current era. The best solution, as
argued in Chapter 11, including a case study from France, would be
for a quick new election.

ABOLISH THE U.S. VICE PRESIDENCY?

It is clear that the U.S. vice presidency, in and of itself, could vanish
and no one would miss it. Vice presidents may at times serve as effective presidential counselors, but presidents do not lack other advisers
and surrogates. It is quite telling that the office has remained empty
for considerable swathes of U.S. history—a total of 16 times for a total
of 40 years, or nearly a fifth of U.S. history. And the existence of a law of
presidential succession, stretching through congressional leaders and
cabinet officers, has already laid out a path beyond the vice presidency.

To spare a word about the role of the vice president as president of
the Senate, it may be enough to say that the chamber is in practice
usually presided over by the president pro tempore, who is, by tradition, the longest-seated member of the majority party. Since a vote
to break a Senate tie by the vice president invariably follows the wishes
of the existing administration, those terribly concerned about the possibility of a tie could simply give the president a special tie-breaking
vote. However, no comparable provision exists in the House, where
the occurrence of vacancies or simply House members not being in
attendance regularly leaves that chamber with an even number of members and thus also the mathematical possibility of a tie vote.

On the central question of presidential succession, which is the
core rationale for the existence of vice presidency, it would be far
more democratic for the people to freely choose their own chief executive through a special election. Of course, the country does always
need to have a president—particularly in times of crisis—and elections
cannot be held instantaneously. Absent a vice president, some provision
does indeed need to exist for short-term replacement, but this would in
practice be unproblematic and will be the theme of the next chapter.

SYNOPSIS

Desirability: 3

If the vice presidency does not do much good, it also usually does not do too much harm. Historically, the overreaching and manipulations of the Cheney years are an anomaly and, it is to be hoped, will remain so. The major reason to wish for the abolition of the vice presidency is to open the way for the people to always have a president whom they have clearly chosen for the role. If other, more important ideas in this book are to be enacted, such as "removal for cause" of the president and special elections, the impediment of the vice presidency must be removed.

Practicability: 5

Abolition of the vice presidency could be easily accomplished by constitutional amendment, a process in which neither the president nor the vice president has an official role. The existing law of presidential succession, which has been reformed in the past yet also offers a powerful precedent, could readily be invoked as the basis for a new succession pattern. Further, both the executive and the Senate could continue their work seamlessly without a vice president, posing no practical barriers to implementation.

Plausibility: 5

As noted, neither the president nor the vice president has an official role in the amending process, and the states have little vested interest in the institution of the vice presidency, making them potentially receptive to a congressional initiative. The vice presidency is not held in high regard but after the Cheney years must be considered no longer a benign anachronism but rather a potentially dangerous, even renegade, part of government. The abolition of the vice presidency would be a logical adjunct to a reform package including removal for cause and special elections, all of which would be the harder elements for which to build support.

CHAPTER 11

Hold Special Presidential Elections

Highlighting Ideas from France

Chapter 8 argues that it should be possible to carry out the "removal for cause" of the president by Congress, probably with some additional layer of approval by the states or by the people. Chapter 9 focuses on the related issue of the abolition of the vice presidency. Under the current rules of American government, this would appear to create a quandary: would it be wise to *raise* the likelihood of a vacancy in the presidency at the same time as *removing* the designated successor?

This quandary is easily enough resolved, however, by returning to the democratic principle that the people deserve a high-functioning president of their own choice. Thus, in cases of removal or death of the president, a new election should be called, allowing the people to once again have a direct say in who will be their chief executive. As discussed in Chapter 5, it would certainly be possible to drastically reduce the amount of time over which a presidential election is held. Still, given the need for continued presidential command and control at all times, some form of temporary presidential succession would be needed, perhaps for 60 or 90 days. Fortunately, a ready model for such a temporary transition followed by a special election can be found in the constitution of America's oldest ally: France.

CASE STUDY: PRESIDENTIAL SUCCESSION IN FRANCE

Although presidents can be found in many European countries, most of them fulfill an almost entirely ceremonial role, filling in for countries that previously had hereditary kings and queens. However, one presidency stands out above all others of Europe: *Le Président de la République française*. This should, perhaps, be unsurprising. France has a long history of strong executive power emanating out of Paris and extending throughout the nation. Indeed, the Sun King, Louis XIV, is often cited as the very embodiment of absolute monarchy, and even in the immediate aftermath of the French Revolution, Napoleon Bonaparte found it possible to install himself as an emperor in his own right. The most recent figure in this succession of strong leaders was Charles de Gaulle, the leader of the French Resistance in exile during World War II.

In 1946, the reconstituted postwar French state established the "Fourth Republic," with a heavy emphasis on the role of the National Assembly led by the prime minister rather than by a strong executive king or president. Although this Parliament-focused government had some notable successes in postwar reconstruction, its proceedings were volatile and chaotic. In the 12 years between 1946 and 1958, there were 25 different governments, and, perhaps more than anywhere else in Western Europe, communists played a prominent and often destabilizing role in government. The dissension and rancor at home left France with little ability to cope with the collapse of its overseas empire in North and West Africa or in Southeast Asia.

As conflict with the independence movement in the colony of Algeria escalated into de facto civil war, de Gaulle stepped once more into the breach. The former general briefly became prime minister but quickly led the call for a new constitution for a "Fifth Republic," which would revolve around a strong executive president with a capacious seven-year term (reduced to five years in 2000). In the words of the 1958 Constitution, the president has a central, if somewhat underdefined, role: "The president of the Republic shall see that the Constitution is observed. He shall ensure, by his arbitration, the proper functioning of the public authorities and the continuity of the State. He shall be the guarantor of national independence, territorial integrity and observance of treaties."

De Gaulle was elected the first president under the new constitution and went on to wield tremendous power. Although the president appoints a prime minister, subject to approval by the National Assembly, to oversee many of the day-to-day tasks of domestic governance, the president remains the leading political figure in the nation with particular control over foreign policy and the military—up to and including sole authority over the use of the French nuclear arsenal.

The president also has the extraordinary ability to unilaterally declare a state of emergency and rule directly by decree for brief periods of time, as de Gaulle did during the Algerian crisis in 1961.

Recognizing that a position as powerful as that of president should always be occupied by the choice of the citizenry, the Fifth Republic makes no provision for a vice president. On a vacancy in the office or the permanent disability of the president, a new election must be scheduled within 20 to 35 days. During this brief interim, the presiding officer of the Senate, who is elected by the members of the upper chamber of the Parliament, serves as acting president with full powers except the ability to initiate a public referendum or to dissolve Parliament. The presiding officer of the Senate may also serve in a caretaker role during periods of temporary presidential incapacity. (An equally viable model would have been temporary succession by another senior figure, such as the prime minister, as is the case in Russia.)

This constitutional provision has been called on twice in the 50-year history of the French Fifth Republic, as it happens in both cases involving the same president of the Senate, Alain Poher. The first time came in 1969, when de Gaulle resigned after the public rejected a referendum that he had endorsed to weaken the powers of the Senate. A political opponent of de Gaulle, Poher attempted to seize the moment and ran for president in his own right but lost to de Gaulle ally George Pompidou. When Pompidou, in turn, died in office, Poher again temporarily took power and once more ceded it seven weeks later to the new duly elected president, Valery Giscard d'Estaing, yet another conservative. Because Poher had only been the acting president, he was able to retain his Senate role and return to it full-time on completion of the transition.

SPECIAL PRESIDENTIAL ELECTIONS IN THE UNITED STATES?

The case of France makes it clear that elections can be held in a month or less after either a resignation or a death, even for the powerful presidency of a major country. In the case of the United States, it is obvious that some unambiguous provision must be made for continuity of executive authority at all times. Should the vice presidency survive as an institution, this temporary replacement role should clearly be played by the vice president. However, abolition of the vice presidency, as advocated in the previous chapter, need not be an obstacle to a special presidential election. Conversely, however, special presidential elections would moot any remaining rationale for a vice presidency.

In the absence of a vice president, some other high-ranking official could be appointed, perhaps making use of the existing Law of Presidential Succession. Traditionally, this law passed the presidential office, after the vice president, to the sitting cabinet members. However, the law was revised in 1947 to place two of the top figures in Congress, the Speaker of the House and the president pro tempore of the Senate, directly ahead of the cabinet secretaries, who follow the congressional leaders in their "order of precedence" (i.e., the order in which their respective departments were originally created). This change in the line of succession was rooted in an entirely valid democratizing impulse to give priority of place to elected leaders ahead of the former first in line, the appointed secretary of state. However, in practice, the placement of congressional leaders before cabinet secretaries poses some significant problems.

The Speaker of the House is, undoubtedly, an important national figure and is elected in much the same manner as a prime minister: by simple majority of the House of Representatives. The president pro tempore of the Senate is a rather more problematic proposition. As currently conceived, the title is an honor bestowed on the longest-seated member of the majority party. This almost ensures that the president pro tempore will be elderly, perhaps not up to the job, and quite possibly not considered a leader in the Senate. A better choice would be to put the Senate majority leader into the line of succession, even though this role is not explicitly established by the Constitution. (Alternatively, the majority leader could also be given the title of president pro tempore of the Senate.)

Either way, however, succession to a member of Congress poses several problems. One involves separation of powers: under current practice, one cannot be a member of Congress and also act as president. Thus, either the Speaker of the House or the Senate president pro tempore would be required to outright resign from his or her legislative office. Were the Speaker of the House or the Senate president pro tempore to be occupying the presidency for a matter of several months or even years, this is a sacrifice he or she would be likely to accept. But what about if the succession were only short term, pending a new election? Would he or she still be willing to give up his or her high office?

A constitutional amendment could clearly allow these officers to fill both roles on a temporary basis; the vice president, after all, already presides over the Senate, so the separation of powers issue is not insurmountable. However, a more important concern would be temporarily transferring political power to someone who was outside the previous administration, perhaps of another political party, and quite possibly antagonistic to the existing presidential administration. At best, this would be unwieldy and disruptive since the new president would necessarily have to rely on the executive branch as it was already staffed and configured, except perhaps adding a few personal aides. At worst, it could lead the temporary replacement to try to ram through his or her own agenda within an already unsettled 90-day period. This possibility would be greatly enhanced if the new acting president had just finished running one of the houses of Congress and thus had his or her own clearly articulated agenda and congressional power base.

In the case of the reform proposed in this chapter—a short waiting period before a special election—it would thus make more sense to return the secretary of state to the head of the line of succession. As the senior appointed official of the existing administration, the secretary of state will be able to provide continuity and stability and will already have working relationships with other executive officers. Further, as a fully briefed specialist in foreign affairs, the secretary of state would be especially well situated to respond to external concerns and would likely already be a household name and a familiar face to the populace. However, lacking his or her own electoral mandate or power base in Congress, a secretary of state would be less likely to abuse the office. Only under very unusual circumstances would the line of succession ever have to pass further down, but even then it would also move to other important senior officials, including the secretary of the treasury, the secretary of defense, and then the attorney general and so on.

It is important to recognize that the period preceding a special presidential election may be a tumultuous one. If the president was removed for cause or impeached, the country may be politically polarized, as during Watergate. If the president were assassinated, the country would likely be traumatized, as with Kennedy in November 1963. Correspondingly, the entire circumstance may be playing out against the backdrop of some national or international crisis, such as when Lincoln was assassinated in office or when Roosevelt died in office during World War II. There will be a need for short-term continuity in the command-and-control functions of the presidency as well as some time to allow any immediate crisis to be alleviated and for emotions to cool.

However, the possibility of disruption should not in and of itself be enough to argue against the very idea of a special presidential election.

The four-year presidential election cycle has frequently coincided with times when the United States has been embroiled in wars, including most recently World War II (1944), Korea (1952), Vietnam (1964, 1968), and Iraq and Afghanistan (2004, 2008), as well as other crises ranging from the Great Depression (1932, 1936) to the civil rights movement (1960, 1964). None of these events prevented or even compromised a presidential election. And even in times of deepest crisis, no leader is as indispensable as he or she might think. While World War II was still under way, the voters of Great Britain seamlessly replaced the great Winston Churchill, and Harry Truman capably succeeded the towering Franklin Roosevelt—and rarely do countries find themselves faced with crises as severe as world war. Still, allowing for the possibility of a truly dire national emergency, it might be judicious to allow Congress to declare an extension of up to, say, 90 additional days although only on a one-time basis and perhaps with the concurrence of the Supreme Court.

What form should a special presidential election take? Chapter 4 argues for an abolition of the Electoral College, while Chapter 5 calls for quicker, more streamlined elections. With these two provisions in mind, there is no great reason that a special presidential election could not be successfully executed on a 90-day timetable, as in France. Special elections to Congress, in specific districts or states, are already held on a similar timetable, and if necessary this could be expanded to a nationwide vote. Without time for a primary season, the kind of two-stage runoff election described in Chapter 3 would be most likely, in which the top two vote earners in the first stage then go head-to-head.

As to who would be eligible to run, the rules would be the same as for any presidential election. If there is a vice president acting as the temporary replacement, voters should have the choice to elevate him or her to the top job—this time in full awareness that they are electing a president and not a vice president. The same would be true of some other short-term acting president, such as the Speaker of the House or the secretary of state. It is worth noting that, on occasion, some congressional leaders or cabinet secretaries might be ineligible to be president by virtue of not being native-born citizens (two modern secretaries of state, Henry Kissinger and Madeleine Albright, were in this situation), but it would in any case be best to eliminate this antiquated requirement. (Surely, the original animating fear in 1787 that a powerful European monarch might install some princeling in the U.S. presidency is hardly a concern today.)

An interesting question arises as to whether a president who has been impeached or removed for cause should be eligible to run again. To the extent that the goal of a presidential election is to install the choice of the people, an argument could be made that they should have the opportunity to choose to return the president to office. This would particularly be true should the method of removal for cause *not* already include a confirmatory vote by the people, which would already be a de facto rejection of the incumbent. On the other hand, if the president has been removed from office based on abuse of power, such as intimidation of rivals or attempts to control the media, the new election might not be fully free and fair. Ideally, the process of removing a president would expose such practices to a degree sufficient to embolden challengers and enlighten voters. In any case, the newly elected president should be bound by the requirements of the Twenty-Second Amendment that no one individual can exceed two full terms in office. The addition of flexibility to the four-year cycle of presidential elections—by virtue of having created special elections in the first place—would make it easier to schedule a new election if a new presidential term would exceed the eight-year term limit.

One potentially serious complication would be the special case of presidential disability, as opposed to removal, death, or resignation. Until the passage of the Twenty-Fifth Amendment in 1967, the vice president had no authority to become "acting president" in cases in which the president was disabled but did not die, such as after Woodrow Wilson's stroke or Dwight Eisenhower's heart attacks. If a president's disability were to last beyond the 90-day mark of the temporary replacement, could the president's term then be ended and a new election called? Or might a still disabled president try to struggle back into office prematurely before the disability has truly lifted? In this case, it would be best to adapt the existing provisions of the Twenty-Fifth Amendment and allow Congress to make the determination of whether the president was fit to return.

SYNOPSIS

Desirability: 5

The president is by far the single most potent actor in the U.S. political system and would continue to be even if many of the reforms in this volume were enacted. It is thus a bedrock principle that the people deserve to at all times to have a president of their own choosing who is functioning reasonably well. If not, the system should provide greater flexibility for a replacement, moving closer to the prime-ministerial model of executive accountability.

Practicability: 4

Special elections are routinely held for members of the House and, in some states, of the Senate, offering an important precedent in the U.S. political tradition. There is no compelling practical reason that a presidential election could not be mounted within about 90 days, a period long enough for an abbreviated campaign season in which candidates could make their case to the public but not so long as to meaningfully deny the people the right to be governed by a president of their choosing. The use of a runoff system, rather than a protracted primary season, would also expedite matters. However, special elections for the president would clearly require a constitutional amendment.

Plausibility: 3

The eventuality of a special presidential election does not particularly pose a threat to any established political actors, as it is designed to address the important yet relatively rare case of a vacancy in the presidency. An impetus toward requiring states to hold special elections in the case of senatorial vacancies (instead of having new senators handpicked by governors) could help lend credence to this idea at the presidential level. This amendment might also garner support if it were a part of a comprehensive package along with such reforms as the abolition of the vice presidency and the approval of removal for cause of the president.

CHAPTER 12

Add Elected Officers to the Executive

Highlighting Ideas from Iceland

One of the great breakthroughs of the constitutional period was the recognition that sovereignty can be subdivided. Until that time, the logic of the European system, as inherited by the nascent United States, was the idea that the "right to rule" was indivisible and was personified in a single individual. The king (or, at times, regnant queen) would reign by "the grace of God" from atop a hierarchy of nobles covering a specified territory that by definition would never geographically overlap with that of any other king.

Perhaps the greatest conceptual breakthrough of the Constitutional Convention was the recognition that sovereignty could be shared at two levels, that is, by both the national and the state governments. This concept of federalism has served the United States well in many ways and indeed is now found in countries around the world. Likewise, the founders had the insight that it was possible to further subdivide the right to rule between the executive and the legislative. Clearly, they were greatly influenced by the example of Great Britain, where absolute monarchy had already begun to be replaced by a formula that situates sovereignty with the "Monarch-in-Parliament."

Where the founders did not succeed in making a conceptual leap was in the concept that executive power could itself be shared. There was some discussion of a "plural executive" at the convention, but the idea was rejected. Perhaps for men learned in the classics, the history of diarchies and triumvirates from the Ancient Roman Republic did not bode well, considering that such rule led to civil strife and ultimately to rule by a single emperor. And at the time of the founding, the contemporary model of the sharing of executive power in a parliamentary cabinet had yet to be invented. At that time, the British prime minister and other ministers were still selected by the monarch, mainly from the House of Lords rather than the elected House of Commons.

As it happens, the founders may indeed have been wise in avoiding a plural executive within which power is shared equally, as this may be an inherently unstable arrangement among ambitious politicians. Caesar's defeat of his rivals, with all its ruinous consequences, might well be more a norm to be expected than an exception to be avoided. Indeed, throughout the democratic world, no country with a full separation-of-powers system has adopted the practice of having two, three, or more executive officers with completely equal authority. (The unique seven-member Federal Council of Switzerland does share equal authority but is chosen by the Swiss legislature rather than being independently elected.) However, an important distinction can be made between a truly plural executive in which lines of authority are murky and power struggles likely and a highly concentrated presidency in which all executive authority is invested in a single individual. Indeed, such overconcentration of power in the executive under separation-of-powers systems leads to three major problems.

The first problem is that it conflates two roles that are in some ways fundamentally different: the hands-on role of "head of government" and the more ceremonial role of "head of state." The American president is expected to be a hard-nosed political operative and the ideological leader of a major political party while at the same time being a symbol of the unity of the nation and the embodiment of the continuity of the state. Inevitably, these two roles often pull the president in opposite directions, giving the office something of a contradictory character.

The second problem is that having only one elected official in the executive provides no internal checks and balances—the branch that it entrusted with the power to enforce the law has no clear way to enforce the law against itself. This is a violation of the spirit, if not the letter, of checks and balances. The two chambers of the legislature are balanced by one another, and in some ways the majority within each chamber is constrained by the minority party. The Supreme Court is composed of nine equal individuals, and its institutional limitations mean that a great deal of the judicial power is carried out by the lower courts. But within the executive branch, the U.S. president is entirely unchecked.

A third consideration is that the president is only a single human being and that in reality executive power is exercised in the name of the president by a variety of other executive officers. Most notable among these are cabinet secretaries and the heads of major administrations, such as the Environmental Protection Agency (EPA) and the Central Intelligence Agency (CIA). While these and many others are in fact important players in the executive, they have no executive authority in their own right—all such executive authority is invested in the president and is merely carried out by other executive actors. Although they wield enormous authority, they are not elected and in fact are not even nominated until after the election, making it impossible for voters to factor in the impact of the entire "team" into their electoral decisions.

The allocation of all executive power and roles to a single individual seems so natural to Americans that most people rarely give it a second thought. The system is designed so that there is a single, extraordinarily demanding role at the very pinnacle of power that one person is expected to fill. However, it is mainly only in the United States and in other presidential systems based on the U.S. model that the executive is composed of only a single individual. In parliamentary democracies, including Western Europe's most recently established independent state, Iceland, the executive is composed of a number of individuals playing distinctive roles.

CASE STUDY: EXECUTIVE AUTHORITY IN ICELAND

Although it has had a form of self-government since the 999 CE, the northerly island nation of Iceland did not achieve full independence from Denmark until World War II. Despite being geographically remote, the small nation has adopted mainstream European democratic institutions by vesting executive power in a cabinet drawn from its Parliament, called the Althingi, and led by a prime minister. In order to fill the constitutional vacuum created by the elimination of the Danish monarchy, the 1944 Constitution of the Republic of Iceland also established the new office of a directly elected president with somewhat vague executive authority. Thus, in Iceland, as in many other republics in Europe, the mainstream parliamentary model of government creates quite distinct elected executive offices of presidents, prime ministers, and cabinet ministers in order to exercise the executive power that is the sole provenance of the U.S. president.

Presidents of Iceland, much like the hereditary constitutional monarchs of other Nordic countries, such as Denmark, Sweden, and

Norway, fulfill the ceremonial role of head of state. On election, they resign from political parties and rise above the fray of politics, acting as dignified caretakers of the enduring values of the state rather than only of the passing government of the day. For most of their term of office, Icelandic presidents serve as goodwill ambassadors abroad, giving speeches and promoting the interests of the nation, while at home they confer titles and awards and host visiting dignitaries. In terms of the work of government, however, their role is limited to making the formal appointment of ministers and to promulgating laws and treaties by signing them once approved by the Parliament.[1]

Unlike hereditary monarchs—and more like the presidents in other parliamentary democracies, such as Austria and Ireland—Icelandic presidents on rare occasions play a small directly political role. The president can recommend legislation, send laws passed by the Parliament to a public referendum for approval, issue regulations in an emergency if Parliament cannot convene, and play a role in the formation of a governing majority should the Parliament be unable to achieve this on its own. However, these so-called reserve powers are extremely rarely employed; for example, by 2010 only two laws had ever been vetoed, both times since 2004. As the head of state, then, the president's principal activities are overwhelmingly symbolic, representing the integrity and continuity of the state without reference to partisan activities or political controversies.

Thus, although the president is directly elected by the people and would appear, on paper, to enjoy considerable authority, all actual executive power resides with the government. In a parliamentary context, the term "government" has a narrower meaning than in the United States, where the term usually refers to the full sprawl of the executive, legislative, and judicial branches. Rather, a "government" simply refers to those senior ministers who enjoy the support of a majority of the Parliament at any given time. Usually, they are also duly elected members of the Parliament themselves and seasoned, well-established politicians, often with their own power base. Collectively, they exercise formal power as the cabinet, which is comprised of ministerial "portfolios," such as finance, foreign affairs, or defense. (For more details on the parliamentary model, see Appendix 2 at the end of this volume.) The senior member of a parliamentary cabinet is the prime (or first) minister, who selects and oversees the other ministers. But in all these cases, including Iceland, prime ministers have no independent electoral mandate from the people and share the same source of support as all other ministers—the support of a parliamentary majority, which can be withdrawn at any time. The precariousness of the prime minister's position was underscored in February 2009 when, amidst the global financial crisis that engulfed Iceland, Prime Minister Geir Haarde was forced from office after less than three years following angry street demonstrations even as President Ólafur Ragnar Grímsson remained securely in office after 13 years as president.

Finally, Iceland has one other officer who plays a quasi-executive role that is unfamiliar in the United States in a government context. Drawing on a tradition that originated in Sweden, the office of "ombudsman" was created in Iceland in 1987. Although not a true elected executive position, since it is filled by a vote of Parliament, the ombudsman nonetheless plays an independent role as a monitor of the actions of the government. With a fixed four-year term, the ombudsman has the ability to investigate complaints by citizens and then to recommend a corrective course of action, which is generally followed although not technically binding in part because it receives media attention. Although this is a fairly weak formulation of a check on the executive—the ability to initiate inquiries and publicize miscarriages of justices—the office of the ombudsman—which is found in other countries throughout the world—helps place limits on the executive branch.

ADD EXECUTIVE OFFICERS IN THE UNITED STATES?

How applicable is the Iceland example and, more broadly, the parliamentary configuration of executive offices to the United States? Certainly, the United States has never been and will never have a parliamentary system, and some of its key features are incompatible with multiple executives. Nonetheless, the Iceland case study can at least shed new light on, if not exactly point to a solution to, the three problems noted earlier in this chapter: (1) the conflation of the head of state and head of government roles, (2) the need for multiple powerful actors in the cabinet, and (3) the need for the executive to enforce the law against itself.

SEPARATING THE HEAD OF STATE AND HEAD OF GOVERNMENT ROLES

The idea of splitting the head of state and head of government roles in the United States is an intriguing one and one worth contemplating if ultimately only as a thought experiment. Notably, such a split is the norm in the majority of successful democracies in the world. Conversely, the presidential position has all too often become a platform for nondemocratic "strongman" rule in countries in which the two roles are fused, notably in Latin America, postcolonial Africa, and several post-Soviet countries. Indeed, when the person who wields the most de facto coercive power through military and police forces is also positioned as the virtual personification of the state, it is all too easy for today's legitimate political opponents to be recast as tomorrow's enemies of the state—and for presidents to believe that they are above the law as long as they argue that they are pursuing the "vital interests of the nation."

The U.S. Constitution is silent on the issue of the head-of-state role. At the time of the founding, the emphasis on popular sovereignty was so great and the disdain for monarchism so intense that no provision was made for symbolic leadership of the new state. In fact, the U.S. president is head of state mostly by default because under the international state system, every country has a head of state, and therefore the United States also logically needs to have one—just as every country has a flag and a national anthem. It would in theory be a relatively straightforward proposition to create a new constitutional position of "ceremonial head of state" in the United States, but it is hard to imagine this new role resonating with the American people in a way that would give it any meaning.

In most parliamentary systems, heads of state gain enormous resonance from the history of the country, either because they are hereditary monarchs or at least because they fulfill the role formerly played by monarchs, often even residing in former royal palaces. But in the staunchly antimonarchist United States, would the creation of some new office really diminish the central role accorded to the presidency not only in power but also in the minds of Americans? The nation's capital would still be called "Washington," and the National Mall at the heart of the District of Columbia would still emphasize the central role of presidents such as Jefferson, Lincoln, and Franklin Roosevelt. Mount Rushmore would remain filled with presidents carved in granite, and could the lore surrounding the White House really ever be replaced with some new head-of-state residence?

The real issue here, then, would be to consistently reemphasize the reality that, under the Constitution, the president is the servant of the law, not its master. The malady of the "imperial presidency" is a recurrent one, seen perhaps most intensely in the overreaching of

President Richard Nixon and his consistent abuses of power and attempts to place himself above the law—most notably during the calamitous Watergate affair. The cure to this malady is equally well known and was seen in abundance during the Nixon years and in its aftermath: the vigorous assertion of congressional and, to a lesser extent, judicial power. The era of President George W. Bush and Vice President Dick Cheney witnessed a major reassertion of the imperial presidency based on the theory that the executive must be essentially unfettered in its operations with regard to security and foreign affairs issues, with Congress and the courts clearly subordinate.

In the aftermath of the Bush–Cheney aggrandizement of the executive, the time is ripe in the United States for a reassertion of the substantive power of the legislative and judicial branches. To this end, symbolism does count, and the parliamentary system offers a striking mechanism for distinguishing between the roles of head of state and head of government in the form of "question time." In many countries, ministers—including prime ministers—are required to appear on the floor of the lower house of Parliament to take questions and to defend their positions. The best known such spectacle takes place in the British Parliament, where prime ministers are cheered and jeered, cajoled, and cross-examined once a week, every week. It requires them to have an impressive command of facts and issues and to be regularly and publicly accountable for their actions on a regular basis. And it serves as a reminder that prime ministers do not personify the state, a role reserved to a monarch who is politically powerless and thus not dangerous to democracy.

Congress does, to some degree, have this power over cabinet secretaries and other executive officers who can be subjected to questioning by committees. These are, however, limited and sporadic events, and the president and vice president are entirely shielded from such questioning under the doctrine of executive privilege. In fact, there is little to stop a president or vice president from completely withdrawing into the White House and even from public sight yet still continue to wield all the powers of the presidency; indeed, Dick Cheney became infamous after 9/11 for retreating to so-called undisclosed locations. A question time for presidents and vice presidents need not be quite as frequent as for the British prime minister, and certainly it should not be as raucous or even a rude event. In early 2010, Barack Obama participated in a question-and-answer session with Congressional Republicans that could form the prototype for future such events. At the same time, the president, as head of state, should not be denied other forums, such as delivering the State of the Union Address with its monarchical tone or issuing official proclamations and presenting medals and awards. Perhaps nothing could do more than the periodic questioning of the president by Congress to reassert that the presidency may be the highest office in the nation but that the president is no king.

ELECTING THE CABINET

Although the same word is used, the "cabinet" means something quite different in the United States than in parliamentary democracies. Under the U.S. Constitution, all executive authority is invested in the president, with the secretaries of the cabinet simply exercising that power on behalf of the president. Far from being elected officials, they are appointed at the discretion of the president and actually must give up any other elected office that they may happen to have, such as a governorship or a seat in Congress.

In a parliamentary democracy, however, not only is it the norm in most democracies that cabinet ministers can be sitting members of the legislature, but it usually is the case that they must be. In parliamentary systems based on the British Westminster model, only sitting members of Parliament are eligible to hold such powerful ministerial portfolios such as finance, defense, and foreign affairs and also a panoply of lesser portfolios and "junior" ministerial positions. The senior ministers collectively form the executive authority—the cabinet—with the prime minister being technically the "first among equals," although prime ministers are often clearly dominant figures.

Admirers of the parliamentary system have from time to time proposed that members of Congress be eligible to serve as cabinet secretaries. While this may at first appear to violate both the spirit and the letter of separation of powers, in terms of constitutional text, the problem could be easily solved. Article I, section 6, does not prohibit sitting members of Congress from being appointed as a cabinet secretary but does require that they resign their congressional seat before joining the executive. In the words of the final clause of that section of the Constitution, "no Person holding any Office under the United States shall be a member of either House during his Continuance in Office."

The constitutional impediment to seating members of Congress in the executive cabinet could thus, technically, be remedied with the deletion of that single clause. However, it is not at all certain that this would be a beneficial or even plausible reform. Unlike in many parliamentary democracies, being a member of Congress is a full-time job with significant legislative work and representative responsibilities. Being a cabinet secretary is likewise a huge task with extensive bureaucratic duties. It is far from clear that any one individual could do both tasks well. To whom would these hybrid legislative-executive officers be accountable: the president or the constituents who elected them to office? Even in the likely case that a congressional cabinet secretary were of the same party and ideology as the president, conflict might likely arise. And how also would these hybrid officers relate to the House or Senate in which they also serve?

Perhaps if such an arrangement were to offer major benefits, such thorny issues could be resolved. But there are two other, much simpler steps that could be taken to address some of the same concerns. One would be to make lines of communication more explicit (and, then, more open to the sunshine of public scrutiny), with cabinet secretaries being granted the right to meet with and publicly address Congress or its committees at any time or perhaps even being designated as ex officio nonvoting members of relevant committees. They might also be empowered to directly introduce legislation, as are ministers in Parliament systems, and also play a more formalized role in the review and amendment of and the debate over laws.

Another reform would be for presidential candidates to nominate an entire slate of cabinet officers before the general election, perhaps during the party nominating conventions at the same time that the vice-presidential selection is announced. This would still make the cabinet secretaries not "elected officials" per se but more like the vice president in that they would still not have an independent mandate from the people—they would share more fully in the president's mandate. While they would still be subject to direction and replacement by the president, cabinet secretaries might gain a greater degree of latitude and discretion were they to be part of an elected team.

Given the importance of the work of some high-level officers, such as the secretaries of state, defense, treasury and health and human services, the American people should have the right to factor the quality of the overall team into their decisions. Citizens in parliamentary democracies already have this right in the form of the shadow cabinet created by the main opposition party. Early announcement of the cabinet might also force the president to choose people who are important and accomplished political figures in their own right. From time to time, presidential candidates have already hinted that they would place particular figures in their administrations, as George W. Bush did with Colin Powell for secretary of state in 2000. This reform would simply formalize and expand the procedure. Such a reform would also enhance the prospects of a greatly shortened transition period between the presidential election and inauguration since the key positions would already have been filled.

A NATIONAL OMBUDSPERSON OF THE UNITED STATES?

A final feature of the Icelandic system—as well as that of numerous other countries—is a single high-profile, independent official empowered to publicly critique the executive. To the extent that such a role exists in the U.S. system today, it is often played by the 535 members of Congress themselves through the function of legislative oversight of the bureaucracy via the committee structure. An important and more individualized form of advocacy occurs through "constituency service," in which congressional staff members intervene with particular bureaucratic offices on behalf of constituents who contact them. Oversight is a valuable, indeed an essential, function of Congress under separation of powers, but constituency service bears little relation to their work as legislators and is in fact a distraction.

A truly neutral ombudsperson would require his or her own independent mandate for action. In this sense, it would be preferable that the figure be elected directly by the people. Appointment by the legislature, as in Iceland, would be another approach, although the national ombudsperson would then need to have a fixed term of office and no further accountability to the legislature. To prevent the national ombudsperson from having too strong a stake in the success or failure of any administration, it might be advisable for the position to be limited to a nonrenewable single term, preferably of a longer duration and on a different electoral schedule than the president.

To be meaningful, however, a national office of the ombudsperson would have to have a wide range of authority and a significant budget, staff, and other resources. Otherwise, the significance of the office runs the risk of being too driven by the personality of the incumbent. Perhaps the closest analogue in the United States is New York City's elected public advocate, an office that provides a cautionary tale in that a potentially significant position has slipped into irrelevance and obscurity in the 2000s because of weak leadership and inadequate resources. At the federal level, the closest the United States comes to an ombudsperson may be the nonpartisan comptroller general of the United States, who is nominated by the president and confirmed by the president for a 15-year term, the length of which does help confer independence. In practice, however, this is a highly technocratic position entirely out of the public eye. The position is focused mostly on overseeing the Government Accountability Office, which provides the useful but very limited service of auditing federal budget statements. Many executive departments also have inspectors general, but their purview is limited to only a single department or agency.

Offices of the ombudsperson are also commonly found in large corporations and universities, making this concept already familiar to many Americans. However, if the creation of an entirely new and unfamiliar position of national ombudsperson is deemed undesirable, it would also be possible to work within the schema of the existing cabinet to diversify the executive and help to render it accountable from within. Indeed, 43 of the 50 states already do this by electing their state attorneys general separately from their governors. In this case, the governor remains the primary executive power—the "president" of the state—but the attorney general has a freer mandate to enforce the laws of the state and in some cases to check executive power. By contrast, when an attorney general is appointed and thus subject to direction and dismissal by an executive, that officer is hard pressed to enforce the law against actions of the very president or governor he or she serves. Although it would be impracticable—and unnecessary—for the United States to separately elect all 15 cabinet secretaries, it would be entirely plausible for the country as a whole to elect its attorney general alongside its president. Directly electing such a powerful and venerable officer, drawing on extensive precedent at the state level, would provide a unique opportunity to check the presidency from within.

SYNOPSIS

Desirability: 1

Although the Icelandic and other parliamentary systems can offer insights into the structure and function of the U.S. executive, few of its features can be directly translated in the U.S. system. Major innovations, such as a separate head of state, an elected cabinet, or placement of sitting members of Congress in the cabinet would be so disruptive as not to be desirable. The creation of a national ombudsperson or direct election of the attorney general could be more viable and constructive if other reforms discussed in this volume have failed to rein in the excesses of the executive but should perhaps not be starting points for reform.

Practicability: 2

Most of these reforms would require constitutional changes, some quite far reaching in terms of the traditional organization and even the basic nature of the U.S. executive. Smaller changes, such as a presidential question time and preelection announcement of the cabinet, however, could be enacted without constitutional or even legislative change.

Plausibility: 1

The reforms in this chapter would likely be opposed by both the president and Congress. Presidents would, understandably, be unwilling to countenance the promotion of potential rivals, such as an elected ombudsperson or attorney general or a ceremonial head of state. Members of Congress value their own role as checks on the executive and appreciate the influence that this affords them. And the general population may be eager to see abuses by the executive curbed but are unlikely to endorse major changes to the essential nature of the office. Small, incremental changes—such as naming a cabinet slate before the election—might be more likely to garner support.

CHAPTER 13

Rein in the President's Legislative and Judicial Powers

Highlighting Ideas from Turkey

Although the American founders established a clear separation of powers, they equally clearly intended for each branch to share in the powers of the others, forming the entire scheme of checks and balances. To this end, Congress has the sole authority to enact laws, but the president is endowed with a role both before and after the passage of legislation. Similarly, the executive cannot intervene directly in the adjudication of cases before the judiciary, but it does play a role in the initiation of charges and the disposition of sentences.

Some of these powers are modest. For example, with regard to the legislature, the U.S. Constitution provides the president with the authority to call Congress into session and to adjourn it (if the two houses disagree between themselves), and the president also is charged with providing Congress "from time to time with information of the State of the Union." The president may also "recommend" (although not formally introduce) legislation, clearly indicating that while there should be lines of communication and interchange between the executive and the legislature, Congress is free to consider or to decline to consider any laws it wishes. In these rather limited powers, then, the president plays a role similar to that of modern heads of state in parliamentary democracies, be they hereditary monarchs or figurehead presidents, who are also charged with tasks such as opening new parliamentary sessions and delivering speeches and providing private advice and counsel to the government. However, the president also retains two other, more clearly monarchical privileges in the form of the veto and the pardon.

As required by the presentment clause of article I, section 7, of the Constitution, any law that is passed in identical form by both chambers of Congress must then be presented to the president. In most monarchies, the king or queen traditionally had the authority to provide or withhold "royal assent," without which the law would not be enacted. This was originally an absolute power but long ago lapsed into a so-called reserve power to rarely, if ever, be used. For example, no British monarch has dared to withhold royal assent since 1708, a time at which kings and queens exerted other significant executive powers. Presentment in the United States—more commonly known as the veto process—is less absolute but still formidable: a bill can be enacted over the objection of the president only if overridden by a two-thirds majority of both houses. This makes the president—the head of the executive—by far the single most important influence over the final enactment of legislation, with as powerful an impact as 290 representatives and 67 senators combined.

In the judicial sphere, the powers of the president are also formidable. The presidency is by far the most powerful long-term force shaping the judiciary, with all federal judges—including justices of the Supreme Court—appointed by the president subject to confirmation by the Senate. Likewise, the president has an essentially unlimited power to pardon any and all offenses under federal law, including individuals or entire classes of people who may not have even been convicted of or even charged with any crime. The pardon power, a clear holdover from the concept of "throwing oneself at the mercy of the king," is one of the few constitutional provisions that is unchecked, with no provision for congressional override or judicial review (although individuals can reject their own pardon). The power is astonishing in scope: hypothetically, the president could release everyone held in federal prison with the stroke of a pen. More typically, however, presidents issue pardons highly selectively. Still, some pardons can have major repercussions, such as in 1974 when Gerald Ford pardoned the disgraced former president Richard Nixon a month after his resignation and in 1977 when Jimmy Carter controversially extended an amnesty to all those who had evaded the Vietnam-era military draft. Both presidents claimed to be acting in the higher interests of the nation, although political calculations were also clearly involved in both cases.

In the American system, it is to be expected that the president will have the vigorous and wide-ranging executive powers needed to fulfill the presidential oath to "take care that the law be faithfully executed" and to "preserve, protect, and defend the Constitution." Much less clear, however, is the appropriate extent of the legislative and judicial powers that should reasonably be wielded by the president as part of the scheme of checks and balances. An examination of other presidencies, including the highly prestigious post of president of the Republic of Turkey, may shed light on alternative or less extensive legislative and judicial roles for the president.

CASE STUDY: THE TURKISH PRESIDENCY

The parliamentary democracies of Europe are full of figurehead presidencies, created to fill the vacuum in the role of head of state created by the abolition of their monarchies but vested with little more than ceremonial duties. One exception has been the presidency of Turkey, which is not the pale imitation of former monarchical offices found in countries such as Italy, Germany, or Austria. Rather, the president of Turkey occupies the office first created and occupied by the revered founder of the modern Turkish state, Kemal Mustapha Ataturk, whose statues dominate town squares across the nation and whose visage appears on the Turkish lira. Previously elected by Parliament for a fixed five-year term, the Turkish president is now directly elected by the people, albeit from a list of candidates nominated by the leaders of the parties in the unicameral Parliament, called the Grand National Assembly.[1]

As Turkish government has evolved since the founding of the modern state in 1923, most executive power is now wielded by a prime minister and cabinet. But the president remains a real political actor, carrying out significant executive, legislative, and judicial functions. However, these are far more limited than in the United States. In practice, the Turkish president cannot exercise executive authority without the approval of the prime minister except in some emergency situations in which the Grand National Assembly may be unable to convene.

On the legislative front, laws also cannot take effect until the Turkish president signs and formally "promulgates" them. The Turkish constitution provides the president with some latitude here: the president may return any piece of legislation to the Grand National Assembly for reconsideration, specifying the reasons for its rejection. However, this is not the "royal assent" of a monarch, which tends to be either an absolute and undemocratic veto or a purely ceremonial and thus politically meaningless formality. Nor is this power the formidable veto of the U.S. president, requiring a daunting two-thirds majority in a bicameral legislature. In this case, the Turkish Parliament can reconsider the law and may change it, but it can also pass it with the same simple majority as the first time. On its second presentment to the president, he or she has a choice about whether to sign it (the usual outcome) or force it to a national referendum. For example, the latter case occurred in 2007 when the government first proposed direct election of the president rather than selection by Parliament. The government went on to win the referendum and enacted the change.

On the judicial front, the president also has powers, but these are also clearly limited and checked. Rather than having an outright king-like right of pardon, the president may unilaterally exercise clemency only on grounds of "chronic illness, disability or old age, [for] all or part of the sentences imposed on certain individuals." This is clearly bounded by circumstance and to specific persons but can be put to creative use. For example, the pardoning of both protesting hunger strikers in 2001 and an elderly former prime minister in 2009 had significant political ramifications. The Grand National Assembly can also enact pardons with a three-fifths majority, which it has done in recent years in order to broker peace with Kurdish rebels and to relieve prison overcrowding.[2]

With regard to another judicial power—the appointment of judges to high courts—the Turkish president appears at first to have even greater powers than the U.S. president since his appointments are not subject to confirmation by the legislature. The major catch, however, is that the president must choose from a list of three candidates chosen by judicial councils themselves. While this provides a certain latitude to the president, in practice it leaves most of the power over judicial appointments within the judiciary itself.

A REDUCED LEGISLATIVE AND JUDICIAL ROLE FOR THE U.S. PRESIDENT?

It bears repetition that, in the U.S. system of separation of powers, it is natural that the American president would have sweeping executive authority, unlike the Turkish president. But the question here is whether the legislative and judicial powers of the president should reasonably be curbed to be brought more in line with the modest presidential authority to recommend laws rather than the more far-reaching and impactful power of the veto, the sole authority to nominate judges, and the unchecked power of the pardon.

A change to the veto process could be enacted with an exceedingly simple textual change in the presentment clause from two-thirds of each house to a simple majority in the procedure for overriding. But would such a change violate an important precept of the Constitution? Not necessarily since the historical record is unclear as to whether the veto was originally intended to be a political or policy tool or rather as a means for the president to try to block an unconstitutional act by Congress. This was indeed how early presidents used the veto, particularly before ability of the courts to invalidate unconstitutional acts through judicial review was fully articulated in 1803. In any case, the founders' original concern that Congress might become tyrannical if not checked by a vigorous executive veto power is scarcely a credible concern today.

Would the override of vetoes by simple majorities of both houses leave the veto a meaningless power? Again, not necessarily. While the simple majority requirement would indeed diminish the legislative role of the president, this power would still be no less, on its face, than the modest authority to "recommend laws"—yet this has not stopped presidents from playing a major role in the initiation of laws. A veto subject to a simple majority override would still enable the president to delay ill-conceived legislation, provide a clear platform for articulating objections, and perhaps sway some members of Congress to reconsider their vote, potentially altering the outcome in close votes. But with a diminished veto, the final decision in legislation would still belong to the legislative branch.

One caveat regarding any reform of the veto is that it would need to be coupled with the elimination—or at least radical restriction—of the use of so-called signing statements through which presidents explain how the executive will interpret a bill being signed into law, including any doubts about unconstitutional provisions. Presidents have sparingly used such statements to constructive ends, but the George W. Bush administration abused this authority, using it far more expansively and twice as many times as all previous presidents combined. Although signing statements have not been recognized as definitively binding, they have considerable potential for abuse. If the constitutional veto is to be reined in, then certainly this "backdoor veto" must be as well.

In addition, a word is in order about the encroachment of the executive into another area that is clearly and unambiguously assigned to the legislative branch: the sole power of Congress to declare war. Since World War II, both of these congressional prerogatives have been significantly compromised. Presidents have increasingly acted unilaterally in the commitment of troops abroad even for extended periods, such as in Korea, Vietnam, Iraq, and Afghanistan. In 1973, Congress reasserted itself through the War Powers Resolution, which gives the president mostly free rein for only up to 90 days. However, this has been resisted by presidents on the grounds that it impedes their authority as commander in chief. Placing the War Powers Resolution into the Constitution as an amendment would resolve this deadlock and restore clear control of the declaration of war to Congress.

What also, then, of the president's judicial powers? The right to nominate federal judges relates closely to the core functions of the executive, namely, to exercise considered judgment in the appointment of government officials. Indeed, a reading of the bare bones of article II of the Constitution would suggest that the major role of the president is to act as a sort of human resources director in chief. Article II provides the president with extensive authority to name executive officers, such as cabinet secretaries and ambassadors; issues the authority to commission them; and allows the president to "require the opinion, in writing, of the principal officer in each of the executive departments, upon any subject relating to the duties of their respective offices." Although there is no explicit power to continue to oversee or dismiss executive officers, the requirement to "take care that the laws be faithfully executed" has been interpreted to invest such authority in the president.

However, the president's relationship to and connection with the judiciary is rather different. Although they are nominated in much the same way as cabinet secretaries, there is no question that judges do not continue to be subject to the authority of the president who appointed them. The power to "require the opinion" does not extend to judges, nor does the president commission them, nor does the work of judges fall into the purview of faithful execution of the law given that their role is interpretation of the law.

Naturally, presidents make an effort to appoint judges who they find ideologically compatible and who they believe will rule in ways they find agreeable, but this by no means always works out. Moderate conservative Dwight Eisenhower regretted his nomination of Earl Warren as chief justice after Warren went to lead the Supreme Court in the case of *Brown v. Board of Education* and then through the highwater mark of its most liberal activist phase. The even more conservative Richard Nixon appointed Harry Blackmun as an associate justice, only to see him within a few years serve as lead author of the ruling in the landmark abortion case *Roe v. Wade*. Likewise, George H. W. Bush appointee David Souter and, to a lesser extent, Ronald Reagan appointee Anthony Kennedy also proved to be far less doctrinaire conservatives than was at first expected. (Interestingly, the reverse pattern of liberal judges drifting rightward seems to be less common.)

The independence of the judiciary thus minimizes the potential for abuse of the judicial nomination power by presidents. A further level of safeguard is added by the requirement of Senate confirmation, particularly in the modern era, when confirmation hearings before the Senate Judiciary Committee have become high-profile events, particularly for Supreme Court justices. While confirmation hearings certainly run the risk of becoming media circuses, as they did most notoriously in the case of Justice Clarence Thomas, the public scrutiny of judges, including extensive media attention, adds a salutary layer of accountability and transparency to the judicial selection process. Further input, particularly at the level of district court nominations, is provided by the informal convention that senators of the same party of the president are allowed to suggest nominees for vacancies affecting their states and also that the Senate will not act on the nomination of a judge if a home-state senator is in opposition. A final important layer of scrutiny regarding the professional skills and qualifications of nominees is provided by the quasi-official role played by the American Bar Association in rating nominees.

One potential area of reform would be to give the judiciary itself some influence over the process of who is initially appointed to the bench and also over who is to be elevated from the lower-level district courts to the circuit court of appeals and ultimately to the Supreme Court. Since federal judges are unelected, it would hardly be a democratic innovation to give them excessive power over this process; there clearly should be a role for the elected officials of the executive and the legislative branches. The Turkish model is one possibility, with judges choosing a limited number of candidates either for initial appointment or for promotion, from which the president must choose. An alternative formulation would be to give the judiciary the ability to veto a nomination.

While the role of the president in judicial nominations already has significant informal checks and balances, the pardon power remains susceptible to significant abuse. However, at present, such concerns seem more theoretical than real. Public opinion and other political calculations have proven fairly effective in holding most presidents in check from misuse of the pardon power, particularly when they are up for reelection; the fact that Gerald Ford probably would have won his 1976 race had he not pardoned Nixon has not been lost on subsequent presidents. The most vulnerable window of time is probably the last few days of an outgoing presidency. George H. W. Bush, after repudiation by the voters in the 1992 presidential election, cleared figures relating to the Iran-Contra scandal, and, even more controversially, Bill Clinton issued several pardons to people who were viewed as contributors or supporters of himself or his wife Hillary Rodham Clinton. Yet, contrary to much speculation, George W. Bush did not make use of the pardon power in his waning days as president in order to shield members of his administration from controversies over the use of torture and the war in Iraq.

Had Bush done so, great attention would unquestionably have been directed to the absolute and unchecked nature of the pardon power. The most obvious and frequently discussed constitutional fix would be to extend the principle of the veto override to presidential pardons, allowing any particular pardon to be reversed by a two-thirds majority of both houses of Congress. Given that the pardon power is such an anomaly in the scheme of checks and balances, this would seem a reasonable step. It would be going too far, however, to outright eliminate any power to pardon. The judicial process can at times be impersonal and imprecise, and the opportunity for intervention into particular cases adds a valuable flexibility to the system. Further, there may be times when political imperatives really do call for setting aside the usual judicial process, such as the ability of the Vietnam-era amnesty for draft evaders to start to bind the wounds of a divided nation. In fact, there may be a case in which the pardon power could be extended to Congress, as in Turkey, where the Grand National Assembly can issue pardon by a supermajority vote.

SYNOPSIS

Desirability: 3

The presidency is already by far the single most powerful institution in American government on the basis of its purely executive authority, which has evolved significantly from the far more modest office originally sketched out in article II of the Constitution. If the other two branches of government are to continue to play their full roles under separation of powers, they should have greater latitude within their designated areas. Greater checks on the veto and the pardon power would diminish the president's ability to act unilaterally. Of the two, reform to the veto power is more pressing, as most presidents have exercised restraint with regard to the pardon power.

Practicability: 4

Since both the veto power and the pardon power are textually based in the Constitution, amendments would clearly be required. As with all constitutional amendments, the president would play no role formal role, hence blocking the single most likely source of objection. Since both changes would enhance the power of Congress, the two-thirds majority required in each house could be achieved were the circumstances to merit it, and the states likewise would have no strong impetus to object.

Plausibility: 3

Changes to the pardon power seem quite unlikely if only because political pressure has been rather effective in limiting the exercise of this authority. Other than a brief flap over some pardons granted by Bill Clinton as he was leaving the White House, the authority has been mostly uncontroversial for decades. The lowering of the threshold for the veto might spark more interest, particularly within the context of other reforms to strengthen Congress and streamline the lawmaking process.

CHAPTER 14

Synchronize the Terms of Congress and the President

Highlighting Ideas from the Netherlands

Separation of powers is perhaps the single most distinctive feature of the U.S. political system when viewed alongside other established democracies. The most obvious manifestation of this separation is the institutional sealing off of the executive from the legislature and of the judiciary from state- or city-level offices. Further, the memberships of the three branches are entirely nonoverlapping since no one can serve simultaneously in more than one branch, albeit with the one peculiar exception of the vice president. To reinforce separation of powers, the framers established differences in the jurisdictions, modes of election, and terms of office for the president, representatives, and senators—all the better to deter collusion among the branches that might lead to tyranny, the framers' great and recurrent fear.

And so the framers chose to create a president with a four-year term, representing all the people but chosen by the ill-defined Electoral College. In this way, the president could represent the entire nation but formally be chosen by electors who might have a greater ability to deliberate wisely than would the overall electorate. The framers endowed senators with lengthy six-year terms, the large constituency of entire states, and (until the Seventeenth Amendment of 1913) selection by state legislatures rather than by the people at large. Although not nearly as insulated from the people as the British House of Lords, on which the Senate was loosely modeled, the long term of office, large constituencies, and indirect election of senators freed them to take a longer and broader view. Finally, representatives—true to their title—were to be elected for brief two-year terms directly by the mass population and representing congressional districts that are generally much smaller than entire states. Representatives would thus be motivated by different electoral incentives than senators, being kept on a short electoral leash and answerable directly to the people of a district that is likely to be far more homogeneous than the diverse population of an entire state.

To the extent that the founders wanted to promote inefficiency in order to prevent tyranny, they were successful—perhaps too much so. Other major developments in American political history have helped reverse some of the disjunctions found within the separation of powers system. Certainly, the most important of these has been the rise of political parties, which play a major role in elections but also in the coordination of relations among the branches. During periods of unified party government, in which the presidency and both houses of Congress are controlled by the same party, coordination is easier, and government can be more efficient in producing public policy. Divided government, on the other hand, may lead to centrist compromise policies but is less likely to produce decisive action and is more prone to gridlock and immobility.

Separation of powers can be seen as a significant contributing factor to a host of circumstances in which problems have been left to fester rather than be dealt with expeditiously. One prominent example is the issue of segregation, which was allowed to persist for generations. Even after the Supreme Court declared segregation unconstitutional in 1954's *Brown v. Board of Education* ruling and even after presidents such as Franklin Roosevelt, Harry Truman, and John F. Kennedy began to take the side of civil rights, progress was thwarted by Congress, largely because of the influence of southern Democratic senators with a great deal of seniority. There proved to be only a brief period of time, aided by the political clout created by the Kennedy assassination, the skills of Lyndon Johnson, and the pressure of the civil rights movement, that breakthroughs finally took place in the form of the Civil Rights Act of 1964 and the Voting Rights Act of 1965. Yet by 1968, the window of political opportunity for progress snapped shut, and the government since then has largely neglected issues of integration and the advancement of minorities.

A more recent example took place in the summer of 2006, when a universal agreement that immigration policy was desperately in need of an overhaul led to complete impasse: neither the punitive measures proposed by House Republicans nor an outright amnesty as advanced in some liberal Democratic quarters nor the middle ground of a guest worker program that won favor in the Senate was able to find a majority. Fragmentation, acrimony, disarray, and inaction were the only products of lengthy debate.

This overfragmentation contributes to another persistent problem in the United States: a lack of accountability to the voters. When there is a major failure of the U.S. system—as in the case of immigration but also health care reform, the maintenance of national infrastructure, the improvement of the educational system, the overhaul of the Social Security program, and many others—each institution and party can point at the other. Republicans blame Democrats and vice versa. The two houses of Congress blame one another or the president, the president blames the Congress, the states blame the national government, and everyone blames the courts. And, to an extent, such blame sharing is warranted since it is exceptionally difficult for any one actor or institution in the U.S. system to act unilaterally.

By contrast, such ineffectiveness and lack of accountability is much less common in parliamentary systems, where gridlock across branches is by definition an impossibility. Since the executive is elected by the majority in the legislature, they are automatically in sync. The legislature initiates the formation of the executive and retains the power to replace it or to trigger new elections through a vote of no confidence. In the interim, the executive guides the legislature, introducing most bills with the assurance that they will become law by instructing their supporters to vote for them. Generally, governments in parliamentary systems are able to promise a political agenda to the voters and then quickly formulate and enact that agenda. All the members of Parliament are elected on the same day and in response to the same set of circumstances and concerns among the voters, and all will serve for the same period of time.

Of course, some problems remain intractable because of their complex or difficult nature, but if these problems are not addressed, it will not be because the government lacks the institutional mechanisms to address them. Thus, come election time, citizens in a parliamentary system are far more able to determine whether the party in power used its mandate well and should be rewarded with reelection or whether it is time to give the opposition a chance. In either case, all the members of at least the lower house of Parliament—from which the government is drawn—will be subject to the election, and the new majority will have a fresh mandate. (Readers desiring a brief refresher on key elements of the parliamentary system may wish to consult Appendix 2.)

Of course, parliamentary systems are not perfect, and reality does not always play out as in the streamlined process outlined here.

When no single party controls a majority of the legislature and thus the formation of coalition is required, efficiency can be undermined by haggling among the parties in the coalition—which some have called a form of "parliamentary gridlock." And in so-called semipresidential systems in which both a president and a prime minister are invested with executive powers, most notably as in France and Russia, tensions within the dual executive can lead to a type of gridlock as well. Other potential impediments include a "backbench revolt" against the policies or priorities of the prime minister, delaying and interference from the upper house, and procedural maneuvers by the opposition.

However, the purpose here is not to critique the pros and cons of parliamentary systems but rather to determine what value lessons, insights, and ideas these can offer the U.S. system. And, indeed, there are reforms that could certainly be undertaken to promote parliamentary-style efficiency and accountability in the United States. The most important of these would be to synchronize the terms of office for president, the House, and the Senate in order to minimize staggered elections that produce divided government and undermine coordination across the branches. Among the established parliamentary systems of the world, the Netherlands comes perhaps the closest to an ideal form of synchronization of terms across both of its legislative houses and the executive.

CASE STUDY: SYNCHRONIZED TERMS IN THE NETHERLANDS

Formally, executive power in the Netherlands resides in a hereditary monarchy, which is not subject to election. In practice, as in most parliamentary democracies, real executive authority in the Dutch system arises from the support of a majority of the members of the lower house of the legislature, in this case known as the Second Chamber. Typically in parliamentary systems, the prime minister and the other senior and junior ministers *must* be sitting members of the legislature who continue to hold their seats while serving in an executive capacity. But in a major modification found in the Netherlands, Belgium, and a few other northern European states, members of the executive are *not* allowed to be sitting members, and ministers must vacate any legislative seats they may hold.[1]

The executive takes the institutional form of the Council of Ministers, the creation of which results from negotiation among the party leaders in the States-General, and its partisan composition reflects that of the majority coalition of parties. Although not specifically appointed or even formally approved by the States-General, the various ministers and the government collectively are subject to removal from office by a vote of no confidence by the Second Chamber. Still, they are a separately constituted branch of government and in no sense part of the Parliament—indeed, when executive ministers come to Parliament, they are seated in a special section separated from legislators. Likewise, the speaker and other leaders of the Second Chamber schedule parliamentary debates and other activities on their own accord, without direction from the prime minister, as is usual in other parliamentary systems. On the expiration of the four-year term of a parliamentary or following a vote of no confidence, a new election is held for the Second Chamber, which will then need to agree to a new government. At the same time, the executive can also dissolve Parliament and call new elections at will, although this authority is rarely used since it will result in the replacement of the executive as well.

Like most Parliaments, the Dutch States-General also includes an upper house called the First Chamber chosen not directly by the people but by the 12 provincial legislatures. Often, such upper houses are ongoing bodies, as in the United Kingdom and Canada (or partly so in the U.S. Senate), or else the upper chamber is filled on a different electoral cycle, as in Belgium and France. However, whenever there is an election for the Second Chamber, the Dutch provincial legislatures must also hold an election for the First Chamber. The First Chamber meets less often than the Second, has no power to initiate or amend bills, and in practice takes a decidedly lower profile than the Second, but its support or at least acquiescence is also necessary for the Council of Ministers to enter and remain in office.

Thus, in many ways, the Dutch political system has attributes that approximate a separation-of-powers system, with three institutionally separate power centers. What it emphatically does not have, however, is the fragmentation of terms that characterizes the U.S. system. The executive and both houses of the Parliament are placed into office at the same time, and all will be replaced at the same time. Further, the entire Second Chamber is chosen in a single nationwide election with no electoral districts, further ensuring that the interests of its members are not fragmented by needing to serve diverse constituencies. And both chambers must support the Council of Ministers, promoting cooperation, collaboration, and coordination.

SYNCHRONIZED TERMS IN THE UNITED STATES?

As noted previously, there is a logic inherent in the differential terms of office, as well as differences in constituency, that is in fact designed to promote differences between senators and representatives. With the Senate being a smaller body, whose members were originally elected by state legislatures, the six-year term adds to the lofty station afforded to senators. Conversely, the two-year term helps prevent representatives from drifting away from the people they represent. Finally, the four-year presidential term gives the president time enough to exercise "energy in the executive," in the famous words of Alexander Hamilton, and to establish a functioning administration. But four years is also not so long that a president will become ensconced in power without having to worry about accountability to the people (or at least to the Electoral College) via the ballot box.

As intended by the framers, giving different elected officials different time horizons and modes of election does make it harder, perhaps too hard, for them to coordinate among themselves. Notably, however, the United States has already dispensed with one of these forms of separation. For nearly a century, senators have now been directly elected by the people, just as House members are, and allocation of votes in the Electoral College is likewise driven by the popular vote (notwithstanding the potential for distortions, as in the election of 2000).

These changes have been driven by the logic of democratic governance itself—the idea that the people should have a direct choice in their elected officials. However, the issue of the length of terms of office does not rise to that level of significance. There is nothing really more intrinsically democratic about a two-year term than a four- or six-year one (or, for that matter, a one- or five-year one). However, if having staggered terms of office contributes to the inability of government to effectively serve the people, then a problem arises.

This problem is most highlighted by the disruption and fragmentation caused by the existence of midterm elections, those that take place two years into a presidential term. At that time, one-third of the Senate and all 435 members of the House would be up for reelection. These midterm elections could greatly alter the composition of Congress in a way that makes it incompatible with the results of the prior election in which a president was chosen. In reality, the powerful electoral advantages of incumbency—everything from fund-raising to the ability to "bring home the pork" to simple name recognition among voters—mean that the legislature is never changed wholesale. Still, it is notable that party control has been particularly volatile and unpredictable over the past quarter of a century, with at least one house of Congress changing party control five times, often in the middle of a presidential term. At the same time, party control of the presidency switched three times. Consider the changing pattern laid out in Table 14.1. As the table demonstrates, the longest that the same configuration of party power remained the same was for two Congresses at a time. Amidst all these swings, both houses, but particularly the Senate, often had razor-thin margins rather than solid party majorities, further muddying the picture regarding the distribution of actual power. Indeed, after the 2000 election, the Senate was evenly divided 50-50, relying on the vice president's veto until one Republican senator, James Jeffords, decided to support the Democrats and thus tilt power to them.

All these swings had significant implications for governance. Ronald Reagan was elected in 1984, Bill Clinton in 1992, and George W. Bush in both 2000 and 2004 with the expectation that they would have a governing partner in either or both houses of Congress, but that situation reversed within two years. Since the Democrats lost control of Congress during only the second of Bill Clinton's eight

Table 14.1   Changes in Divided Government, 1987–2009

Year	Congress	President	Senate	House
1987	100th Congress	R	D*	D
1989	101st Congress	R	D	D
1991	102nd Congress	R	D	D
1993	103rd Congress	D*	D	D
1995	104th Congress	D	R*	R*
1997	105th Congress	D	R	R
1999	106th Congress	D	R	R
2001	107th Congress	R*	D*	R
2003	108th Congress	R	R*	R
2005	109th Congress	R	R	R
2007	110th Congress	R	D*	D*
2009	111th Congress	D*	D	D

Note: An asterisk marks a change in party control.

years in office, the entire trajectory of his administration was altered. Similarly, losing Congress in George W. Bush's sixth year in power meant the abrupt truncation of his agenda, particularly on the domestic front.

As part of the search for more effective governance, then, the adoption of a parliamentary-style uniform term of office such as that found in the Netherlands should be considered. The most straightforward reform would be to "average out" the two-year terms of both representatives and the six-year terms of senators to the same four-year term as the president. Under this scenario, Senate terms would also not be staggered, but the entire Senate would be elected at the same time, as are members of the House. The shortening of the six-year term to a four-year one for senators would likely go unmourned (except perhaps by senators themselves). One measure of the anomalous character of this lengthy term is that no other legislative office in any state carries a term longer than four years. The increase of the House term to four years could also address the often-expressed concern that a two-year term for members of the House is simply too short. Consider that a representative elected in the fall of 2008 takes office in January 2009, has to receive party renomination in mid-2010, and then stand for reelection in the fall of 2010. Giving representatives a four-year term would allow them three full years within which to focus on their actual work without becoming preoccupied with reelection activities.

As for the presidential term, there are critics of the four-year renewable term. In this case, though, the criticisms relate not so much to the number of years as to the complications of reelection. Would it be better, some wonder, if the president had only a single term and was thus freed from maneuvering for reelection and to concentrate on governing and making the most of the single term? Historically, it can be observed that many second-term presidencies do not work out well when the initial surge of energy has dissipated, when scandals have begun to accrue, and when there is no possibility of reelection. It was during second terms that the Watergate scandal ended the Nixon presidency, the Iran-Contra affair marked the low point of the Reagan administration, Bill Clinton was impeached, and George W. Bush's popularity and support plummeted after poor performance in Iraq and in the aftermath of Hurricane Katrina. However, this pattern could just as readily be interpreted as either an argument for a single term or an argument against term limits for life, allowing a president back into office but only after at least four years had elapsed, as is the practice for some state governorships, city mayoralties, and a number of foreign presidencies.

Whichever approach is taken, there is a much greater likelihood that the voters would elect the members of a single party to control all three institutions. What would be the impact of this reform, which would essentially allow the voters to make a determination of the party control and thus the direction of public policy all at one time? The executive and the legislative branches could be synchronized, with all three chosen on the same day, by the same means of direct popular vote, and for the same period of time. The reversals, interruptions, and inconclusive stalemates of staggered and midterm elections would be eliminated, and greater effectiveness and accountability would result.

While on the subject of synchronizing terms, it would also be worthwhile to consider adding a fixed period of service for justices of the Supreme Court. Federal judges, in general, serve for a term of "good behavior," which, barring the extremely unlikely event of an impeachment for malfeasance, means until they die or voluntarily retire. The life term allows judges to be insulated both from political pressure and from public opinion and thus protects the integrity of the judiciary as a whole. To the extent that the Supreme Court draws its democratic credibility from appointment by an elected president and confirmation by an elected Senate, however, it is problematic for justices to remain on the bench for decades at a time, often distantly removed from the circumstances in which they were originally appointed. The U.S. Constitution is mostly silent as to the composition of the Supreme Court, for example, nowhere specifying that it must be composed of nine justices. It is thus plausible that Congress might legislate a nonrenewable fixed term for Supreme Court justices of perhaps 12 or 16 years, after which they would remain federal judges but at a lower level. Such a term would be long enough for justices to still be mostly insulated from undue pressure but also allow the frequent replenishment of the Court by presidential appointment. A 12- or 16-year term could also help synchronize the Court to the cycles of presidential elections, providing greater predictability in terms of new appointments.

All the reforms outlined in this chapter would still not, of course, move the American political system all the way to the effectiveness and accountability of a parliamentary system. Even if terms and modes of election were to be coordinated, with the resultant effect of greater party cohesion and policy coordination, there would remain major *institutional* barriers. The House, the Senate and the president would still each have formidable powers and their own agendas. James Madison's original vision of "ambition countering ambition" would remain in force. Nothing short of the elimination of the presidency as a separately elected institution and replacement by a prime-ministerial executive chosen by and answerable to Congress could achieve that. As noted in this book's introduction, such a thoroughgoing overhaul of the system is beyond the scope of this book—and probably also beyond the pale of contemplation for the U.S. constitutional system. Yet there are still other ways to streamline and simplify the process of governing while enhancing its democratic accountability. One of these ways, weakening the Senate relative to the House, is the subject of the next chapter.

SYNOPSIS

Desirability: 3

To the extent that gridlock is a major impediment to the effective functioning of the U.S. government, any steps that tend to promote greater coordination and efficiency are welcome. The synchronization of terms of office of the president, senators, and representatives would allow the voters to choose a more coordinated "team." Because the two chambers of Congress remain institutionally separated from one another and both from the presidency, the potential for conflict still exists. But coordinated time horizons and simultaneous election could have considerable impact. Beyond synchronization, there is also value to the idea of freeing representatives from their short terms and making senators more regularly accountable than their lengthy terms now require.

Practicability: 3

This change would require a constitutional amendment but a fairly straightforward one. Members of the House of Representatives would likely be in favor of a longer term, although a two-thirds majority in the Senate would be harder to muster, particularly if senators would be required to immediately give up their seats. A temporary exception for sitting senators might soften this blow; a similar exception for the incumbent president was built into the Twenty-Second Amendment limiting presidents to two terms. Given that coordinated four-year terms are fairly common in state legislatures, ratification by the states would seem less problematic.

Plausibility: 3

Since about 1968, American voters have seemed—for a panoply of reasons—to accept or perhaps even prefer divided government, with only a total of 10 of the following 40 years (1977–81, 1993–95, and 2003–7) marked by unified control of government. This period also overlapped, however, with deep skepticism about the idea of energetic, activist government. If there is a renewed desire of the American public for government that is more able to deliver, the model of parliamentary Western European social democracies may become more appealing. With the interests of House and Senate members opposed in terms of a change to a uniform four-year term, pressure would probably have to come mostly from below.

CHAPTER 15

Weaken the Senate

Highlighting Ideas from India

At the time of the founding, the new nation had very little experience with elected officials in executive office and thus was uncertain about how to structure the new presidency. However, the framers of the U.S. Constitution had a far better idea of what they wanted in a legislature, drawing directly on the experience of the Confederation Congress and the Continental Congress as well as that of state legislatures and the colonial assemblies that had preceded them. The range and scope of legislative powers outlined in article I were carefully considered and have endured over time. The same approbation cannot be provided with regard to some of the *structures* of Congress, however, which were part of the pragmatic negotiations that took place at the convention. These may have been necessary for approval and subsequent ratification of the new Constitution and perhaps were unavoidable for that reason.

Fortunately, historical developments have eradicated the most odious of the compromises, namely, the Constitution's silence on slavery and its provisions for the return of fugitive slaves. The Three-Fifths Compromise that included 60 percent of the enslaved population when apportioning seats in the House has also been rendered moot by time. The argument has already been made in Chapter 4 for the abolition of another ill-considered compromise: the Electoral College. Yet the "Great Compromise" with regard to Congress—equal representation in the Senate—has long been not only accepted but even lauded as a creative breakthrough.

The idea of bicameralism itself is rooted partly in the founders' experience of Great Britain, in which the lower house represented the commoners, while the upper house was reserved for the nobility.

Similarly, in many colonial and, later, state legislatures, membership in the upper house included property requirements that gave it a more upper-class characteristic. When fashioning a new Congress, the founders adopted a bicameral structure in part as a check against tyranny— by subdividing Congress, they created a sort of internal check within the legislature, which they expected to be the strongest of the branches. Another was to provide balance to the presumably more impetuous House of Representatives. With fewer members enjoying a six-year term and (until the Seventeenth Amendment of 1913) election by state legislatures rather than directly by the people, the Senate would prevent rash action.

The principle of equal representation in the Senate, however, was harder to justify on the basis of democratic theory. James Madison, in Federalist 62 and 63, goes to great lengths to justify the Senate as the chamber that reflects the "federal principle." But far from being a logical deduction from democratic theory, equal representation was more a question of bowing to reality: small-population states like Rhode Island and Delaware might be willing to concede more powers to a new central government than they had under the Articles of Confederation, but they would not permit themselves to have a vanishingly small voice. So important was this issue to the founders that equal representation in the Senate is one of only two provisions in the entire Constitution that is *entrenched*, meaning that it is explicitly excluded from the possibility of amendment in article V. The only other entrenched provision, a 20-year moratorium on congressional legislation regarding slavery, lapsed naturally in 1808, but the Senate equal representation clause has no expiration date.

Thus, what was difficult to defend—except on pragmatic grounds— in the 1780s has remained with us but has become even more difficult to defend as the differential in population size has grown. At the time of the founding, the free population of the smallest state, Rhode Island, had just one-seventh of the free population of the largest state, Virginia. Today, to take the similarly most extreme case, California has 35 million people, while Wyoming has half a million, yet both states have two U.S. senators. Thus, Wyoming residents have 70 times more senatorial representation per capita than do Californians. Likewise, per capita North Dakotans have 37 times the influence as Texans, Vermonters have 30 times the clout of their neighbors in New York, and Floridians have just one-twentieth the voice of the fine citizens of Delaware. In fact, the largest nine states include more than half the nation's population but only 18 seats in the Senate. The 26 smallest states hold a majority, 52 seats, in the Senate but less than 18 percent of the overall U.S. population, leaving 82 percent of the population represented by a minority of just 48 senators. This picture gets even worse when one considers that any 41 senators is enough to sustain a filibuster, yet the senators from these states represent not even 12 percent of the national population (see Table 15.1).

The antidemocratic qualities of such "malapportionment" were noted by the Supreme Court in its 1964 ruling in the case of *Reynolds v. Sims*, which established the "one-person, one-vote" standard for legislative districting. Because of this ruling, those state senates that had once been apportioned as the U.S. Senate is—such as with one state senator from each county—were forced to reapportion districts on the basis of population. Ironically, however, the one-person, one-vote standard was *not* applied to the U.S. Senate precisely because of the entrenchment of equal representation in article V. Since the power of the Supreme Court derives from the Constitution, it had no ability to reverse this undemocratic feature of the U.S. Senate.

Of course, the larger states do continue to have drastically more representation than do the smaller states in the House and thus in Congress overall. But since every piece of legislation, every budget authorization, and every constitutional amendment must pass both chambers, the enhanced power of the smaller states should not be understated. Worse still, the Senate has important extra powers, including the ratification of treaties, the confirmation of presidential nominees to high office,

Table 15.1   The Nine Largest States

State	2008 Population
California	36,756,666 (11.95%)
Texas	24,326,974 (7.81%)
New York	19,490,297 (6.31%)
Florida	18,328,340 (5.97%)
Illinois	12,901,563 (4.2%)
Pennsylvania	12,448,279 (4.06%)
Ohio	11,485,910 (3.75%)
Michigan	10,003,422 (3.29%)
Georgia	9,685,744 (3.12%)
Total:	155,422,195 (52.1%)
All 50 states:	298,141,399 (100%)

and final say in the impeachment process. The policy implications of this can be great, with federal funding being provided to smaller states in amounts far out of proportion to their populations and laws routinely being bent in the direction of sparsely populated rural areas often to the detriment of the nation's cities.

Given the seeming impossibility of changing the standard of equal state representation in the Senate, what can be done? The most drastic change would be the outright abolition of the Senate since article V would become defunct should the Senate itself cease to exist. And there are certainly many countries that get by with a unicameral legislature—about a third of the countries of Europe, for example. And within the United States, the state of Nebraska and even the largest U.S. cities have done perfectly well with unicameralism.

Although the United States certainly could function with just a single-chambered legislature, the complete abolition of the Senate is probably going too far. Bicameralism does provide a valuable internal check within the legislative process as well as a balance created by a second house with different characteristics. Likewise, having a second legislative chamber serves the democratic goal of a greater diversity of voices and perspective to be heard and allows for "sober second thought" to help guard against quick passage of ill-considered laws. Further, the valuable additional layer of oversight of the federal bureaucracy, through the standing committees of the Senate, would be lost. And the notion of federalism at the national level would also be undermined, with the smallest state left vulnerable. For example, in a unicameral House, the 12 smallest states would have only 17 representatives in the *entire* legislature. From a comparative perspective, it is also noteworthy that among the 25 federal states in the world, nearly all have traditionally had a bicameral legislature in order to provide a voice to representatives of the federal units.

Fortunately, the comparative approach also offers a ready-made model for reform: an upper house that plays a distinctive role but that is decisively weaker than the lower house. Indeed, in parliamentary systems throughout the world, this is the norm. In some case, this asymmetry has been codified into law, as in the Parliament Act of 1911, which gave the British House of Commons the ability to overrule the traditionally hereditary House of Lords, which now can only delay legislation. In Canada, the appointed Senate technically has the same powers as the House of Commons but by convention accepts a subordinate role. This British inheritance has also extended to other former colonies, including the world's most populous and diverse democracy: India.

CASE STUDY: ASYMMETRIC BICAMERALISM IN INDIA

In the aftermath of the independence movement led by Mahatma Mohandas K. Gandhi, the new Indian state chose to broadly adopt the British Westminster parliamentary model. The president, elected by Parliament, is a ceremonial figurehead not unlike the British monarch. The lower house, the Lok Sabha, or "House of the People," was modeled on the House of Commons, with direct election of 552 representatives by voters in single-member districts from throughout the country; this popularly elected chamber produces a prime minister and cabinet who wield effective executive authority and can be removed by the Lok Sabha through a vote of no confidence.

Less obvious, however, was how to adapt the British tradition for a new upper house. Like Britain, India had an established aristocracy of maharajahs and other nobility that could have formed a House of Lords. But by 1947, that chamber had become something of an embarrassing anachronism and would have been even more so in a new Republic of India based on popular sovereignty. Instead, India looked to the experience of other federal countries, including the United States, for ways to use the upper house to reflect the enormous diversity of a country with (today) more than 1.2 billion people with a dizzying array of cultural, linguistic, religious, caste, and other heritages. Thus, they crafted the Rajya Sabha as the "Council of States" in order to reflect the interests of all parts of the sprawling country. As in the United States until 1913, members are chosen by the state legislatures rather than directly by the voters for a term of six years. Unlike in the United States, a PR system is used to fill the chamber's 238 seats among 30 states and territories, with apportionment based on population rather than on equal representation. An additional 12 members are named directly by the president of India and are usually prominent social or cultural figures.

Perhaps the most important difference between the Rajya Sabha and the U.S. Senate, however, is that in India the upper house is not a full partner in the legislative process since the constitution allows it to be overridden by the Lok Sabha. Indeed, on finance-related matters, the Lok Sabha's decisions are final, with the upper house having only 14 days to register its opinion. By contrast, the U.S. House has only the comparatively minor authority to initiate all finance-related bills, all of which still require the consent of the Senate. On legislation regarding nonfinancial questions, the Rajya Sabha technically has an equal say but in practice defers to the Lok Sabha. In part, this is because, as in the United Kingdom and Canada, the lower house has greater democratic credibility since its members are directly elected by the voters and since it has the sole responsibility for constituting the government.

But the upper house also defers because it knows that should an impasse continue for more than six months, it will be broken by a vote taken in a joint session of the two chambers. Since the Lok Sabha has more than twice as many members, there is all but a guarantee that its wishes will prevail. Remarkably, since the founding of the Rajya Sabha in 1952, a joint sitting has been forced only three times. The first two times occurred more than three decades ago, involving a dowry bill in 1954 and a banking bill in 1977. In 2002, the Rajya Sabha refused to go along with a Prevention of Terrorism Bill that they considered draconian and abusive of civil liberties. The government based in the Lok Sabha forced the issue by convening a joint session and formally overriding the upper house. Notably, the bill was repealed less than two years later in part because of the initial widespread opposition from the Rajya Sabha and from opposition leaders in the Lok Sabha.[1]

Although the Lok Sabha may have the final say, in practice the Rajya Sabha continues to play a substantive role, partly because of its ability to delay nonfinancial legislation for up to six months. In fact, the mere threat of this delay has often caused the Lok Sabha to withdraw or rewrite legislation, the latter sometimes through a joint committee with upper house members. As a result, the recommendations of the Rajya Sabha often become part of the law. Members of the upper house also play a significant role in the overall legislative process, including introducing legislation, offering amendments, and conducting debates. In addition, the approval of the Rajya Sabha is required for such weighty although infrequent matters as constitutional amendments, declarations of war and national emergency, and presidential impeachments. It is thus only in the case of a true showdown that the lower house unambiguously prevails.

A WEAKENED SENATE IN THE UNITED STATES?

Although the Indian Rajya Sabha may seem a weak body in the American context, it is in fact a "middle-of-the-pack" chamber when compared to upper houses in other countries. In a number of parliamentary democracies, the upper house plays a merely advisory or consultative role. At the weakest end are chambers such as the British House of Lords and the Irish Senate, which look over legislation, hold hearings, and offer suggestions but little more. A bit more active would be the senates of France and Canada, which sometimes initiate legislation and have more bargaining power. Outside the Western Hemisphere, however, it is unusual for both houses of a national legislature to have truly equal power, and when this does occur, the results are not always desirable. For example, the ability of the Italian Senate to stymie the government—including bringing it down with a vote of no confidence, as happened in January 2008—has contributed to that country's chronic governmental instability.

So how, then, could the value of the U.S. Senate as a second chamber be maintained but still reconciled to the reality that its method of equal representation to all states grossly violates the one-person, one-vote standard? At first glance, the system established by the United States in the Federal Republic of Germany after World War II might seem to have promise. Under this system, the Bundestag, or upper house, has an absolute veto over any legislation involving the federal states but can be overridden by the Bundesrat, or lower house, on matters of national-level policymaking.

On closer examination, however, two crucial elements present in Germany are not found in the United States. First, the members of the Bundestag are not elected but rather appointed by the state governors and subject to their direction. They are essentially ambassadors to the federal government, and as such the Bundestag far more directly reflects the will of the German states than the U.S. Senate represents the will of the American states, even before 1912, when U.S. senators were elected by state legislatures. This robust element of federalism was imposed on Germany precisely to prevent an overcentralization of power in the capital as had occurred under the Nazis. But it would surely be a step in the wrong direction for American democracy for U.S. senators to be placed under the control of state governors. A related problem is that while the German constitution—formally called its "Basic Law"—clearly articulates the areas of authority involving the states, the U.S. Constitution is much murkier, and the interwoven practices of "cooperative federalism" practiced in the United States has blurred the distinctions even further. To give the U.S. Senate a special role with specific regard to issues involving the states, then, seems to be a practical and theoretical nonstarter.

The approach used in the Indian Parliament would probably be more viable—a joint sitting in which the will of the 435 votes in the

House of Representatives would almost certainly override that of the 100 votes in the Senate. Joint sittings of Congress are not unheard of, such as for ceremonial occasions like the State of the Union Address. But the idea of joint *lawmaking* would be a complete innovation, and the procedural rules would need to be crafted from scratch. For example, who would preside—the Speaker of the House, who has considerable power over that chamber, or the vice president, who plays only a ceremonial role in the Senate? Would they include debate and amendments or just an up-or-down vote? How often would such joint sittings occur, and how would they be initiated? Extensive new rules would have to be created ex nihilo.

The comparative record also does not provide much reason to embrace this approach. As we saw previously, in more than 60 years of independence, India has used the approach only three times. A similar provision for such a joint sitting exists under the Australian constitution, but it can be held only after an immediate "double dissolution" of both houses of Parliament and a new "snap" election. For politicians eager to hold their seats in office, this certainly creates great disincentives for resorting to such an approach very often. In fact, it has been used even less frequently than India—exactly once in all of Australian history, in 1975, when the Senate refused to pass the government's budget and reached a deadlock that spiraled into the country's biggest constitutional crisis.

A simpler and less problematic approach, then, might be to adapt the existing congressional override procedure for presidential vetoes. Currently, a two-thirds majority of both chambers is needed to override a presidential veto. But this could first be altered so that an override could take place with a two-thirds vote of just the House, thus strengthening that chamber with regard to the president. Then the same standard of two-thirds of the House could be applied to the Senate. Under this procedure, should the Senate have rejected a piece of legislation or an appropriations bill or failed to act on one at all, it could become law purely with a two-thirds majority in the House.

This would greatly strengthen the more democratically representative House over the Senate without going to the extreme of eliminating the upper house and the distinctive layer of representation it offers. Such a constitutional approach would also not violate the equal representation protections of article V since each state would still have two senators with exactly one vote. However, the *overall* power of the Senate as a chamber would be reduced, bringing U.S. practice in line with that most commonly found throughout the democratic world. (The role of the Senate and indeed of Congress itself in the constitutional amendment process is discussed further in Chapter 20.)

And what of the other special powers of the Senate, such as treaty ratification and confirmation of presidential nominees? One possibility would be to simply transfer these powers to the House; another would be to require a vote of both Houses, subject to the same two-thirds House override of the Senate. Another major function of the Senate, the conducting of oversight and the launching of investigations into the actions of the executive, should be maintained in full form—an extra layer of scrutiny of the executive can only be beneficial. Finally, regarding the Senate as the final arbiter in the removal of the president or other executive or judicial officeholders, the current system may work well enough. Few issues require greater deliberation than the decision to reverse the results of an election, and the "sober second thought" offered by the Senate may continue to serve the country well. As discussed in Chapter 9, "removal for cause" of the president should also be added as an option for Congress.

Weakening the Senate could also provide an opportunity for other reforms that have been discussed in that chamber. One important reform would be eliminating the bizarre and profoundly undemocratic practice in which Senate vacancies that arise between elections can be unilaterally filled by state governors. The 2008 elections highlighted this scattershot process, with governors in five states simultaneously filling seats left empty when sitting senators, including the new president and vice president, joined the Obama administration. The most sordid chapter of this process was the scandal involving Governor Rod Blagojevich's alleged attempts to "sell" the Senate seat vacated by Obama, leading to Blagojevich's quick removal from office by the Illinois legislature. Governors have filled dozens of powerful Senate seats since they gained this authority under the Seventeenth Amendment of 1912, and in late 2009 one in eight Americans was represented by at least one appointed senator. Fortunately, the more democratic practice of holding a special election can be enacted by the individual state legislatures and would require no amendment to Constitution. In 2009-2010, Massachusetts used a combination of an interim appointment followed by a quick election, a possible compromise practice.

Another innovation that has from time to time been proposed is granting former presidents and perhaps vice presidents who have honorably completed their terms the option of a lifetime seat in the Senate.

This is the practice in, for example, Italy, where former presidents of the republic take their place for as senators for life. The advantage would be to give these former officeholders a continuing stake in government and a dignified, ongoing platform from which to share their unique experience and prestige for the betterment of the nation. It might also have the effect of curbing potentially troublesome freelance activities; we cannot be assured that the benign postpresidential careers of Jimmy Carter, George H. W. Bush, or Bill Clinton will always prevail in the future. One obvious argument against such a move is that it could impact close votes in the Senate, but if the House is empowered to override the Senate, this problem becomes less acute. Further, it would be possible to make this an honorific post as is done in Paraguay, where former presidents can serve on committees and give speeches but cannot cast a vote.

Meanwhile, the House remains the national institution that can most clearly reflect the mass preferences of the public. Yet its ability to do so is compromised when the electoral system that puts representatives into office is skewed in a way that gives one side an unfair advantage. This problem of partisan redistricting, or gerrymandering, is the subject of the next chapter.

SYNOPSIS

Desirability: 2

In principle, the U.S. Senate egregiously violates the standard of one person, one vote; hence, in principle, it would be desirable to weaken it relative to the House. In practice, however, the Senate plays a role that is at least as constructive as the House and often provides a moderating influence. Longer terms of office and larger constituencies provide many (though not all) senators with a broader view than many (though not all) members of the House. The smaller size and more freewheeling style of the body also allow senators to provide balance to a potentially volatile and majoritarian House. Ironically, however, the very *possibility* of weakening the Senate may be enough to avoid needing to carry through on the threat.

Practicability: 2

Extending an override authority to the House or even more unprecedented changes such as joint legislative sittings would clearly require a constitutional amendment. Thus, mustering two-thirds of the Senate would be difficult to say the least; similarly, enough smaller states gain outsized benefits from their "overrepresentation" in the Senate. A more subtle change could come through the evolution of a "convention" of deference or restraint from the upper house, which could conceivably emerge should public awareness grow of just how malapportioned the Senate is relative to state populations.

Plausibility: 2

Once previously in U.S. history, we have indeed witnessed the Senate—and the state legislatures—acquiescing to a major change regarding the upper house: the Seventeenth Amendment of 1912. This amendment, requiring senators to be elected directly by the people and not by the state legislatures, was originally strongly opposed by many powerful political insiders who benefited from cronyism. Massive public pressure during the Progressive Era—up to and including the threat of a constitutional convention—eventually got the Senate to reform itself. In the context of a larger democratic movement, then, this reform is not entirely implausible.

CHAPTER 16

Depoliticize the Creation of Congressional Districts

Highlighting Ideas from Japan

Chapter co-authored with Brandon L. H. Aultman

In a democracy, the voters are supposed to choose the officials who will represent them—elected officials are not supposed to choose the voters they wish to represent. Yet all too often, elected officials do indeed have the opportunity to manipulate their jurisdictions by having partisan influence over the composition of their districts, a process known as "gerrymandering." This is not the case in the U.S. Senate, where the lines of state boundaries are clearly and permanently fixed. But in most other legislative bodies, it is officeholders themselves who can stretch, skew, alter, and manipulate the boundaries of jurisdictions so as to maximize the support for the party in power and to minimize the gains of the opposing party.

The heart of the matter is that the exercise of drawing districts is not pure arithmetic or the work of dispassionate political philosophers who are intent on upholding democratic tenets. There may in fact be some officials who participate in drawing district lines with such an aim in mind, but, on balance, these high-minded aims are preempted by the immediate needs of parties, the incumbents, or even the desires of state legislators to design a district for their own potential future bids for Congress. Yet redistricting has a major impact on representation and forces several questions. Who is being represented? What groups are left out? What groups, as a result of redistricting, prevail in national and state representative bodies? The active manipulation of these geographical boundaries becomes grist for ongoing partisan struggles in Congress—and certainly within each state—for control over the policymaking process.

Usually drafted every 10 years following the decennial national census, redistricting plans are mostly products of the respective legislature of each state. The official purpose of redistricting plans is to promote the "one-person, one-vote" principle that permeates the contemporary understanding of democracy as reflected in the Fourteenth Amendment to the U.S. Constitution. However, with census data in hand and increasingly powerful mapping software, state legislators are able to contort these geographical districts into a number of self-serving iterations. For example, homogeneous districts of rural areas in the Southwest and the South may have the effect of diminishing the vote of a black or Hispanic voter. Other states, like North Carolina, may want to create a black-majority district to winnow out past electoral discrimination and institutionalized racism—such moves, however, have been declared unconstitutional by the Supreme Court (explained later in this chapter in the case of *Shaw v. Reno*). Heterogeneous districts that encapsulate broad urban sprawls can be reshaped to fit the needs of a particular candidates. For instance, when the Republican Party ascended to power in the Texas state legislature in 2002, their first move was to redraw district lines—a full eight years before the next census. A strategy of the then–majority leader of the House of Representatives, Tom DeLay, the plan sought to maximize the number of prospective Republican seats in Congress. Although fiercely contested, the plan was eventually adopted, and several new Republicans were elected in 2004.

The shaping of districts with electorally deleterious consequences for certain voting blocs and aggrandizing electoral effects for majority-party candidates is a long-established feature of American government. The term "gerrymandering" was coined in the *Boston Gazette* in 1812 to describe an oddly shaped electoral district in Massachusetts. The story goes that the district boundary in question clearly favored the party of then-incumbent governor Elbridge Gerry and had the shape of a small salamander. Adding a tale, head, and claws to the creature, the author of the now famous cartoon exclaimed that it was not a salamander but a "gerrymander."

Although the United States prides itself on a one-person, one-vote maxim, gerrymandering is still practiced in a number of permutations and occurs surprisingly more often than one might think. Before the civil rights era, redistricting was often used to dilute the African American vote amidst the white majority throughout the South.

Thus, racial gerrymandering had the effect of muting the power of black voters just granted the electoral franchise under the Fifteenth Amendment. Following the 1965 Voting Rights Act, most districts in the South came under the U.S. Justice Department's scrutiny, where the need for redistricting to ensure the reenfranchisement of black voters rose to political importance. After this period, redistricting came at times to be used in order to increase rather than dilute the minority vote, resulting in significantly increased numbers of black and other minority officeholders.

However, in the landmark case of *Shaw v. Reno* (1993), the Supreme Court established limitations on redistricting plans whose primary effects were to enhance minority voting blocs. The shape of the district in question was, in contrast to the larger, more amorphous shapes around it, a skinny, lightning-shaped district that spanned diagonally. The majority held that district lines could be redrawn, consciously aware of race as a tool in the process, as long as the districts were not so "bizarre" as a result of *only* enhancing the likelihood of a minority candidate's victory. White voters, therefore, had legal grounds for suing the state as victims of racial gerrymandering.[1] Thus, race could be a *motivating* factor in the redrawing of district lines but not the *predominant* factor. While curbing the use of race as a factor, however, partisan composition or other political considerations remained valid factors in the redistricting process.

Other repercussions exist at a national party level in Congress outside of pure interpretations of representation of issues, race, and gender. The overall makeup of party membership of the House is essentially the result of state legislatures, all of which are influenced by local and national party concerns. But in light of the fact that districts can inaccurately and unethically dilute and concentrate votes depending on majoritarian partisanship, congressional composition may not really reflect the composition of the state's electorate. If that is the case, are there alternate avenues for drawing up district plans in the states? An answer is suggested by Japan, whose method of shaping the districts for its national assembly, called the Diet, may be instructive.

CASE STUDY: NONPARTISAN REDISTRICTING IN JAPAN

A number of key changes in representative arrangements in Japan took place as a result of the new constitution in 1947: the establishment of two legislative chambers collectively known as the National Diet—the lower house consisting of a House of Representatives (of 480 members) and the upper house consisting of a House of Councillors (of 242 members). Japan's electoral districts, as a result of electoral arrangements in 1925, were originally multimember in makeup. Voters, casting one vote under the single nontransferable vote system, elected three to five representatives in their districts. The mapping of electoral districts, inevitably, became a political issue.

By the 1970s, because of growing population shifts, political competition, and criticism of corruption and excessive influence by campaign contributors, the system came under attack. Reform finally was enacted in 1994 and changed the landscape of both the numbers of elected officials in the Diet and how the districts were actually shaped. Japanese political geography is subdivided into more than 40 prefectures and those into smaller units of cities and towns. To handle the ponderous task of parsing electoral districts equitably from such a tangle of jurisdictions, the Diet ruled that a parliamentary boundary commission be created. The prime minister was empowered to determine the membership of the commission, with the consent of both houses of the Diet. As in the United States, districts were to be redrawn with every decennial census. The districts had to maintain as close as possible an equitable ratio of representatives to population and, with very few exceptions, the boundaries of small towns and counties could not be divided. Finally, social configurations and and naturally occurring geographic considerations were to be factored into the in the drafting of districting plans.

The original commission in 1994 faced a major problem in the six-month time allotment they were granted: to what extent is the equal population standard feasibly applied without concentrating power in the larger cities and diluting the influence of smaller prefectures? Such concerns eventually prompted many party leaders to call for the previous system of PR, dismantling the single-member district system altogether and thus abolishing the need of a boundary commission. The group lost political momentum after being criticized not only by a swell of voters but also by the prime minister—and a new redistricting plan was adopted at the end of 2001, one that arguably settled the ratio issue and buffered the shifts in population, at least for now.

Although the perennial problem for the parliamentary boundary commission is the massive shifts in population throughout Japan, the lack of clear partisanship in the drafting of these electoral districts is instructive. Inevitably, voter ills will bubble up as the numbers come in from the next Japanese census—but, on the surface, a system whose commission's concerns revolve around equal representation and mathematical ratios is a far cry from a U.S. system that can spawn scenarios like that of Texas in 2002. The Japanese commission will have to grapple with issues ranging from the sort of boundaries needed when cities and towns merge, all while respecting a proportional ratio to neighboring, much smaller prefectures. No doubt, the politics of the coming years will again concern the extent of urban over rural representation. But the upshot seems to be that the voter is ever in the mind of the commission, not necessarily the majority party and its wishes for more seats in the Diet.

NONPARTISAN REDISTRICTING IN THE UNITED STATES?

Could the Japanese system work in the United States? A major hindrance here is the basic difference between the relationship of local and national political organs in Japan and the United States. Japan is a unitary state, with most of its policymaking emanating from its capital. The United States, conversely, operates under a federal system in which the states are not fully subordinate to the national government and can determine many of their own policies. This kind of state self-governance makes difficult the establishment of any national electoral body responsible for drawing districts. However, a combination of coordinated state actions and federal actions, potentially up to and including a constitutional amendment, could prevail.

Already, a few U.S. states, acting as laboratories of policy and democracy, utilize third-party groups, nonpartisan commissions, or panels of judges to draw up districts every 10 years. In theory, these individuals are free from the political pressures facing the active party members of representative bodies. Iowa has a five-member nonpartisan commission, the composition of which is selected by the various caucuses of the state's legislature. The members are civilian, and the initial responsibility for drawing district plans falls on them. In Iowa, for example, two decades of partisan bickering over the appropriate drafting of district lines finally led to a nonpartisan redistricting scheme. Taking effect in 1980, Iowa's scheme sets up the Legislative Services Bureau, which is tasked with initiating the redistricting process. The bureau must create three separate draft plans that can be either accepted or rejected by the legislature and makes four separate considerations in statutory order of importance: (1) population equality, (2) contiguity, (3) unity of counties and cities, and (4) compactness. Aside from these provisions, the bureau is forbidden by law to use political affiliation, election results, and other electoral data in their considerations. To make the process more transparent, public hearings are conducted to inform the electorate—moreover, voters may request maps of the proposed district changes. Although the bureau's proposals are sometimes met with hostility, its proposed changes have been generally accepted—even when, as in 1991, it meant that members of the majority Democratic Party were put in areas of greater partisan competition, losing seats as a result.[2]

If the states were to each adopt nonpartisan, third-party commissions to draw their respective legislative districts, the potential for voter dilution would be very much diminished as a result of partisan demands. Statutory ratios relating to the size of the population of each district, like those used in Japan, would reinforce this. Although states like Iowa accord the Legislative Services Bureau with the opportunity to make decisions based on "equality," legislation providing a baseline minimum ratio would be helpful. Other statutory provisions, also like those in Japan and Iowa, would seek to preserve some element of "home rule" for localities and cities, contiguousness of the districts (avoiding oddly shaped districts like those found unconstitutional in North Carolina) and social matters like race, ethnicity, and economic status. And although partisanship may naturally result from the governors of each state nominating those to the commission, outlawing the use of political affiliation and previous electoral data limits the role of such potential partisanship. Politically neutral data would be used in the drafts by the commission, sent to the governor or legislature-appointed chairperson, who would then propose a "boundary bill" before the legislature as a whole. And if the state legislatures had the sole responsibility of naming those on the commission, the statutory provisions requiring neutrality among the members of the redistricting board would still serve as positive restrictions.

With the power to redistrict out of the hands of pure majoritarian politics, voters are no longer left to the self-interested whims of partisan redistricting. A system with a nonpartisan redistricting commission still maintains the checks and balances that naturally occur as a result of the dynamic between executive and legislative branches—the need for the legislature to agree with the districting bill and the executive's signature are intact. And, as Iowa's case has demonstrated, even majority parties sign onto nonpartisan bills that potentially cost them seats.

But perhaps they should, whatever the electoral expense, because the bottom line to nonpartisan redistricting is the voter—a principal player quickly forgotten in the political games that our elected representatives often play in their contests for reelection.

SYNOPSIS

Desirability: 5

The right of the people to choose their representatives is fundamental in a democracy, and to the extent that partisan districting violates this right, reform would be highly desirable. When the redistricting process is subjected to undue partisan influences, it renders less democratic the results of not only specific House elections but also the overall composition of the House and, by extension, the entire legislative branch. Just as the distorting influence of the Electoral College should be purged from the voting process for president, partisan redistricting should be eliminated from congressional elections.

Practicability: 5

As evidenced by the example of Iowa, this reform is one of the most readily practicable in this volume—no Constitutional amendments would be required, nor, in fact, would any national-level action at all. It is already within the purview of each of the state legislatures to delegate responsibility for redistricting to a nonpartisan commission. The practice in Iowa, in which the legislature must approve the recommendations of the nonpartisan commission, preserves the democratic accountability of the process and also meets the existing constitutional standard that state legislatures have ultimate responsibility for creating congressional districts.

Plausibility: 3

On first examination, this might seem to be an implausible reform, if only because those with power are generally unwilling to give up the instruments of that power. On closer examination, however, this reform would seem somewhat plausible were there to be enough public pressure for its enactment. In states that skew heavily toward one party or the other, the effect of nonpartisan redistricting is unlikely to be great. In those with a less clear-cut partisan profile, a nonpartisan process of congressional redistricting may be as likely to produce gains as losses for any given party.

PART THREE

REFORMING AND REVITALIZING THE COURTS AND THE CONSTITUTION

Allow Legislative Overrides of Judicial Opinions

Empower Courts to Issue Advisory Opinions

Add Social and Economic Protections to the Constitution

Streamline the Constitutional Amendment Process

Call a Constitutional Convention

CHAPTER 17

Allow Legislative Overrides of Judicial Opinions

Highlighting Ideas from New Zealand

Among the many, often convoluted "rules of the game" of American politics, one seems strikingly clear: the courts are the referees, with the Supreme Court having final say. As is well known to even casual students of American constitutional law, one can search in vain for a clear statement of this power of "judicial review" in the text of article III of the U.S. Constitution. It was not until the 1803 case of *Marbury v. Madison* that Justice John Marshall authoritatively articulated the view that judicial review is inherent in the very logic of a written constitution. Given that there are times at which a president or a Congress will seek to overstep the powers provided them in the Constitution, unless the courts have the ability to declare an action "unconstitutional," the very idea of a written constitution—and indeed of democratic, limited government—is an exercise in futility.

For more than 200 years, the logic laid out by Marshall has remained compelling to most Americans. It is true that debates still rage over the proper role of judges, in particular whether they should be "restrained" and defer to the original intent of the founders or more "activist" in applying the Constitution as an evolving, "living" document. But nearly all have accepted that the protection of democracy itself requires that the federal court system, with the Supreme Court at its pinnacle, should be able to override and reverse actions of both the executive and the legislative branches that violate the Constitution.

It may thus come as a surprise to many to find that most democracies do not invest their court systems with anywhere near such sweeping powers. In some countries, such as Italy and Austria, a single constitutional court has been established to resolve certain constitutional issues. But such courts work within a very limited institutional capacity since they cannot share their case burden with an entire system of lower courts. Likewise, bringing cases before some constitutional courts is a narrow and technical process, with only certain political actors or institutions—and often *not* members of the general public—able to initiate proceedings. And in a substantial number of countries, including such long-established democracies as France, the Benelux nations, and Scandinavia, there is a strong tradition of parliamentary supremacy, with *no* court having the right to even review, much less strike down, acts of parliament.

CASE STUDY: PARLIAMENTARY SUPREMACY IN NEW ZEALAND

The principle of parliamentary supremacy has also been a long-established tradition in Great Britain and in many of the now-independent countries that were founded as part of the British Empire. In Britain, the official formulation of sovereign power is that of "the monarch in Parliament," which in modern practical terms means that the country is governed by the House of Commons, with the monarchy and the House of Lords playing primarily ceremonial roles. The courts play an independent role but are formally agents of the Crown, and even the highest courts are limited only to deciding cases appealed from lower courts—never to reviewing laws passed by Parliament or acts taken by the government (although they may review bureaucratic misapplications of the law). Any attempt by British courts to interpret constitutional issues is further complicated by the reality that the "British Constitution" is not a single written document as in most countries but rather a welter of different historical acts, traditions, conventions, and established practices.

In recent decades, however, the clarity of parliamentary supremacy has become somewhat blurred by British participation in the European Union (EU), the reach of which has expanded dramatically, particularly since the Maastricht Treaty of 1992 linked the member nations much more closely together. Today, British courts, as well as the European Court of Justice in Luxembourg, have the ability to identify laws passed by Parliament that conflict with EU law. The British government is not, in theory, bound by these rulings, but in practice it is since the only way around a violation of EU law would be the enormous step of withdrawing the country from the EU. Thus, the British Parliament is left with little choice but to bow to such court rulings.

For this reason, perhaps the clearest example of the tradition of parliamentary supremacy to be found in the world today is no longer that of Britain but that of one of its offspring: New Zealand. This nation of some 4 million in the South Pacific has often been described as being "more British than Britain," maintaining social conventions, traditions, and practices that have been overtaken by more rapid change back in the mother country. As in Britain, New Zealand has no single written constitution. Instead, its constitution incorporates traditions and laws from Britain alongside acts of the New Zealand Parliament as well as distinctive legal instruments, such as the Treaty of Waitangi, which enacted a settlement between the British colonizers and the indigenous Maori people. There is also a Bill of Rights Act, but this was passed by—and can be changed by—a simple majority vote of Parliament.

Thus, even more so than in Britain, the Parliament plays a clear-cut and dominant role in New Zealand.[1] Parliament is unicameral, consisting of a single House of Representatives, its ineffectual upper house having been abolished in 1950. The monarchy is a remote, historical institution, even more clearly marginal and powerless than in Britain proper. Unlike Britain, where significant power has been devolved to regional legislative assemblies in Scotland, Wales, and Northern Ireland, New Zealand remains an undiluted unitary state, with all political power concentrated in the national capital city of Wellington. New Zealand also does not belong to any supranational organizations comparable to the EU, providing no outside layer of judicial scrutiny. The Supreme Court has no authority whatsoever to review acts of Parliament or the government. Hence, there are literally *no* institutional checks and balances on the power of the House of Representatives or of the prime minister and cabinet it elects.

In all, devotees of separation of powers in general and of robust judicial review in particular are likely to be appalled and to expect New Zealand to be in a situation ripe for dictatorship. Such critics would, of course, be wrong. Perhaps by sheer force of tradition, legal inheritance, social custom, international pressure or by simple recognition of the value of democratic self-government, New Zealand is one of the world's most robust and stable democracies. Parliament is characterized by coalition governments and consensus politics, and opposition parties are free to contest—and regularly win—elections. In fact, Parliament freely undertook the introduction of an element of PR in the electoral system in 1996, resulting in a larger number of viable political parties and greater power sharing. Civil liberties likewise remain strong; for example, as with many nations after September 11, 2001, New Zealand passed laws to identify and detain terrorists but ones that were notably balanced and careful. Minority rights also flourish, with strong antidiscrimination laws and Parliament seats reserved specifically for Maori representatives. And in a 2007 index of corruption by the nongovernmental organization Transparency International, New Zealand was ranked the least corrupt country on the planet.[2]

LEGISLATIVE SUPREMACY IN THE UNITED STATES?

If the country with the most extreme case of parliamentary supremacy can also be among the world's most democratic, might it also be desirable for the United States to curb or even outright eliminate the power of judicial review? Certainly, to hear some critics of the courts, this would be a positive outcome. An entire generation of conservative critics have derided "judicial activists" who "legislate from the bench" by failing to defer to the elected branches. They view the courts as elitist institutions, removed from democratic accountability, in which liberal judges run amok by inventing new rights and reversing the will of Congress, the president, and state legislatures.

From this perspective, the courts have gone from being, in Alexander Hamilton's famous phrase, the "least dangerous branch" to an arrogant, overbearing, even tyrannical body that needs to be reined in for the sake of democracy. Conservatives tend to cite any number of particularly vexing examples of supposed judicial activism, such as the 1966 ruling in *Miranda v. Arizona* that strengthened the rights of those being arrested for crimes; the 1973 *Roe v. Wade* decision, which prohibited most restrictions on abortion on the basis of due process for women; the 1989 ruling in *Texas v. Johnson*, which found that flag desecration laws violated the First Amendment right to freedom of expression; and the 2003 ruling in *Lawrence v. Texas*, which invalidated anti-gay "sodomy laws" on privacy grounds. Of course, progressives tended to find these same rulings salutary for democracy because they promoted equality for vulnerable groups and reinforced basic civil liberties.

Both conservative detractors and liberal promoters of an activist judiciary tend to view the courts in general and the Supreme Court in particular as a dynamic, independent force in American politics. And the judiciary is, indeed, at least partially freed from some of the constraints of the other branches. Never subject to election, much less reelection, federal judges with lifetime appointment do have greater independence and insulation from public opinion than elected officials. They also tend to deal with arcane principles and to operate out of the public eye; with regard to the Supreme Court, only one small part of its deliberative process—hour-long oral arguments— are held in public, and these are never videotaped, and the audiotapes are made public only later. And the Supreme Court does, in a very real sense, have the "final say" on constitutional issues since only the extremely arduous process of amending the Constitution itself can invalidate a Supreme Court decision.

But this perspective emphasizes the strengths of courts while over-looking their many institutional weaknesses. Indeed, the very reasons that Hamilton called the judiciary the "least dangerous branch" con-tinue to exist down to the current day. For example, judges have no influence over changes in the composition of the judiciary since they are appointed or promoted solely at the will of presidents in concert with the Senate, which must confirm them. Thus, the composition and direction of the judiciary remains under the control of the elected branches, albeit with a certain degree of time lag. Likewise, judges must wait for cases to come to them either through lawsuits at the lower trial court levels or via the appeals process to higher courts. Even the Supreme Court cannot "seek" cases but must wait for them to slowly and methodically make their way to it, and then it must decide on the basis of the idiosyncrasies of the particular case before it. Nor can the Supreme Court issue advisory opinions while legisla-tion is still being crafted (the subject of the next chapter).

Even more importantly, the courts were and still are, in Hamilton's language, denied both the "power of the sword," namely, the enforce-ment authority of the executive, and the "power of the purse," or the funding authority of the legislature. Supreme Court rulings are thus not self-executing and must rely on the cooperation of the other branches, the support of the lower courts, and the acquiescence of the general public for the principles laid out in its rulings to be truly carried out. Courts that find themselves too far ahead of the other branches, as well as American society itself, run the risk of seeing their rulings disregarded or outright opposed. Further, Congress has the ability to limit the jurisdiction of the Supreme Court to hear appeals from lower courts about certain types of cases—a controversial and somewhat murky process called "jurisdiction stripping," which in theory could be used to narrow the scope of the Supreme Court's power. That Congress has only very rarely—and to limited effect— exercised this power is testimony to the generally constrained and constructive role played by the Supreme Court.

The courts are thus but one player in a much more intricate system, hardly the unilateral actors that their detractors claim. Even one of the most sweeping and influential decisions of the twentieth century— *Brown v. Board of Education*, which invalidated racial segregation—was only a single factor in a complex debate that encompassed the civil rights movement, claims of "states' rights," massive popular resistance in the segregated South, advocacy by presidents Kennedy and Johnson, and ultimately legislation by Congress. *Brown* may indeed have been catalytic, but it hardly dictated the course of future events.

Even if it is clear that the power of judicial review does not—and indeed cannot—lead to tyranny, might there still be gains for democracy to be had from putting some curbs on judicial review? The case of Canada offers an intriguing example. Working with a written Charter of Rights and Freedom introduced in 1982, the Canadian Supreme Court has a stronger basis on which to apply judicial review than its counterparts in Britain or New Zealand. Canada's highest court can, and regularly does, issue decisions that have the effect of invalidating or modifying acts of Parliament or the government. In deference to the British tradition of parliamentary supremacy, however, as well as the rights of provinces under Canadian federalism, section 33 of the Charter contains the so-called "notwithstanding clause." This unique provision allows that even if the courts have struck down a law, the federal Parliament or the legislature of any province "may expressly declare . . . that [the law] shall operate notwithstanding" the court's ruling. This feature has the function of allowing a legislative override of the courts for a period of five years, subject to repeated renewal. Although the national government has never invoked the clause, the government of Quebec has done so at times to protect a preferred status for the French over the English language within the boundaries of that province.

This would seem to be a reasonable middle ground for a branch of government that, as it is unelected, suffers from what has been called the "countermajoritarian problem," that is, the ability to function in a way that runs against the will of the majority. However, the very phrasing of the term "countermajoritarian" obscures that the actual practice of democracy is as much about individual liberty and political equality as it is about carrying out the will of any particular majority, especially a "simple majority" of 50 percent plus one of the population. In the cases cited previously in this chapter, ranging from *Brown* to *Roe* to *Lawrence*, the operative principle behind the Supreme Court's ruling was to promote liberty and equality even if majorities in some states might disapprove. Were there to be a notwithstanding clause in the United States, many states and perhaps Congress would likely have overridden these rulings to the detriment of disempowered groups.

Further, a robust Supreme Court can play a critical role in a separation-of-powers system, particularly with regard to overreaching by the executive. In a parliamentary system, the prime minister and cabinet may be quite powerful, but they continue in office only as long as they retain the support of a majority in the lower house. Presidents, who are institutionally separate and have their own electoral mandate directly from the people, are not so easily restrained. In the United States, the Supreme Court has served as a critical safeguard against excessive executive authority, whether it be reining in Richard Nixon's claims of "executive privilege" during the Watergate scandal or George W. Bush's denial of due process guarantees as part of the so-called War on Terror.

The Supreme Court has not always succeeded in this task. For example, its upholding of Franklin Roosevelt's internment of Japanese Americans during World War II remains a singular blight on its record. Still, the decisive authority of the Supreme Court has nonetheless played an important role in balancing the power of the branches and avoiding the sorts of excessive executive authority found in other separation-of-powers systems. Of the two dozen countries in the Western Hemisphere with a president who is institutionally separated from the legislature, only one—the United States has never experienced either one-party rule or executive dictatorship. These collapses of democracy have occurred when the rule of law has been abused and when no high court enjoyed the institutional stability, public prestige, and impartial reputation needed to constrain overreaching executives.

SYNOPSIS

Desirability: 1

A "rogue" Supreme Court in which unelected, life-tenured judges seize control of the country would be a dire development for democracy. But such a scenario could exist only in fiction: in reality, courts have none of the tools that could enable them to enforce a truly unreasonable set of rulings. Instead, they would be faced with massive outright resistance alongside passive noncompliance. The individual justices of such a rogue Supreme Court would also be subject to impeachment and removal by Congress. Aside from such an extreme scenario, there is little to be gained and much to be lost by impeding the ability of the courts to play their proper role.

Practicability: 4

From a technical perspective, asserting legislative supremacy could readily be achieved through the section in article III of the Constitution that the Supreme Court only has "appellate jurisdiction . . . with such exceptions, and under such regulations as the Congress shall make." While this concept of "jurisdiction stripping" is a largely untested and controversial provision of the Constitution, a case could be made that Congress does in fact have a form of the Canadian notwithstanding clause but, like the Canadian Parliament, sees the merits of a fully functioning and independent judiciary.

Plausibility: 2

Barring an outlandish scenario of attempted tyranny by the judiciary, it seems unlikely that serious attempts will be made to eliminate the power of judicial review. In particular, wide-ranging jurisdiction stripping, although not a violation of the letter of the Constitution, would widely be viewed as a violation of the spirit of the Constitution and of the established role of the courts. Further, Congress may well see a strong and independent court system as an ally in the face of an actor with far greater capacity to abuse its power: the president.

CHAPTER 18

Empower Courts to Issue Advisory Opinions

Highlighting Ideas from Bulgaria

Chapter co-authored with Brandon L. H. Aultman

One of the significant limitations on the Supreme Court discussed in the previous chapter is that it can only obliquely choose which issues to address and when to address them. The U.S. Constitution limits the jurisdiction of the federal courts to "cases and controversies," and precedent was set as early as the Washington administration that this means that the Supreme Court must wait for specific cases to reach it through the lengthy and convoluted appeals process or through its very limited purview of original jurisdiction. However seemingly urgent the issue, there is no provision for questions to be brought to the Supreme Court in hypothetical terms. Congress may not draft a controversial bill and send a copy to the Supreme Court to determine whether it passes constitutional muster, nor can actors in the executive branch confer with the justices to be sure that they are not over-stepping the constitutional bounds of their office. The Supreme Court may only adjudicate; it may not advise.

However, there is nothing inherent in the nature of the judicial power to prevent such an advisory role. The supreme courts of half a dozen U.S. states—as well as numerous foreign countries—have more far-reaching authority to issue advisory opinions that enable these courts to bring clarity to important constitutional questions on a timely basis and also before any damage can be done to the integrity of the constitution. For example, the Canadian federal government uses advisory opinions by asking "reference questions" of the

Supreme Court. When Canada was considering the legalization of same-sex marriages throughout the provinces, a member of Parliament asked the Canadian Supreme Court three different reference questions pertaining to governmental authority and religious liberty: whether the Parliament of Canada had the authority to define marriage in the first place, whether legislation allowing religious institutions to decline marrying same-sex couples violated civil rights protections, and whether requiring religious officials to solemnize marriages for same-sex couples violated the Canadian charter's protection of religious liberty. As one can see, the diversity of such questions and the power to answer them allow the Canadian Supreme Court to be an active participant and not merely a referee in the policymaking process. An even more far-reaching power to issue advisory opinions can be found in an ancient land that has one of the newer constitutions in Europe: the former Soviet satellite state of Bulgaria.

CASE STUDY: INTERPRETIVE DECISIONS IN BULGARIA

Bulgaria, under complete communist control until the Soviet Union's collapse, had begun its democratic transition by 1990. Although still under control of former communists, rebranded the Bulgarian Socialist Party, the country established a democratic constitution in 1991. The elaborate new document articulated the constitution as the nation's supreme law, laid out the new institutions of government, and outlined basic human and political rights for Bulgarian citizens. A new constitutional court was charged with safeguarding this new structure as well as liberties and rights.[1]

The Constitutional Court of Bulgaria (CCB) is unique in design.It is among three distinctly national Bulgarian courts, the others being the Supreme Court of Cassation and the Supreme Administrative Court. Instead of being a part of any one national judicial apparatus, the CCB has proclaimed itself separate and distinct. Indeed, the Bulgarian constitution even reads that the CCB "guarantees the supremacy of the Constitution and is independent of the legislative, executive, and judiciary branches." Unlike the U.S. Supreme Court, its members are not selected solely by the president. Instead, the 12 members of the CCB are elected by the National Assembly and the president, among other prominent officeholders. Moreover, they are not life members;

they hold their positions for staggered nine-year terms and are not eligible for reelection.

The CCB's interpretations of the constitution and findings in a case are an ultimate ruling of law, binding in every capacity. For example, the Bulgarian constitution reads, "[A]ny act found to be unconstitutional shall cease to apply as of the date on which the ruling shall come into force." The Bulgarian constitution also gives the CCB the ability to render what are known as "interpretive decisions" on abstract or hypothetical matters of policy as authoritative as a decision rendered in a case or controversy—in other words, binding advisory opinions.

The advantages of a system of binding advisory opinions in the Bulgarian context are manifold. First, as in many continental European countries, the process itself is "inquisitorial" rather than "adversarial," that is, that the courts are not neutral referees but rather active partners in attempting to determine the facts in a case. While this is an idea that is foreign to the common law tradition best exemplified in the United Kingdom and former British colonies (including the United States), the inquisitorial system leads to greater efficiency in the courtroom and higher visibility for judicial decision making. It is efficient in that this process is comparatively quicker than its adversarial counterparts, in which months are dedicated in pretrial procedure alone. It is less costly for parties involved, including the state, as the need for counsel is less urgent and justices render decisions independent of an elaborate adversarial process.

Second, "interpretive decisions" give the CCB a critical and proactive role in bringing predictability and order to the Bulgarian government process. Because the CCB's decisions are binding, its promulgations have a lasting and stabilizing impact on the political structure. Such a binding advisory power also provides the CCB with a unique opportunity to develop jurisprudence outside a rigid judicial and legislative process, which has led to greater protections for the media, clearer constitutional rules for presidential selection, and a strong political bulwark for opposition parties. This last condition was particularly important when the Socialist Party ascended to dominance in the legislative chamber in the mid-1990s. Sweeping reforms were proposed, some of which included diminishing the role of the courts as well as curtailing the ability of the media to report on government policies. On request, the CCB unsurprisingly issued interpretive decisions that maintained and reinforced the integrity of the judicial branch—to the chagrin of socialist reformers. Furthermore, it renounced the authority of the legislature to curtail media rights by reiterating the supremacy of the constitution and its explicit protections of press-related liberties.

Finally, the CCB is able to stem controversies by addressing potentially crippling constitutional questions in the abstract. Besides saving time for both the government and the parties involved, handling abstract questions of constitutionality engages the broader interested community. Indeed, the CCB is required by law to inform all "interested parties" of the prospective subjects and statutes under review. In fact, they even provide an invitation for a written submission by interested parties as "briefs" for the consideration by the judges, giving outside actors the opportunity to weigh in and inform the CCB's decision. The U.S. legal system has similar mechanisms by which the submittal of amicus curiae, or friend-of-the-court, briefs take up a particular side of a case and provide compelling arguments. However, U.S. courts are not required to issue statements or open invitations to inform interested or affected parties concerning the potential litigation. Unlike the United States, where litigation is wholly private and oral arguments (at least in the Supreme Court) are barred from televised coverage, Bulgaria allows public scrutiny of information and hearings pertaining to prospective interpretive decisions. Abstract considerations also allow the CCB to handle constitutional questions that adversarial approaches would strictly prohibit because they would not meet standards for justiciability, such as standing, ripeness, and mootness. This leads to rather progressive and, for most of the CCB's history, protective decisions regarding areas from from citizen rights to the organization of government.

ADVISORY OPINIONS IN THE UNITED STATES?

The question of advisory opinions in the U.S. federal government was first answered in the early days of the republic. America's first secretary of state, Thomas Jefferson, wrote to John Jay, the first chief justice of the Supreme Court, providing a list of 29 legal questions to be answered by the Court. In response, John Jay wrote that the Court, to his estimation, was bound by the Constitution's cases and controversies clause in article III, limiting the Court to addressing issues arising out of only those cases that took the form of formal lawsuits and had proceeded through proper judicial procedure. Determining the law, then, requires that a controversy pass along appropriate judicial channels before the Supreme Court can proffer any kind of decision.

As interpreted, Jay said that the Constitution does not allow advisory opinions.

This interpretation of the cases and controversies clause of article III has been solidified through case law. More than a century after Chief Justice Jay denied Jefferson's request, *Muskrat v. United States* (1911) determined "[t]hat judicial power [to determine the constitutional validity of an act of Congress] ... is the right to determine actual *controversies* arising between adverse litigants, duly instituted in courts in *proper* jurisdiction" (emphasis added). The Supreme Court has instituted other formal rules of standing to limit the kinds of cases that can even be presented before the federal justice system. Such rules winnow the number of cases that could potentially seek the attention of the Court.

It is also true, however, that nowhere in article III of the Constitution does it make explicit the ability of the Supreme Court to review and thus potentially void acts of Congress and the president, and yet that power is now clearly established. Article III does, however, allow participation by the Supreme Court in resolving "controversies"— could this provision be interpreted to include advisory opinions and break with tradition more than two centuries old? American political culture has come to expect the power of the judiciary as a "natural" check on legislative and executive authority, and advisory opinions could be an excellent tool to work around controversial constitutional issues relating to separation of powers by promoting cooperation among executive, legislative, and judicial branches.

Take, for example, the case of *Employment Division v. Smith* (1990), in which the constitutionality of a law banning the use of controlled substances for religious rituals was questioned. Although the Supreme Court ultimately ruled that such a law does not violate the free exercise of religion, Congress disagreed and passed the Religious Freedom Restoration Act (RFRA) in 1993 forbidding federal and state agencies from restricting a person's free exercise of religion. A stark political battle ensued, with the Supreme Court having the final say (at least so far) in striking down the RFRA in the mid-1990s. Perhaps advisory opinions could have proffered a less costly, nonadversarial outcome.

There are further benefits in terms of promoting government efficiency and predictability. What if, for example, the legislature is evaluating a possible new tax but fears that if the tax came under constitutional fire and was struck down, the refund suits would have a crippling effect on revenue? Clearly, under the current interpretation of the cases and controversies provision of article III, Congress is stuck—it cannot pass a law without some basis of constitutionality but cannot know with absolute certainty until after it passes the law. Advisory opinions would alleviate such problems. Another concrete example would be the aftermath of the *Goodridge* decision in Massachusetts, a state that permits its high court to submit advisory opinions to the legislature or the executive. The 2003 *Goodridge* decision had the effect of legalizing marriages for same-sex couples and invalidating the state's then-current marriage statute restricting marriage to only different-sex couples. In deliberating the social and economic changes the decision would require, the state legislature proposed a bill in the senate, named Senate Bill No. 2175, that would have created civil unions for same-sex couples purportedly "equal" to marriage in all areas except the word itself. To avoid overtly counter-manding the most recent legal decision concerning marriage for same-sex couples held in *Goodridge*, the legislature asked the Massachusetts high court to give its opinion on the matter of Senate Bill No. 2175's constitutionality. The court held that its decision in *Goodridge* made clear that marriage for same-sex couples could not be curtailed and that Senate Bill No. 2175 violated the state's equal protection and due process clauses. Clearly, advisory opinions are an invaluable tool for representative government, as the adversarial pro-cess in the Massachusetts case was totally avoided.

One interesting point is that advisory opinions would not neces-sarily have to be absolutely binding or final in order to still be useful. Congress and perhaps the state governments could pose questions to be addressed by the Supreme Court or appellate courts to circumvent the costly and time-consuming litigation that would inevitably ensue from controversial legislation. The nation would have an answer to constitutional quandaries before a law even reached the president's desk for signature, the Supreme Court would not be obligated to hear and answer every question posed to it, much as it is not legally obligated to agree to hear every case that is appealed to it. And in any case, since it takes only half the cases it heard a generation ago, a mere 70 or so per year, the institutional capacity of the Supreme Court is far from overtaxed. Alternatively, Congress could establish a new inferior court, reporting directly to the Supreme Court, that might be tasked with issuing advisory opinions on matters of lesser significance.

One historical argument against advisory opinions is that the legis-lative and executive branches already have the ability to obtain the informed opinions of scholars and official counsel, thus making the need for a court's nonbinding opinion superfluous. But this approach has been seen an underhanded acceptance of wealthy interests interfering with the policymaking process. Moreover, there is a clear difference between the opinions of scholars and the decisions of law courts, especially the Supreme Court. There is certainly no law professor in the country who can predict with 100 percent accuracy how the Supreme Court will rule on a given issue, particularly with new justices entering the picture. Advisory opinions ultimately offer a particularly valuable tool in the process of adopting policy. Rather than relying on vested interests in the outcome of a case alone, judicial bodies could be tasked with identifying constitutional weaknesses of prospective legislation in a temperate and well-reasoned manner. After all, these are the same entities whose opinions on matters of law are final—so who better to proffer those kinds of legal conclusions and help guide policymakers in their pursuit of upholding the Constitution?

SYNOPSIS

Desirability: 3

Granting the power to issue advisory opinions would not in and of itself have a major transformative impact on American politics. The judicial branch already labors under too many institutional weaknesses to enable it to ever be the true engine of change in the United States. However, to the extent that coordination across branches, efficiency, and predictability are important goals, this could be a modest reform that could avoid long, protracted battles over the meaning of the Constitution and streamline the legislative process.

Practicability: 4

The silence of the literal text of the Constitution on this question leaves open the possibility of change either through judicial interpretation or through legislative action by Congress based on its power to structure the federal court system. A system of nonbinding advisory opinions might pass muster more easily, If mere interpretation of the Constitution is not enough, Congress and the states would have to be willing to amend article III either by loosening the language around the cases and controversies provisions or by simply adding the power of advisory opinions to the short list of actual powers at the judiciary's disposal.

Plausibility: 3

A reform of this type would be steadfastly opposed by those who already believe that the courts are "out-of-control activists." However, most Americansr recognize the legitimate role of the courts in interpreting the law, which could include a role before the law is actually enacted. As part of a larger package of reform designed to produce better laws more quickly and efficiently, the idea of advisory opinions could well find champions within both Congress and the states.

CHAPTER 19

Add Social and Economic Protections to the Constitution

Highlighting Ideas from South Africa

Throughout most of the foregoing chapters, reforms were proposed that would require an amendment to the U.S. Constitution, usually just the alteration of an already existing practice that could enhance and promote democracy in the United States. Yet some possible reform could go further, bringing about changes not just *to* the Constitution but *of* the Constitution itself. This is not at all to disparage the Constitution or to deny that in many ways it is a remarkable document. Indeed, the 1780s where in many ways the "Big Bang" of constitutionalism, the brief period during which the very idea of government based on a single written constitution was formalized and implemented. Prior to the 1780s in the United States, governing institutions and practices had mostly just evolved incrementally with little prior planning and few strategic decisions, often in crazy quilt patterns.

The U.S. Constitution and other closely affiliated documents such as the Articles of Confederation and the new postrevolutionary constitutions of the various states, reflected a major breakthrough in both the theory and the practice of democratic governance. Of course, the framers were heavily influenced by the thinkers of the European Enlightenment, drawing more famously on such ideas as Thomas Hobbes's ideas about the need for strong government, John Locke's notions of how to limit the reach of government, and the Baron de Montesquieu's theory of separation of powers. To this they added homegrown elements, perhaps most notably the concept of federalism. Yet few of them could have imagined that the constitution they drafted would become virtually synonymous with the American polity and that it would endure with minimal changes for more than 220 years, becoming the oldest continuously functioning written constitution in the world.

The U.S. Constitution is notably strong in its protections of the constellation of political and personal freedoms, commonly called civil liberties, that offer protections of individual liberty from the arbitrary use of power of the government. Although not part of the original document ratified in 1789, the Bill of Rights must be considered part of the original constitutional process because it was largely a promise to enact such a breakwater against government abuse that persuaded sufficient number of skeptics to support ratification.

The powerhouse First Amendment in one sweeping gesture prohibits an established religion like the Church of England while also protecting religious free exercise, then launches into extraordinarily broad protections of freedom of expression, including speech, the press, assembly, and petition. As subsequently interpreted by the courts, these are robust freedoms that are as close to absolute as those enjoyed anywhere else in the world. The Fourth Amendment's ban on unreasonable search and seizure is nearly as dramatic and in the modern era has served as the principal basis for the concept of personal privacy. Collectively, the Fifth through the Eighth Amendments guarantee multiple protections for those accused of a crime and being tried in a court of law. And, to the chagrin of many left-leaning civil libertarians, the Second Amendment vigorously defends a right to keep and bear arms.

The very expansiveness of the Constitution's political protections, however, serves to highlight its near silence on social and economic protections. The preamble allows that one of the aims of the Constitution is to "promote" the general welfare, and article I allows Congress to tax and spend for the general welfare. But the idea of "general welfare" is never developed further or even mentioned again. In fact, social and economic status is only obliquely mentioned again in the original text of the Constitution in terms of an absolute ban on titles of nobility. Beyond this prohibition on the erection of hierarchical social structures, however, the Constitution remained essentially silent on issues of equality until the Fourteenth Amendment of 1868, which requires "equal protection of the law." This simple phrase has proven a powerful tool for advancing social and economic equality, but it is hardly self-evident in meaning or self-executing in action; indeed, the Supreme Court, in *Plessy v. Ferguson* in 1896, managed to find racial segregation compatible with equal protection. It would take the Court until 1954, in *Brown v. Board of Education*, to declare that "separate is inherently unequal" and Congress until 1964 to enact a truly comprehensive Civil Rights Act to fully enforce the Fourteenth Amendment.

The absence of social and economic protections in the Constitution is hardly surprising given the context in which it was written. At that time, advancing the well-being of the citizenry was at best an indirect goal of government, which sought mainly to create a stable and just framework within which society could function. Later concepts such as income redistribution, antidiscrimination protections, or affirmative action were far from the minds of the founders. Much to the contrary, many influential historians—most famously Charles Beard in *An Economic Interpretation of the Constitution of the United States* (1913)—have argued that the Constitution was designed primarily to protect those who were already wealthy and powerful and in this sense was to some degree a repudiation of the more radically egalitarian vision of the American Revolution.

It is clear that whatever its original intentions, the Constitution also does not *prevent* the passage of ordinary legislation or the enactment of regulations to promote social and economic protections. But even during the New Deal of the 1930s, President Franklin D. Roosevelt and the Democratic Congress had to threaten to increase the number of Supreme Court justices, thereby "packing" the Court with new liberal justices, in order to get the sitting Supreme Court to agree to a larger role of government in promoting the welfare of citizens and the regulation of the economy. And, as is often noted in comparative studies, social and economic protections in the United States have remained rather limited and grudging when compared to the capacious welfare states of most industrialized democracies. By virtually every measure of social protection, the United States offers comparatively minimal protections in employment, such as job security, minimum-wage laws, unemployment and disability benefits, and maternity leave, and quite limited social benefits, such as universal health care, low-cost higher education, and subsidized transportation.

Many bookshelves have been filled with analyses of why the United States historically has had a minimal social safety net. Was it because Americans, marked by high levels of social mobility and the absence of an entrenched landed aristocracy, never developed an acute sense of class consciousness and thus never developed a domestic strain of socialist ideology? Did the institution of slavery cause class conflict to be displaced by racial conflict, thus preventing the development of solidarity between poor whites and nonwhites, both of whom could benefit from government help? Did the national history of initial settlement, then westward expansion, and then immigration all breed a culture of individualism and self-reliance rather than a focus on building the apparatus of government? Or did an ethos of egalitarianism spawn a universe of voluntary and charitable associations that provided the social welfare functions performed elsewhere by governments?

For any or all of these reasons, the United States has long had a peculiarly blinkered view of the nature of democracy. Few would argue that freedom of speech, freedom of religion, or the right to a fair trial are fundamental to the maintenance of a free society. In recent decades, voting rights have come to be viewed in a similar light, with few contesting the right of all unincarcerated adult citizens to participate in the political process by casting a ballot and, for that matter, by being elected to public office. Indeed, the commitment in these areas, which are often placed under the rubric of *procedural democracy*, is quite firmly established in the United States.

Yet the same Americans who are incensed if someone is denied the right to attend the house of worship of their choice often display far less concern if that same person has no literal house within which to live. The right to speak freely may be inviolable, but protections against the hunger and illness and poor education are unpredictable, unreliable, and often the first lines to be cut from state and federal budgets at the first sign of fiscal duress—and sometimes even when the economy is flush. But without greater attention to and care for the basic needs of life, procedural democracy can seem a rather hollow construct with limited meaningful substance. Indeed, among the world's wealthy democracies, it is uniquely in the United States that the concept of *substantive democracy* remains so vociferously debated. The historical trends and patterns that have led to this shortcoming cannot, obviously, be changed today. However, there is another reform that could still be undertaken, one based on the seemingly simple observation that many modern constitutions contain clear-cut social and economic protections, while that of the United States does not.

SOCIAL AND ECONOMIC PROTECTIONS IN THE SOUTH AFRICAN CONSTITUTION

Inequality and exploitation are ills found in every corner of the world, but perhaps no modern country—and certainly no country that

seriously tried to call itself a democracy—ever systematized and institutionalized inequality and exploitation as thoroughly as South Africa
during the era of apartheid from 1948 to 1994. After World War II,
when most countries, including the United States, began moving
toward a more liberal stand on issues of race and ethnicity, South Africa
tacked hard to the right. With fierce escalation, the white Afrikaner-led
government used ever more repressive means to separate and subordinate nonwhites, including harshly segregated "group areas" and internal passport laws, extensive police surveillance and intimidation, and
the outright torture and massacre of political resisters. Although their
behavior made them global pariahs and provoked militant resistance
among people of color, white South Africans continued to dominate
socially and prosper economically. With just 20 percent of the population, they filled every significant corporate and political office and by
the end of the apartheid period earned more than half the national
income, with the bottom 40 percent accounting for less than 4 percent
of national income.[1]

But despite outward appearances, by the 1990s the country had been
drained economically by the costs of maintaining a police state as well
as by the impact of international trade sanctions and withdrawn invest-
ments. It was also exhausted by the functional equivalent of a long-
term low-level civil war. By 1994, a compromise was reached, in large
part through the towering leadership of Nelson Mandela, in which
the whites agreed to black-majority rule and blacks agreed not to
expropriate existing white wealth, as had happened in many other
African colonies. As part of the process of reconciliation, a lengthy
deliberative process was initiated that culminated in the enactment of
a new constitution in 1996 that is widely considered the most
progressive in the world—and is also one of the longest and most
detailed, at more than 140 pages.

In addition to laying out the structure of government and politics,
the constitution spells out a tremendous range of rights and freedoms
accorded to all citizens of the "New South Africa." Many of these are
classic civil liberties found in the United States and other democracies,
such as freedom of expression and religion, due process protections for
those accused of crimes, protections against unreasonable search and
seizure, and property rights. But the document goes much further,
sketching out a vision of substantive democracy by affirming the
"democratic values of human dignity, equality and freedom" and the
respnonsiblity of government to "respect, protect, promote and fulfill

the rights" in the constitution. Its specific social and economic protections include the following clauses:

- "The state may not unfairly discriminate directly or indirectly against anyone on one or more grounds, including race, gender, sex, pregnancy, marital status, ethnic or social origin, colour, sexual orientation, age, disability, religion, conscience, belief, culture, language and birth."
- "Everyone has the right to bodily and psychological integrity, which includes the right: to make decisions concerning reproduction; to security in and control over their body; and not to be subjected to medical or scientific experiments without their informed consent."
- "Everyone has the right to an environment that is not harmful to their health or well-being; and to have the environment protected, for the benefit of present and future generations."
- "Everyone has the right to have access to adequate housing . . . no one may be evicted from their home, or have their home demolished, without an order of court made after considering all the relevant circumstances. No legislation may permit arbitrary evictions."
- "Everyone has the right to have access to: health care services, including reproductive health care; sufficient food and water; and social security, including, if they are unable to support themselves and their dependants, appropriate social assistance. No one may be refused emergency medical treatment."
- "Everyone has the right to a basic education [and] to receive education in the official language or languages of their choice in public educational institutions where that education is reasonably practicable. . . . Everyone has the right to use the language and to participate in the cultural life of their choice."

The scale and scope of the protections enshrined in the South African constitution are without parallel and are the unmistakable product of a movement—that of the African National Congress—that is deeply committed to human rights for all, in no small part because their own rights were so badly abused for so long. Of course, enshrining guarantees in a legal document cannot in itself produce the prosperity needed to overcome mass poverty, to heal the wounds of a traumatized society, or to end all other legacies of apartheid. South Africa remains very much a work in progress, with stunning inequalities and major problems with violent crime, including sexual assault.

Yet the placement of key social and economic guarantees directly in the constitution itself, where they are not open to denial or even much debate, has had a significant impact. In the country with the world's largest population of people living with HIV/AIDS, it was the constitution's right to health care that ultimately forced the government to pay for antiretroviral medications for all. Likewise, the existence of a specific textual ban on discrimination on the basis of sexual orientation—a provision unique among the world's constitutions—led to a Supreme Court ruling allowing same-sex marriage in South Africa, the only government outside Western Europe or North American to enact such a policy.

SOCIAL AND ECONOMIC PROTECTIONS IN THE U.S. CONSTITUTION?

If social and economic protections can be enacted through ordinary law, as they have been in the case of Social Security, Medicare, Medicaid, and other programs, why go to the seemingly extreme step of placing them into the text of the Constitution? The reason, of course, would be for the same reason that any right or freedom is enshrined directly as part of the supreme law of the land: to provide it with the highest priority and to establish it as a settled matter beyond the reach of transient forces of public opinion, simple legislative majorities, and the ordinary law-making process. If full democracy encompasses both procedural and substantive aspects, then should both not be fully and equally respected and advanced?

Reframing the issue in terms of long-standing political freedoms may be illuminating. One could ask: why enshrine protections against unreasonable search and seizure into the Constitution? Police forces and the mayors and governors they serve can be counted on to respect policies regarding the need to have probable cause and to seek warrants from judges as long as a clear policy is laid out. Likewise, it could be argued that there is no need to make it a constitutional issue that newspapers cannot be censored. It is understood that there is freedom of the press, and, besides, politicians seek the support of newspaper editorial pages. And some might contend that freedom of religion goes without saying—everyone can participate in the religious rituals that they prefer, provided, of course, that they are not too offensive to the beliefs of the majority. And since fairness and impartiality will emerge naturally through the striving of individuals in the market-place, it could be said that it is unnecessary and redundant to pass an amendment proffering "equal protection of the law."

Few contemporary Americans would make the arguments in the preceding paragraph; indeed, they probably strike many as not only odd but even un-American. Freedom of speech and the press, free exercise of religion, and equal protection of the law are viewed as bedrock attributes of American democracy. Yet, equally urgent social and economic protections are regularly violated in the United States. Courts since the 1980s have eviscerated school integration require-ments, such that most black and Latino children remain in schools as deeply segregated and inadequately financed as they were in 1970. President Bill Clinton colluded in 1996 with a newly elected Republican Congress to "reform" welfare by imposing draconian and punitive time limits and other conditions on the meager cash transfers made to the poorest Americans. President George W. Bush in 2007 to issued just the fourth veto of his presidency to deny an expansion of health insurance for underprivileged children, ostensibly because it would promote socialized medicine. And, of course, despite permanent legions of the homeless and unstably housed, there was no "housing crisis" in the United States until it began to directly threaten the middle class during the meltdown of 2008. Speech, religion, and due process, it seems, are regarded as fundamental constitutional rights, while sound education, basic income, adequate health care, and decent housing are treated as expendable luxuries.

In what way, then, might social and economic protections be shielded from such reckless disregard? As is so often the case in areas of social justice, the ideas of Franklin D. Roosevelt can help point the way. In 1944, the United States had largely recovered from the Great Depression through a combination of New Deal reforms and the turbocharging of the economy caused by the total mobilization of World War II. By January 11 of that year, victory in the war seemed increasingly likely, so Roosevelt took part of his State of the Union Address to lay out a vision of the postwar domestic scene.[2] "This Republic had its beginning, and grew to its present strength, under the protection of certain inalienable political rights—among them the right of free speech, free press, free worship, trial by jury, freedom from unreasonable searches and seizures. They were our rights to life and liberty," said Roosevelt. "We have come to a clear realization of the fact, however, that true individual freedom cannot exist without economic security and independence."

In a bold stroke, Roosevelt then presented his idea for a "Second Bill of Rights" that would parallel and reinforce the original. "In our day these economic truths have become accepted as self-evident. We have accepted, so to speak, a second Bill of Rights under which a new basis of security and prosperity can be established for all—regardless of station, or race or creed." Among these, he argued, are the following:

> "The right to a useful and remunerative job in the industries or shops or farms or mines of the Nation;
>
> The right to earn enough to provide adequate food and clothing and recreation;
>
> The right of every farmer to raise and sell his products at a return which will give him and his family a decent living;
>
> The right of every businessman, large and small, to trade in an atmosphere of freedom from unfair competition and domination by monopolies at home or abroad;
>
> The right of every family to a decent home;
>
> The right to adequate medical care and the opportunity to achieve and enjoy good health;
>
> The right to adequate protection from the economic fears of old age, sickness, accident, and unemployment;
>
> The right to a good education."

"All of these rights spell security," stated Roosevelt. "And after this war is won we must be prepared to move forward, in the implementation of these rights, to new goals of human happiness and well-being. America's own rightful place in the world depends in large part upon how fully these and similar rights have been carried into practice for all our citizens. For unless there is security here at home there cannot be lasting peace in the world."

As brilliantly presented by law professor Cass Sunstein in *The Second Bill of Rights: FDR's Unfinished Revolution and Why We Need It More Than Ever*, Roosevelt's ideas did not involve the literal amending of the Constitution.[3] He had, after all, enacted a vast panoply of reforms through the New Deal without changing a word of the Constitution. "I ask the Congress to explore the means for implementing this economic bill of rights—for it is definitely the responsibility of the Congress so to do, and the country knows it," Roosevelt said. But subsequent history clearly indicates that Congress cannot be counted on to reliably or consistently offer sufficient social and economic protections to achieve true substantive democracy. As Sunstein documents, the federal courts had begun the process of enacting the Second Bill of Rights through judicial interpretation throughout the 1950s and 1960s. But that process ground to a halt after the turn to the political right that began with the election of Richard Nixon in 1968 and accelerated with Ronald Reagan's election in 1980 and the Republican takeover of Congress in 1995. When Congress did enact the Obama healthcare plan in early 2010, more than one commentator noted that it was actually more limited than what Nixon had proposed three decades earlier.

Thus, it seems clear that the enlightened goodwill of a particular Congress or the humane vision of a particular court is clearly not enough: placement directly into the Constitution is called for. While the Constitution has no provision for enacting an entire slate of reforms at once, it has in fact done so before. The original Bill of Rights is composed of 10 separately proposed and separately ratified amendments, and so too a Second Bill of Rights might require several separate amendments covering such discrete areas as housing, employment, basic income, education, and health care. Alternatively, a single powerful Amendment, like the Fourteenth, could clearly enunciate a principle of social and economic equity from which certain basic rights would logically flow and task the government with enacting and advancing these rights. Both approaches have their pitfalls. The first runs the risk of legislating policy via amendment, which the Prohibition amendment clearly demonstrated to be a bad idea, since legislation requires a degree of precision and flexibility impossible in an amendment. Conversely, a principle that is too broad or abstract would remain susceptible to dilution and evasion. Perhaps the best combination would be a single amendment with broad principles enacted in the first clause and then specific domains and their basic definitions spelled out in subsequent clauses or, if necessary, separate amendments.

Needless to say, this is all far more easily said than done. Earlier reforms proposed in this volume, including PR, a multiparty system, runoff elections, and a streamlined electoral process, would promise to energize now quiescent segments of the population that would most benefit from a Second Bill of Rights and thus build political support for it. But the arduous process of constitutional amendment remains a major impediment, one whose reform is addressed in the next chapter. And the ultimate mechanism for promoting constitutional change—a new convention—is the subject of the final chapter.

SYNOPSIS

Desirability: 5

Because this volume focuses on institutions and processes rather than on policy, most of its focus has been on procedural democracy rather than substantive democracy. But to the extent that procedural democracy rings hollow without basic further guarantees to protect the human dignity and bodily integrity of citizens, placing critical basic social and economic protections in to the Constitution could do more than any other single step to reinforce the promise of American democracy.

Practicability: 3

At several points of ferment in American history—at the time of founding, after the Civil War, amidst the Progressive Era, and during the Civil Rights Movement—three or more constitutional amendments have been ratified at a single time. Whether enacted via a single amendment or several, enshrining the equivalent of a Second Bill of Rights into the Constitution would be a straightforward proposition that would gain credibility from its explicit parallel to the revered original Bill of Rights.

Plausibility: 3

A certain proportion of Congress and the state legislatures might be well inclined to support comprehensive social and economic protections, perhaps more so post-2008 than at any time in the prior 40 years. Still, such wide-ranging changes would probably need to be deferred until later in a reform agenda, perhaps as one of its crowning achievements, once other reforms, such as PR and a multiparty system have increased the voice and influence of currently disempowered segments of the population.

CHAPTER 20

Streamline the Constitutional Amendment Process

Highlighting Ideas from Australia

Considering its impact and durability, the U.S. Constitution is a remarkably brief document. Its original form ratified in 1789 includes only about 4,600 words; add in the Bill of Rights passed two years later but essentially as part of the same historical process, and the word count increases only another 600 words. The reasons for this brevity are several. First, as noted in the prior chapter, the Constitution does not substantively address social and economic protections. It also omits many features that are essential to any careful understanding of politics, notably political parties, as well as government, such as the congressional committee structure.

Rather than seek to provide detailed guidelines for governance, it was intended as a simpler "citizen's charter" that sketched out only the bare bones of what the founding generation felt was truly essential to establishing an effective but limited government structure and to striking the pragmatic compromises needed to promote ratification by the states. It should also be understood against the backdrop of a common law system, in which much about government and politics was assumed to be already understood. The detailed statues of the Napoleonic Code, which would so influence the design of the next generation of constitutions in western Europe, still lay more than a decade into the future at the time of the U.S. founding.

But another important reason that the Constitution can be so functional and yet still concise was that the generation of the founders was under no illusions that they had all the answers that the country would need in perpetuity. Rather, in a stroke of creativity as well as humility, they devoted one of the document's seven articles to establishing a procedure to undo their handiwork by providing a clear mechanism for amendment. Underscoring the central role they envisioned for Congress, they required amendments to be initiated by that branch, with no veto or other formal role envisioned for the president or the judiciary. Mindful of the central role of the states, they required further ratification by a proportion of state legislatures or special conventions while also allowing the states to introduce amendments through the vehicle of a constitutional convention. Thus, rather than attempt to bind the hands of their successors, the founders—still imbued with some of the spirit of the American Revolution—allowed for each generation to reconstruct government as they saw fit. Only two issues that were seen as likely deal breakers for the ratification process—prohibition of slavery and equal representation of the Senate—were formally "entrenched" or put beyond the reach of amendments.

Still, the amendment process has taken place only rarely and usually in brief, concentrated bursts. Holding aside the first 10 amendments, which were enacted almost immediately in part as a way to reassure those concerned that the new government would be too powerful, only 17 additional amendments have ever been enacted. Of these, two (the Eighteenth, introducing Prohibition, and the Twenty-First, rescinding it) are essentially inoperative. And of the remaining 15, only two can be said to have had a huge impact on U.S. history, the Thirteenth, abolishing slavery, and the Fourteenth, guaranteeing equal protection under the law. Of the others, only a small subset are even particularly noteworthy, including the Fifteenth, Nineteenth, and Twenty-Sixth, which expanded voting rights on the basis, respectively, of race, gender, and age, and perhaps also the Sixteenth, authorizing a federal income tax. The others mostly tinker with the mechanics of government or regulate aspects of the electoral process.

In part, it has been possible for the amending process to be used so rarely because the very brevity of the Constitution allows flexibility for interpretation without textual alteration. Powers such as the judicial review of legislative and executive acts and the the president's ability to terminate executive officers, for example, were established by court rulings based on the logic rather than the literal text of the Constitution itself. Other times, key historic events have led to widely accepted new understandings of the Constitutional order, such as the redefinition of federalism that followed the Civil War and the expanded scope of government activity that followed the Great Depression. Yet one barrier to amendments that cannot be underestimated is the sheer difficulty of garnering the consensus needed to enact them.

Under the Articles of Confederation, major changes could only be made by the *unanimous* consent of all the states. This unanimity requirement was far from the only severe shortcoming of the Articles but may have been the one that kept it most hamstrung. Yet it was also clear that the founders wished the Constitution to be a form of higher law that could not easily be tampered with by transient majorities in Congress or the states. Their challenge was thus to establish a formula for supermajorities that would insulate the Constitution from capricious revision without allowing it to ossify into brittle rigidity. They thus struck on the formula of two-thirds of each house of Congress followed by fully three-quarters of the state legislatures, which was not coincidentally also the proportion of states originally required for the new Constitution to take effect. In the modern union of 50 states, this means the support of 38 state legislatures.

However, the founders may have set the bar too high. While amendments have been introduced into Congress more than 10,000 times, only the tiniest of proportions have actually been enacted. And those that did were usually in periods of exceptional political ferment, including the original Constitution-making period (Amendments 1–10, all in 1791), the Civil War (Amendments 13–15, 1865–70), the Progressive Era (Amendments 16–19, 1913–20), and the Civil Rights period (23–26, 1961–71). The onerous burden of garnering even a two-thirds majority in Congress has led to only two amendments being proposed by Congress to the states since 1971, one regarding equal rights for women and the other regarding expanded voting rights for Washington, D.C., neither of which received the support of 38 states required for ratification by the deadline established by Congress. Thus, for the *third* time in U.S. history, we have passed two or more full generations without the proposal and ratification of a textual alteration to the Constitution. The first time was the 61 years between 1804 and 1865, the second the 43 years between 1870 and 1913, and the most recent the 39 years and counting since 1971. (The highly anomalous and fairly trivial Twenty-Seventh Amendment limiting congressional pay raises took effect in 1992 but was first proposed by Congress in 1789, forgotten for decades, and then resurrected.)

Countries whose constitutions can be amended too easily face problems of their own in which those constitutions may too volatile and subject to passing whims and passions. In Brazil, for example, the constitution can be amended by a mere 60 percent majority vote held twice in each chamber of Congress, and eight constitutional amendments were passed between just December 2004 and March 2006.[1] A few other countries have even more rigid formulas for amendment than the United States. In fact, in Argentina, a full constitutional convention must be called for any change. But most countries have struck a more manageable process, including one of the closest cousins of the United States: Australia.

CONSTITUTIONAL AMENDMENTS IN AUSTRALIA

First colonized by the British in the 1770s, Australia did not become a separate country in its own right until 1901. By that time, it had a variety of examples and precedents on which to draw in structuring its new political system. Some of these were derived from the British tradition, including keeping the British monarch as head of state (represented by a governor-general), maintaining a bicameral parliament, and vesting effective executive authority in a prime minister and cabinet drawn from the lower house. In other realms, however, it adapted practices from the American example, such as adopting a federal structure and having two elected parliamentary chambers that resembled those in the United States: a House of Representatives with members allocated by population and a Senate with an equal number of members from each state.

Australia also broke with practice in Britain as well as in neighboring New Zealand by adopting a written constitution embodied in a single document with a fixed process for amendment. As in the United States, the Australian constitution requires the assent of the legislature for initiation and then a specialized majority for ratification. However, the threshold for consent to constitutional change is considerably lower. Ordinarily, the proposal must garner just a simple majority in both houses of Parliament. In the case of an amendment passed by the House of Representatives but rejected by the Senate, if the House passes it a second time, the prime minister may advance the amendment for state ratification without Senate approval. Although this has never happened, a constitutional amendment could at least in theory thus be proposed by Parliament with the assent of just 76 of its 226 members, as long as that majority included the prime minister.

The next step drew on practices in the highly decentralized country of Switzerland, which has an unusual "double-majority" requirement for constitutional amending. The formulation of the double majority in Australia requires that an amendment be endorsed both by a simple majority of the entire voting population and by majorities within half the states. Thus, the consent of the majority of the population (including those living in territories rather than states) is required, while the federal principle is maintained by requiring majority assent to ratification to constitutional change. In cases in which a particular state would be specifically impacted, majority approval from within that state is also necessary, a requirement sometimes dubbed a "triple majority."

In practice, the Australian system actually does require a high level of consensus; with only six states, a majority is in fact four states, which works out to a full two-thirds of the total number of Australian states. Further, since more than half the population resides in the two largest states—New South Wales and Victoria—it is highly unlikely (though mathematically possible) that a national majority could be garnered without the majority support of at least one of those two large states. In part because of this high threshold, the Australian constitution has been amended even less than the U.S. Constitution— just eight times in 108 years versus 27 times in 220 years.

A STREAMLINED AMENDING PROCESS IN THE UNITED STATES?

The particular circumstances in Australia mean that the double-majority rule there does not in fact necessarily facilitate easier constitutional change than in the United States. But what if the formula were to be transposed to the U.S. situation? Regarding the first stage of congressional approval, the necessary numbers in the United States for two-third majorities are currently 292 House members and 67 senators. Under the Australian system, the requirement would drop to 218 in the House and 51 in the Senate. If the House were given the ability to act without Senate approval, as is possible in Australia, then the required total would drop from the current 359 of 535 members of Congress to 218 of 535 members, or just 41 percent. (The case for the House having enhanced powers over the Senate is made in Chapter 15.)

Of course, Congress's role is limited to only the proposal of amendments, not their full enactment. Both the United States and Australia, along with most other federal countries, require a further step of ratification. But in Australia, this is carried out by means of popular referendum, with the people themselves having the opportunity to approve or disapprove constitutional change. In the United States, the people are bypassed in favor of votes by the members of the legislatures of three-quarters (38) of the states, meaning that an amendment could be blocked by just 13 states. Yet the smallest 13 states make up just over 4 percent of the national population, enabling them to thwart the will of more than 95 percent of the population! A further irony of the three-quarters requirement in the United States is that it still does not mathematically guarantee approval by a majority of the overall U.S. population since the 38 smallest states, which could in theory vote together as a bloc, have just under 40 percent of the national population.

Yet another major complicating factor is that every state but Nebraska has a bicameral legislature and that state ratification requires a confirmatory vote in *both* chambers. Thus, failure to pass just 13 of the 99 state legislative chambers could effectively block ratification.

True, there is an alternate procedure allowed under the Constitution that could get around the problem of bicameralism. At the time it proposes an amendment, Congress can determine whether ratification will be carried out by three-quarters of the state legislatures or by three-quarters of specially elected unicameral ratification conventions, which would be elected by the people of each. This procedure has been used only once, for the Twenty-First Amendment, which repealed the earlier Prohibition amendment, but does exist as a mechanism for streamlining ratification that is worth considering.

The previously mentioned numbers may have become a bit abstract, so a brief case study may help illuminate matters. The Equal Rights Amendment (ERA), the most important guarantee of rights for women ever proposed in U.S. history, would have added to the Constitution the simple but powerful statement that "equality of rights under the law shall not be denied or abridged by the United States or by any State on account of sex." In 1971, the amendment was passed with support in both houses of Congress, exceeding a remarkable 80 percent. The amendment was then ratified by both houses of the legislatures in 35 states and by one house in eight states. Yet, despite this significant national consensus, the amendment fell short. Under the Australian system of ratification by referendum, the amendment would almost certainly have been enacted, particularly since public opinion polls at the time showed the support of a national majority for ratification. (The full story of the Equal Rights Amendment is rather more complicated, it should be noted, because of controversies over a deadline extension and also attempts by five states to rescind their approval.)

It thus seems clear that the formula used in Australia would allow the United States to more readily amend its Constitution. In fact, it could be done with the same relatively low majorities that have elected presidents in some recent years. For example, in 2008, Barack Obama won 53 percent of the vote and 28 states, and in 2004, George W. Bush took 31 states and nearly 51 percent of the vote. The same basic electoral coalitions—if also supported by a majority in Congress— would likewise be able to amend the Constitution under the Australian formulation.

But how desirable would this be? The counterargument is apparent: lowering the bar for approval *too* drastically would enable transient majorities to enact wide-ranging changes. In the wake of September 11, 2001, for example, Congress acquiesced readily to proposals from the White House for enhanced executive power, notably the far-reaching PATRIOT Act. On the wind of popular passions, even an ill-considered amendment might quickly be approved by a double majority of the people and of the states. This could enshrine dangerous elements directly into the Constitution that would place them beyond even the scrutiny of the judiciary,which cannot overturn amendments.

What then is the ideal balance? Is 50 percent too low? Is 75 percent too high? Is the current 67 percent best? Why not 60 percent? The Australian model offers one possibility, but the democratic world offers many others. Canada requires approval of Parliament and then a majority of provinces that themselves represent a majority of the population. Major changes in the European Union require 55 percent of the member states, which must make up at least 65 percent of the union's population. France allows a legislative supermajority or a simple majority in a referendum. Rather than tinker with such specific formulas, however, it may be best to conclude this chapter by returning to a few basic observations.

The first is that two or more generations should not pass without a polity being effectively able to amend its fundamental constitutional arrangements. If this happens, as it has repeatedly in U.S. history, then something is not working properly. The founders did not put the document they created on such a pedestal, nor should we. The second is that constitutional law should remain higher than ordinary law and should continue to require supermajorities to adjust basic protections of individual civil liberties or make fundamental alterations to the machinery of government. The third is that too small a minority of the population should not be able to thwart the will of a robust majority. Surely, the status quo allowing 13 of the nation's state legislative chambers to block the expressed will of the other 86 is too disproportionate, as is allowing states with less than 5 percent of the national population to frustrate the desires of 95 percent of the population. Finally, the process should not be so focused on elite actors that the will of the people themselves is not fully accounted for. One mechanism for popular input is certainly the nationwide public referendum, though for reasons outlined in Chapter 8, this option does have its pitfalls. The other mechanism already exists, a dormant yet still viable seed buried in the text of the Constitution itself: a new constitutional convention, which is the subject of the next and final chapter of this book.

SYNOPSIS

Desirability: 4

The ability of a people to adjust the basic conditions of their government is a fundamental attribute of popular sovereignty. To the extent that the U.S. formula for amendment excessively frustrates that ability, it is in need of reform. Conversely, for a constitution to have lasting and durable value, it should not be changed too easily or too frequently. While arguments may exist over the specifics of various possible formulas, the weight of the evidence is that the amendment formula in the United States is clearly not optimal.

Practicability: 2

In technical terms, it would be a simple matter to insert some new language into article V of the Constitution—the current amending process could be used to adjust the amending process for the future. The process of refining the exact formula would be rather more challenging, but various proposals could be aired in the marketplace of ideas until a single best approach could be identified.

Plausibility: 2

Simplification of the amendment procedure does not necessarily have many "natural enemies" at the federal level. In fact, if part of the provision were to be to reduce the legislative majorities in Congress and the states, this move could actually enhance the ability of those bodies to shape constitutional change. Hence, a great deal of the plausibility of a reform to the amending process would probably depend on the political context and the expectation of how the new procedure would be used. As discussed in the next chapter, the very threat of a constitutional convention might be enough to spark reform in the amending process.

CHAPTER **21**

Call a Constitutional Convention

Highlighting Ideas from the Philippines

Although best known for its sweeping statements of the unalienable rights of life, liberty, and the pursuit of happiness, the U.S. Declaration of Independence also boldly asserts that the people have a right of revolution. "Governments are instituted among Men, deriving their just powers from the consent of the governed," wrote Jefferson and his compatriots, adding "that whenever any Form of Government becomes destructive of these ends, it is the Right of the People to alter or to abolish it, and to institute new Government, laying its foundation on such principles and organizing its powers in such form, as to them shall seem most likely to effect their Safety and Happiness."

Such was the antiauthoritarian mood of 1776, but by a mere 11 years later, the Constitutional Convention was faced with a starkly different challenge. The country had languished under the enfeebled government of the Articles of Confederation, and so the founders were faced with the task of imposing order while avoiding tyranny. In some respects, the establishment of the U.S. Constitution was a reversal of the more radically egalitarian and decentralized vision of the Revolution. Certainly, the Constitution makes no allowance for a right of revolution, with its attendant images of violent uprising and rebellion from below. But it does contain a mechanism—never used but preserved down to the current day—by which the Constitution itself could be radically altered or even abolished. Embedded within article V is a requirement that Congress, "upon the Application of the Legislatures of two thirds of the several States, shall call a Convention for proposing Amendments."

While ostensibly just another way to initiate amendments, the calling of a constitutional convention could have much more far-reaching implications. Indeed, the framers at the Constitutional Convention of 1787 could not help but be aware that they had far exceeded the limited mandate with which they first assembled, namely, to find ways to merely adjust the Articles of Confederation. They also proposed that the new document would take effect with just three-quarters of the states (9 of the 13) rather than the unanimous consent clearly required under the Articles. Similarly, it is far from unclear that the writ of a modern constitutional convention could be restricted only to certain topics rather than more fundamental change.

Throughout U.S. history to date, other forms of constitutional change have been relied upon. In 27 cases, this has meant textual alterations to the original Constitution, with several amendments covering multiple subjects. In countless other cases, it has meant the development of practices and precedents that "fill in the blanks" left unaddressed by the Constitution, be it that there will be 435 members of the House or nine members of the Supreme Court or that the rules of the Senate but not of the House will allow filibusters. Still other constitutional norms have evolved through judicial interpretation, such as the changing conception of whether the Fourteenth Amendment permits segregation. But what if such changes prove insufficient or, worse yet, invidious to democracy? And what if it is the political establishment in Washington itself that is in need of deep reform but resists calls for change? The last resort, a sort of "controlled revolution," would be the convening of a new constitutional convention following a call by the legislatures of 33 states.

Critics of this idea often raise the specter of a "runaway" convention in which an entirely new system of government could be foisted on an appalled nation. If a convention were to be somehow captured by special interests or a particular ideological faction, they argue, the result could be a transformation of the United States into a theocracy, an outpost of communism, an anarchist state, a dictatorship, or perhaps some other dire outcome. Such scenarios are overstated at best and outlandish at worst, but it remains a valid observation that there would be better ways and worse ways to establish and carry out the work of a constitutional convention. The case of a former U.S. territory, the Philippines, provides two such examples: a scandalous 1971 convention under dictatorship and a laudable 1986 convention under democracy.

CASE STUDY: CONSTITUTIONAL CONVENTIONS IN THE PHILIPPINES

Taken by the United States from Spain after the Spanish-American War in 1898, the island nation of the Philippines was an American commonwealth territory for nearly half a century. In 1935, the United States introduced a commonwealth constitution based closely on the U.S. model, including a separation-of-powers system with a president limited to two terms. This constitution saw the country through independence all the way to 1971, the waning years of the second and constitutionally final term of the increasingly authoritarian presidency of Ferdinand Marcos.

Unwilling to cede power, Marcos initiated a constitutional convention with the goal of either eliminating term limits, extending his current term of office or perhaps transferring power to his infamous though well-shod wife, Imelda. Delegates to the constitutional convention were elected through a flawed process, and both bribery and intimidation of the delegates were openly practiced by the Marcos regime. The convention as a whole proved less pliable than the regime expected, but the biggest problem from Marcos's perspective was that it moved so slowly that its work would not be completed before the end of his term. Threatened with the loss of power, he unilaterally invoked the presidential power to declare martial law and ruled the country by decree.

With his hand thus greatly strengthened, Marcos and his allies commandeered control of the convention and pushed through the creation of a new prime-ministerial role that would control all executive functions, including command of the army. By definition, a prime minister is the leader of both the executive and the legislative branches and in most countries can stay in office for as long as he or she retains the support of the majority of the legislature. Thus, in one cynical power grab, Marcos was able to create a new locus of power that could dominate the entire government indefinitely, subject only to the continued rigging of legislative elections. Of course, he engineered his election as the first prime minister under the new system.

By the start of the 1980s, Marcos had become a full-blown dictator, arresting or exiling his political opponents, curbing press freedoms, imposing a curfew system, encouraging graft and corruption, and cultivating an outright cult of personality, with his photo placed ubiquitously throughout the country. Popular discontent brewed for years but reached a critical point when the main opposition leader, Benigno Aquino, was assassinated in broad daylight when disembarking from a plane on his attempted return to the country in 1986. In a few short days, a remarkable and mostly nonviolent "People Power Revolution" took shape, combining mass street demonstrations, open opposition by the Catholic Church, agitation by the military, and the resignation of senior members of the Marcos regime. Marcos was quickly forced into exile, and one of the first actions of his successor—Aquino's widow Corazon—was to promulgate interim changes to the existing constitution and to call for a new one.

Although the 1986 process was deemed a "constitutional commission" rather than a convention per se, the process was widely hailed as open and inclusive. The commission's members were appointed by Corazon Aquino but in the spirit of the People Power Revolution included representatives from across the entire political spectrum, even including Marcos loyalists. The main thrust of the entire process—which was carried out in a few months, enabling the quick consolidation of the People Power Revolution—was built around the principle of opposition to dictatorship. As such, the new constitution shifted significant power back to Congress, placed limits on the use of martial law, created a human rights commission, lengthened the working sessions of Congress, and limited the president to a single nonrenewable term. In a subsequent ratification referendum, the new constitution was approved by 76 percent of the Filipino public.[1]

A CONSTITUTIONAL CONVENTION IN THE UNITED STATES?

The example of these two Filipino constitutional conventions offers important lessons for the United States and not only because the Philippine constitution is so close to that of the United States. From a purely procedural perspective, one might have expected the 1971 convention to have been more successful than the 1986 convention. In 1971 the delegates were elected, but in 1986 they were appointed by the president, and in 1971 they had a long time frame for deliberation but in 1986 worked under pressure during a turbulent situation. Yet the truly crucial difference was that in 1986, unlike in 1971, there was a genuine spirit of consensus building, and the participants had the political will to achieve a democratic outcome.

This observation is particularly significant for the idea of a constitutional convention in the United States because the Constitution itself provides no guidance whatsoever about the how a convention should be organized and conducted. Further, U.S. political history offers scant precedents for a federal constitutional convention beyond the rather eclectic examples offered by various state constitutional conventions. Thus, many fundamental questions have no clear-cut answers. For example, could the mandate of a new convention be limited only to certain subjects, or, once convened, would it have latitude to cover other topics, and how would this be determined? Would the delegates be elected or appointed, and how would this be decided? Would those delegates be closer to electors in the Electoral College and bound to support a particular position, or would they be more like members of Congress, who can freely vote as they wish? Would it be a standing body that might exist for many months or even years, or would it be strictly time limited? And could the convention propose a method for ratification of its proposed amendments via some path, such as popular referendum, or would it be bound by the methods that currently exist in article V of the Constitution?

The examples from the Philippines become interesting here since they suggest that an emphasis on procedural issues might lead to poor results. Rather, in this case, the "letter of the law" might be important but less so than the "spirit of the law." It is usually an overstatement to say that "context is everything," but it may not be in this situation. A convention called with a genuine goal of building an improved political system through democratic deliberation and meaningful citizen input could be a powerful means to further drive reform. But because the ground rules are so imprecise and thus subject to manipulation, a constitutional convention could just as easily become a retrogressive tool to reinforce the status quo or even to roll back rights and liberties.

It thus is hard to say much more about the idea of a constitutional convention in the United States without specifying the particular rules under which it would be conducted and the specific political context within which it would occur. The topic of the complexities of calling and conducting a twenty-first-century convention is given excellent treatment in a recent work by Larry J. Sabato titled *A More Perfect Constitution*.[2] After plumbing the issues, Sabato proposes a convention in which the formula for allocation of seats in the House of Representatives would be used to allow each state to elect a number of delegates on the basis of its population. These 435 delegates, from which sitting members of Congress should be excluded, would begin working with the mandate provided by the original state petitions and some basic rules established by Congress but would then be largely autonomous. Amendments proposed by the convention would then be submitted to the states for ratification by three-fourths of either state legislatures or specially convened ratifying conventions (the latter method being the one used in the case of the Twenty-First Amendment). Other proposals have included more or less random selection of citizens as delegates, an idea being pondered for a state constitutional convention in California, or perhaps some more broadly participatory process, perhaps making use of new information technologies, such as the Internet.

With regard to the political context, it is clear that it would be better to have no constitutional convention than to have one likely to produce bad results. If a constitutional convention were to be called in a moment of political crisis such as after an assassination or a popular insurrection or amidst a devastating disaster such as a crippling terrorist attack or ecological catastrophe, the results might be hastily produced and poorly conceived. True, the need for approval by three-fourths of the states could serve as a brake, but some other amendments have swept through the ratification process in mere months. The George W. Bush administration was able to do considerable violence to the Constitution in the aftermath of the 9/11 terrorist attacks simply using the tools it already had at hand within the executive branch. A constitutional convention that captured a more widespread moment of fear or anger or social tension could hastily produce a document that might inflict far more permanent damage to basic constitutional principles.

However, a constitutional convention that served as the culmination rather than the catalyst for change could consolidate a new consensus and enshrine it in the Constitution in a well-considered and clearly conceptualized manner. In the Philippines, it was not constitutional change that spurred on the People Power Revolution. Rather, the 1986 constitutional revisions flowed neatly and cleanly from basic demands and principles that had been percolating in Filipino society for years. This would strongly suggest that a constitutional convention, if one is needed at all, could be used to facilitate the proposal of a range of constitutional amendments—such as those outlined throughout this book—that had already taken shape through democratic deliberation and discussion over the course of years.

It may also be the case that the credible *threat* of a constitutional convention, with all its attendant uncertainties, could in and of itself prove to be a spur for reform. Indeed, this was the case of the

Seventeenth Amendment, which significantly changed the character of the U.S. Senate by providing for the direct election of senators by the people of each state rather than by the respective state legislatures. This change, perhaps along with limiting presidents to two terms, was the biggest alteration to the structure of the federal government ever enacted through the amendment process. Given that large numbers of both senators and state legislatures had to assent to this change, its passage would seem to be rather implausible. But popular pressure during the Progressive Era built to such a point that, by 1913, nearly two-thirds of the states had submitted applications to call a constitutional convention focused on this issue, and Congress found it simpler just to propose an amendment itself than to allow a Pandora's box to be opened. And if senators can be convinced to place their fates in the hands of the voters rather than their cronies in the state legislatures and if those legislatures could be persuaded to give up their power to directly influence one chamber of Congress, then many other far-reaching reforms are also eminently plausible.

SYNOPSIS

Desirability: 2

In theory, the substance of a reform agenda in the United States could be carried out without the extreme step of a constitutional convention either through the existing constitutional amendment process or through a streamlined process as proposed in the previous chapter. Because of its uncertainty as well as its susceptibility to manipulation, a constitutional convention should be a last resort and is not a step that is particularly desirable in its own right. If meaningful change proves otherwise impossible, however, or if a slate of reforms had already been clearly articulated and simply needed to be enacted, then the argument for a constitutional convention becomes more compelling.

Practicability: 4

The means for calling a constitutional convention are fairly clear, and the near miss in the early twentieth century demonstrates that the participation of two-thirds of the states is possible. However, the utter lack of clear-cut guidelines for constituting and conducting the convention would likely be repeatedly invoked in states that might otherwise be inclined to join the call for a new convention.

Plausibility: 2

The complexities and uncertainties of a constitutional convention render it a not particularly plausible event. However, as in the Progressive Era, popular support and pressure at the state level could prove sufficient to spur action. If Congress proved recalcitrant long enough, if problems became severe enough, or if a clear enough reform agenda had been articulated through grassroots activism, a sufficient number of state legislatures might be willing to submit a petition. As in the case of the Seventeenth Amendment, Congress might undercut this by proposing its own amendment, but in the end much the same result would have been achieved.

Conclusion: Rankings of the Ideas and Priorities for Reform

The 21 preceding chapters of *Importing Democracy* have laid out ideas from around the world that could potentially facilitate the reform and revitalization of American democracy. With more than 190 countries in the world, there are inevitably many other features of other political systems that are not addressed in this volume. Some common features, such as a political role for the military or rule by a single party, are manifestly antidemocratic and as such were excluded a priori. Other features that are commonly found in established democracies would distort the existing American system to such a great degree that the disruption caused by reform would likely be counterproductive; the establishment of a full parliamentary system or the demotion of the judiciary to a clearly subordinate role would fall into this category. Further, in some areas, such as the robust American system of federalism and the impressive judicial protection of freedom of expression, the U.S. model already is among the best in the world and thus does not require major reform. Finally, the focus of this book is on political institutions and processes rather than public policy, although a parallel volume could certainly be written—and, indeed, some have been written—on lessons that the United States could learn from the specific public policies enacted in other countries.

Despite these parameters, the preceding chapters do lay out the contours of a sweeping reform agenda, particularly in the brief synopses and scores at the end of each chapter. The scoring system used in this book is not driven by the quantification of data or the analysis of statistics. As such, they do, inevitably, have a subjective dimension. (No attentive reader would by this point have failed to discern the author's center-left political orientation, high regard for majority rule alongside protection of minority rights, or concerns about an over-bearing executive.) Further, each idea was considered more or less in isolation from the others, and they do not necessarily all fit together well or lead to entirely consistent conclusions.

Each idea was scored separately and independently as the chapter was finalized, without any overall plan or manipulation of scores to produce certain outcomes. Further, the scores were derived from processes of inductive reasoning based on the actual experience of each issue in other countries and sometimes in U.S. states alongside deductive reasoning based on the *desirability*, *practicability*, and *plausibility* of each reform. To reiterate the criteria laid out in the introduction, these three variables were defined and operationalized in the following ways:

- The variable "desirability" considers how well any given reform, on balance, advances four key characteristics of democratic systems: (1) offering meaningful input by all citizens on a regular basis to the workings of government, (2) balancing the promotion of majority rule with the protection of minority rights, (3) producing governments that are strong enough to be effective but limited enough not to be tyrannical, and (4) advancing both individual liberty and social equality among their citizens.

- "Practicability" refers to the difficulty of achieving a goal given the existing constraints of American politics. Particularly relevant here are two dimensions: (1) whether it would require a major constitutional change or could be enacted through ordinary legislation, regulations, or policies and (2) whether there are multiple actors throughout the political system with the motivation and ability to block a change.

- The related but still distinct variable of "plausibility" assesses how likely existing political actors might be to actually implement such a reform. Once again, two dimensions are particularly salient: (1) whether political actors would be prone to adopt the change, in whole or part, mostly of their own accord and (2) how possible it would be to build public awareness of the issue and to generate sustained public pressure for the change.

Table C.1 summarizes the 21 ideas reviewed in this book. They are organized into three tiers based solely on their desirability score. The reason for this is that, on closer scrutiny, a number of potential reforms

Table C.1   Desirability, Practicability, and Plausibility Scores

	Practicability Score	Plausibility Score	Practicability/ Plausibility Composite Score
Reforms with Desirability Score of 5			
Adopt proportional representation	3	2	5
Move toward a multiparty system	3	2	5
Simplify and shorten the electoral process	5	3	8
Allow "removal for cause" of the president	4	3	7
Hold special presidential elections	4	3	7
Depoliticize the creation of congressional districts	5	3	8
Add social and economic protections to the Constitution	3	3	6
Reforms with Desirability Score of 4			
Establish runoff elections for executive offices	3	3	6
Abolish the Electoral College	3	3	6
Advance minorities and women in elected office	2	3	5
Streamline the constitutional amendment process	2	2	4
Reforms with Desirability Score of 3			
Abolish the vice presidency	4	3	7
Synchronize the terms of Congress and the presidency	3	3	6
Rein in the president's legislative and judicial powers	4	3	5
Empower the courts to issue advisory opinions	4	3	7
Reforms with Desirability Score of 2			
Weaken the Senate	2	2	4
Allow legislative overrides of judicial opinions	4	2	6
Call a constitutional convention	4	2	7
Reforms with Desirability Score of 1			
Introduce compulsory voting	5	3	8
Establish national referenda	2	2	4
Add elected officers to the executive	2	1	3

proved to *not* in fact be particularly desirable no matter how practicable or plausible they might be. Similarly, some of the most desirable reforms might not be particularly practicable or plausible but might still deserve a place in a reform agenda and be worth the great effort they may require. The last column in the table provides a composite of the practicability and plausibility scores, which can serve as a proxy for how difficult each idea would be to enact—the lower the composite score, the more challenging that reform would be to carry out.

THE LOW-RANKED REFORMS

In reviewing the scores in the table, several potential reforms— those with desirability scores of 1 or 2—can safely be excluded from a reform agenda and should probably even be opposed by those inter- ested in advancing democracy. Perhaps the weakest of all the ideas proved to be the idea of adding elected officers to the executive. For better or worse, the presidency is a singular institution, and it would fundamentally alter the nature of the office, to little concrete gain, to diversify executive power. Still, the observation that most other estab- lished democracies have dispersed their executive roles among multi- ple individuals could help promote smaller reforms, such as the naming of the cabinet before the presidential election.

Another low-ranked idea was that of weakening the Senate. Although this is appealing on its face because of the malapportionment of Senate seats among large and small population states, the Senate in actual practice has usually proven to be a constructive partner to the House of Representatives and a benignly moderating influence in Congress. Nonetheless, this is a reform that should be held in abey- ance only for as long as the Senate continues to perform well.

Slightly stronger but still problematic would be two reforms that might advance democracy in terms of raw *quantity* of participation but at the potential risk of undermining the *quality* of that democracy. National referenda are appealing at first glance and might be used in a confirmatory role in some contexts, such as a streamlined constitu- tional amending process. But as a tool of public policymaking, the referendum is far too blunt an instrument in a mass, complex modern society. The record of referenda is poor at the state level and when elevated to the national level could prove disastrous. Similarly, the idea of compulsory voting would be a brute force way of attacking the com- plexities that lead to the low voter turnout rates that are endemic to the

U.S. system. Far better than focusing on coerced turnout would be an emphasis on giving more voters stronger reasons and greater incentives to bother to vote, which could indeed be the effect of some of the higher-ranked reforms identified in the following sections.

Finally, a full-scale constitutional convention would seem to be unwarranted or at least premature. In fact, constitutional conventions may bear a certain similarity to nuclear weapons—useful as a threat but best left unused. This is not to say that a constitutional convention might never be warranted or that it would necessarily produce bad effects. But other reforms, notably a streamlining of the constitutional amending process, could be vigorously pursued long before the more drastic step of a new convention would become a top priority.

THE MID-RANKED REFORMS

Another set of reforms, ranked with scores of 3 or 4, fell into the middle of the pack. The more readily attainable of these might well be worth prioritizing in a reform agenda, while the more arduous may not be worth the effort. Among the mid-ranked reforms, perhaps the simplest and most important to enact would be the abolition of the Electoral College. There is widespread agreement that this institution is cumbersome, anachronistic, and anomalous. It has failed to deliver the White House to the candidate who won the popular vote as recently as 2000, and also remains fraught with other potential pitfalls. Direct election of the president is a clear-cut reform with a simple goal that would likely be widely popular with the electorate were it to gain some political momentum.

The abolition of the vice presidency is perhaps of lesser urgency but could also gain considerable support given the overall poor image of the office, especially after the Cheney years, and the constitutional ambiguity of its status. Abolishing the vice presidency would probably best be carried out in the context of other reforms to the presidential election process, notably "removal for cause" of the president and special presidential elections that are ranked higher.

Curbing the president's legislative and judicial powers was also mid-ranked. While in theory the president's pardon power could be greatly abused, actual practice makes its reform less than pressing, and in any case the most likely reform would simply be a congressional override rather than outright abolition since the pardon power does have a legitimate role to play. Any diminishment of the presidential veto would be far more controversial, but few steps could place power more clearly back in the hands of Congress, where the founders intended, than enabling that body to more easily prevail over the president. Were other steps to curb excessive executive power to prove unsuccessful, the credible threat of this reform might be enough to influence a recalcitrant president. Another change, allowing the Supreme Court to issue binding advisory opinions, might be packaged with a change in the veto power in order to ensure that Congress does not itself become *too* unencumbered by checks and balances.

The idea of aligning the offices of members of Congress with the president is the single reform that would do the most to infuse the U.S. government with the spirit of the parliamentary system and has been broached repeatedly throughout American history. At a time in which divided government has become far more common than in other eras, this reform has a certain appeal in terms of *partly* overcoming the problems of gridlock in Washington. But it is also a major step away from the separation-of-powers concept inherent in the Constitution, and, unlike with some other reforms, this change would have some clear downsides. The varying political time horizons created by two-, four-, and six-year terms do indeed contribute to different political priorities and perspectives, and thus a diversity of perspectives could potentially be lost by synchronizing terms. Enacting this reform would likely be complex and cumbersome and could divert energy and attention from more imperative reforms. The gains it would accrue might also not be that great, given that it is already the case that every time the president is up for election, so too are all but 66 or so of the 535 members of Congress.

With regard to elections, two mid-ranked reforms—increasing the number of women and minorities in office and holding runoff elections—are also worth pursuing but would be far more tenable after other reforms, such as the introduction of PR and the development of a multiparty system. Under PR rules, women and minorities would be likely to automatically be elected to public office in greater numbers, and the procedures of PR party lists would be more amenable to even further ensuring diversity. However, even short of PR, there is still a great deal that could be done within existing political structures to advance and support women and minority candidates, a process that is already under way, albeit moving at far too slow a pace. Similarly, runoff elections would be of limited use in the existing two-party system but would flow logically as an integral part of any larger reform agenda, including PR and multiple parties.

Finally, the idea of streamlining the amendment process is one that not only should be part of any extensive reform agenda but also could help advance many of the other reforms that would require constitutional amendments for their enactment. That said, neither the example of the U.S. states nor that of other countries suggests a single best model for an optimal system of amendment, one that would allow greater flexibility without undermining the basic integrity and stability of the document itself Perhaps this change should come a little later in the reform process, however, since a great deal could be accomplished through existing mechanisms of change.

THE TOP-RANKED REFORMS

Of the top-ranked reforms, two relate to the functioning of government and in particular to the quality of the executive. For better or for worse, the United States for decades has had a system that has become increasingly centered on the presidency, and the executive is called on to carry out a tremendous range of domestic programs and an even broader array of responsibilities with regard to foreign and military policy. Sometimes, presidents and their administrations assume office and turn out not to be up to the task, as was the case with Jimmy Carter and George W. Bush. Other times, circumstances emerge in which a president can no longer function well, either because of scandal, as with Richard Nixon and to a lesser extent Bill Clinton, or because of old age, as with Ronald Reagan toward the end of his second term. Whatever the circumstances, it is far too difficult to remove a president from office for reasons relating to performance rather than to the "high crimes and misdemeanors" now required under the process of impeachment.

It is no light matter to reverse the mandate of a democratic election, but it is an even more serious matter for the term of an incompetent executive to drag on and on, placing the country in, at best, a holding pattern and, at worst, a sharp downward decline. There would undoubtedly need to be a very carefully designed system to prevent the abuse of the removal-for-cause process, but such a reform of government is urgently needed. In parliamentary democracies around the world, a poorly performing executive can be removed with relative ease, and the U.S. electorate deserves no less protection from incompetence than their counterparts in other countries. No other single change to the institutions of government is more compelling than this.

A necessary extension of the idea that the people deserve a high-functioning executive is that they deserve a president of their own choice. Rather than falling back on a vice president who was all too likely to have been chosen for electoral considerations rather than on the basis of ability or policy positions, it would be far preferable to hold a quick special election to select a new president. This change would also be likely to secure the reform of abolishing the vice presidency. In practical terms, these reforms are made somewhat more likely by the fact that neither the president nor the vice president has any formal role to play in the constitutional amending process and that several other amendments, including the Twelfth, Twentieth, Twenty-Second, Twenty-Third, and Twenty-Fifth, establish precedents for adjustments to the election or term of these two officers.

All the other top-ranked reforms relate to the electoral process, and the "lowest-hanging fruit" here, that which could be most readily enacted, would be to streamline the electoral process and to depoliticize the creation of congressional districts. Neither of these reforms would require significant constitutional action but rather could be carried out largely by the application of political will, the passage of ordinary legislation, and the enactment of new rules by political parties. If articulated clearly for the public, both reforms would be likely to garner widespread support and also to find a receptive audience among elected officials. Even beyond the creaking, antiquated Electoral College, the presidential election process cries out for simplification and reform, while the depoliticization of congressional districts would be a quick way to ensure greater party competition, greater diversity among officeholders, and a higher-quality caliber of representation.

The other two reforms related to the electoral process—PR and a multiparty system—are rather more challenging, as they would be harder to enact and would be likely to feel more unfamiliar, even foreign or threatening, to many American voters. However, if the conceptual leap could be made from the deeply entrenched notion that "elections can only have one winner," the idea of sharing legislative seats in proportion to votes cast should resonate with preexisting American notions of basic fair play. The entrenchment of the idea of PR (or perhaps a mixed-member system as in Germany) could also propel support for the use of runoff elections for executive offices, a reform discussed in this book and one that already has precedent in the U.S. system, as it is employed in the state of Louisiana and some cities.

A PR system in and of itself would have various constructive effects, such as increasing the numbers of women and minorities in public office. But its major impact would be to shift the United States from a two-party system to a multiparty system. No other reform would be more likely to dislodge the counterproductive status quo, introduce new perspectives, bring in new voters, and overall empower the mass electorate than the proliferation in the number of parties from which voters could choose. Of course, it would be important to avoid hyperfragmentation, particularly given that federalism and separation of powers are already sources of fragmentation in the U.S. system. But by employing a mixed-member system and by imposing an electoral threshold of about 5 percent, the number of viable parties could be limited to about four to six.

The introduction of a multiparty system would undoubtedly be disruptive, perhaps more disruptive than any other single reform. But to the extent that a democracy thrives only when it is delivering on the policy preferences of the people, such disruption, if well managed, could be one of the most promising political developments in American history. The current two-party system abjectly fails to represent the entire leftward side of the political spectrum, leaving many of the poorest and most disenfranchised citizens to exist on the margins of society and alienated from the "American dream." A multiparty system could only help extend the promise of true equality to all Americans.

Another mechanism for extending true equality would be the last of the top-ranked reforms, which would bring the United States into line with other established democracies by taking certain basic social and economic protections out of the sphere of public debate and enshrining them as fundamental constitutional rights. In a patchwork fashion, the United States has already established some social and economic rights, be it through free public education and public libraries, minimum-wage laws, Social Security, public sanitation services, and Medicare. The idea of further extending such social and political protections may, among the ill informed or the reactionary, raise the specter of a form of "socialism" that has too long been derided as alien and even un-American. In fact, a greater regard to the social welfare of all would not be the negation of the promise of the American republic but rather the affirmation of its highest aspirations.

APPENDIX 1

Key Excerpts from the Constitution of the United States of America

⟶

Constitutional provisions referred to in the text of this book are presented here. Commentary in brackets is not part of the text of the Constitution. The complete text of the Constitution as provided by the National Archives can be accessed at http://www.archives.gov/exhibits/charters/constitution .html.

[Preamble]

We the People of the United States, in Order to form a more perfect Union, establish Justice, insure domestic Tranquility, provide for the common defence, promote the general Welfare, and secure the Blessings of Liberty to ourselves and our Posterity, do ordain and establish this Constitution for the United States of America.

[Composition and Officers of Congress]

Article I, Section 2

The House of Representatives shall be composed of Members chosen every second Year by the People of the several States, and the Electors in each State shall have the Qualifications requisite for Electors of the most numerous Branch of the State Legislature. . . .

The House of Representatives shall chuse their Speaker and other Officers; and shall have the sole Power of Impeachment.

Article I, Section 3

The Senate of the United States shall be composed of two Senators from each State, chosen by the Legislature thereof for six Years; and each Senator shall have one Vote. *[Modified by the Seventeenth Amendment]*

Immediately after they shall be assembled in Consequence of the first Election, they shall be divided as equally as may be into three Classes. The Seats of the Senators of the first Class shall be vacated at the Expiration of the second Year, of the second Class at the Expiration of the fourth Year, and of the third Class at the Expiration of the sixth Year, so that one third may be chosen every second Year; and if Vacancies happen by Resignation, or otherwise, during the Recess of the Legislature of any State, the Executive thereof may make temporary Appointments until the next Meeting of the Legislature, which shall then fill such Vacancies. . . .

The Vice President of the United States shall be President of the Senate, but shall have no Vote, unless they be equally divided.

The Senate shall chuse their other Officers, and also a President pro tempore, in the Absence of the Vice President, or when he shall exercise the Office of President of the United States.

[Prohibition from Executive Branch Employment]

Article I, Section 6

No Senator or Representative shall, during the Time for which he was elected, be appointed to any civil Office under the Authority of the United States, which shall have been created, or the Emoluments whereof shall have been encreased during such time; and no Person holding any Office under the United States, shall be a Member of either House during his Continuance in Office.

[Presidential Veto Power]

Article I, Section 7

Every Bill which shall have passed the House of Representatives and the Senate, shall, before it become a Law, be presented to the President of the United States: If he approve he shall sign it, but if not he shall return it, with his Objections to that House in which it shall have originated, who shall enter the Objections at large on their Journal, and proceed to reconsider it. If after such Reconsideration two thirds of that House shall agree to pass the Bill, it shall be sent, together with the Objections, to the other House, by which it shall likewise be reconsidered, and if approved by two thirds of that House, it shall become a Law. But in all such Cases the Votes of both Houses shall be determined by Yeas and Nays, and the Names of the Persons voting for and against the Bill shall be entered on the Journal of each House respectively. If any Bill shall not be returned by the President within ten Days (Sundays excepted) after it shall have been presented to him, the Same shall be a Law, in like Manner as if he had signed it, unless the Congress by their Adjournment prevent its Return, in which Case it shall not be a Law.

Every Order, Resolution, or Vote to which the Concurrence of the Senate and House of Representatives may be necessary (except on a question of Adjournment) shall be presented to the President of the United States; and before the Same shall take Effect, shall be approved by him, or being disapproved by him, shall be repassed by two thirds of the Senate and House of Representatives, according to the Rules and Limitations prescribed in the Case of a Bill.

[Ban on Titles of Nobility]

Article I, Section 9

No Title of Nobility shall be granted by the United States: And no Person holding any Office of Profit or Trust under them, shall, without the Consent of the Congress, accept of any present, Emolument, Office, or Title, of any kind whatever, from any King, Prince, or foreign State.

[Electoral College Provisions]

Article II, Section 1

The executive Power shall be vested in a President of the United States of America. He shall hold his Office during the Term of four Years, and, together with the Vice President, chosen for the same Term, be elected, as follows. *[Modified by the Twenty-Second Amendment]*

Each State shall appoint, in such Manner as the Legislature thereof may direct, a Number of Electors, equal to the whole Number of Senators and Representatives to which the State may be entitled in the Congress: but no Senator or Representative, or Person holding an Office of Trust or Profit under the United States, shall be appointed an Elector.

The Electors shall meet in their respective States, and vote by Ballot for two Persons, of whom one at least shall not be an Inhabitant of the same State with themselves. And they shall make a List of all the Persons voted for, and of the Number of Votes for each; which List they shall sign and certify, and transmit sealed to the Seat of the Government of the United States, directed to the President of the Senate. The President of the Senate shall, in the Presence of the Senate and House of Representatives, open all the Certificates, and the Votes shall then be counted. The Person having the greatest Number of Votes shall be the President, if such Number be a Majority of the whole Number of Electors appointed; and if there be more than one who have such Majority, and have an equal Number of Votes, then the House of Representatives shall immediately chuse by Ballot one of them for President; and if no Person have a Majority, then from the five highest on the List the said House shall in like Manner chuse the President. But in chusing the President, the Votes shall be taken by States, the Representation from each State having one Vote; A quorum for this purpose shall consist of a Member or Members from two thirds of the States, and a Majority of all the States shall be necessary to a Choice. In every Case, after the Choice of the President, the Person having the greatest Number of Votes of the Electors shall be the Vice President. But if there should remain two or more who have equal Votes, the Senate shall chuse from them by Ballot the Vice President. *[Modified by the Twelfth Amendment]*

The Congress may determine the Time of chusing the Electors, and the Day on which they shall give their Votes; which Day shall be the same throughout the United States.

No Person except a natural born Citizen, or a Citizen of the United States, at the time of the Adoption of this Constitution, shall be eligible to the Office of President; neither shall any Person be eligible to that Office who shall not have attained to the Age of thirty five Years, and been fourteen Years a Resident within the United States.

[Vice-Presidential Succession]

In Case of the Removal of the President from Office, or of his Death, Resignation, or Inability to discharge the Powers and Duties of the said Office, the Same shall devolve on the Vice President, and the Congress may by Law provide for the Case of Removal, Death, Resignation or Inability, both of the President and Vice President, declaring what Officer shall then act as President, and such Officer shall act accordingly, until the Disability be removed, or a President shall be elected. *[Modified by the Twenty-Fifth Amendment]*

[Powers and Responsibilities of the President]

Article II, Section 2

The President shall be Commander in Chief of the Army and Navy of the United States, and of the Militia of the several States, when called into the actual Service of the United States; he may require the Opinion, in writing, of the principal Officer in each of the executive Departments, upon any Subject relating to the Duties of their respective Offices, and he shall have Power to grant Reprieves and Pardons for Offences against the United States, except in Cases of Impeachment.

He shall have Power, by and with the Advice and Consent of the Senate, to make Treaties, provided two thirds of the Senators present concur; and he shall nominate, and by and with the Advice and Consent of the Senate, shall appoint Ambassadors, other public Ministers and Consuls, Judges of the supreme Court, and all other Officers of the United States. . . .

[Removal of the President]

Article II, Section 4

The President, Vice President and all civil Officers of the United States, shall be removed from Office on Impeachment for, and Conviction of, Treason, Bribery, or other high Crimes and Misdemeanors.

[Term of Federal Judges]

Article III, Section 1

The judicial Power of the United States shall be vested in one supreme Court, and in such inferior Courts as the Congress may from time to time ordain and establish. The Judges, both of the supreme and inferior Courts, shall hold their Offices during good Behaviour, and shall, at stated Times, receive for their Services a Compensation, which shall not be diminished during their Continuance in Office.

[Jurisdiction of the Courts]

Article III, Section 2

The judicial Power shall extend to all Cases, in Law and Equity, arising under this Constitution, the Laws of the United States, and Treaties made, or which shall be made, under their Authority;—to all Cases affecting Ambassadors, other public Ministers and Consuls;—to all Cases of admiralty and maritime Jurisdiction;—to Controversies to which the United States shall be a Party;—to Controversies between two or more States;—between a State and Citizens of another State,—between Citizens of different States,—between Citizens of the same State claiming Lands under Grants of different States, and between a State, or the Citizens thereof, and foreign States, Citizens or Subjects.

In all Cases affecting Ambassadors, other public Ministers and Consuls, and those in which a State shall be Party, the supreme Court shall have original Jurisdiction. In all the other Cases before mentioned, the supreme Court shall have appellate Jurisdiction, both as to Law and Fact, with such Exceptions, and under such Regulations as the Congress shall make.

[The Amendment Procedure]

Article V

The Congress, whenever two thirds of both Houses shall deem it necessary, shall propose Amendments to this Constitution, or, on the Application of the Legislatures of two thirds of the several States, shall call a Convention for proposing Amendments, which, in either Case, shall be valid to all Intents and Purposes, as Part of this Constitution, when ratified by the Legislatures of three fourths of the several States, or by Conventions in three fourths thereof, as the one or the other Mode of Ratification may be proposed by the Congress; Provided that no Amendment which may be made prior to the Year One thousand eight hundred and eight shall in any Manner affect the first and fourth Clauses in the Ninth Section of the first Article; and that no State, without its Consent, shall be deprived of its equal Suffrage in the Senate.

[Ban on Religious Tests for Public Office]
Article VI

The Senators and Representatives before mentioned, and the Members of the several State Legislatures, and all executive and judicial Officers, both of the United States and of the several States, shall be bound by Oath or Affirmation, to support this Constitution; but no religious Test shall ever be required as a Qualification to any Office or public Trust under the United States.

[Ratification of the Constitution]
Article VII

The Ratification of the Conventions of nine States, shall be sufficient for the Establishment of this Constitution between the States so ratifying the Same.

[Freedom of Expression and Religion]
Amendment I *[1791]*

Congress shall make no law respecting an establishment of religion, or prohibiting the free exercise thereof; or abridging the freedom of speech, or of the press; or the right of the people peaceably to assemble, and to petition the Government for a redress of grievances.

[Right to Gun Ownership]
Amendment II *[1791]*

A well regulated Militia, being necessary to the security of a free State, the right of the people to keep and bear Arms, shall not be infringed.

[Protection from Unreasonable Search and Seizure]
Amendment IV *[1791]*

The right of the people to be secure in their persons, houses, papers, and effects, against unreasonable searches and seizures, shall not be violated, and no Warrants shall issue, but upon probable cause, supported by Oath or affirmation, and particularly describing the place to be searched, and the persons or things to be seized.

[Protections in Legal Proceedings]

Amendment V *[1791]*

No person shall be held to answer for a capital, or otherwise infamous crime, unless on a presentment or indictment of a Grand Jury, except in cases arising in the land or naval forces, or in the Militia, when in actual service in time of War or public danger; nor shall any person be subject for the same offence to be twice put in jeopardy of life or limb; nor shall be compelled in any criminal case to be a witness against himself, nor be deprived of life, liberty, or property, without due process of law; nor shall private property be taken for public use, without just compensation.

Amendment VI *[1791]*

In all criminal prosecutions, the accused shall enjoy the right to a speedy and public trial, by an impartial jury of the State and district wherein the crime shall have been committed, which district shall have been previously ascertained by law, and to be informed of the nature and cause of the accusation; to be confronted with the witnesses against him; to have compulsory process for obtaining witnesses in his favor, and to have the Assistance of Counsel for his defence.

Amendment VII *[1791]*

In Suits at common law, where the value in controversy shall exceed twenty dollars, the right of trial by jury shall be preserved, and no fact tried by a jury, shall be otherwise re-examined in any Court of the United States, than according to the rules of the common law.

Amendment VIII *[1791]*

Excessive bail shall not be required, nor excessive fines imposed, nor cruel and unusual punishments inflicted.

[Revised Provisions of the Electoral College]

Amendment XII *[1804]*

The Electors shall meet in their respective states and vote by ballot for President and Vice-President, one of whom, at least, shall not be an inhabitant of the same state with themselves; they shall name in their ballots the person voted for as President, and in distinct ballots the person voted for as Vice-President, and they shall make distinct lists of all persons voted for as President, and of all persons voted for as Vice-President, and of the number of votes for each, which lists they shall sign and certify, and transmit sealed to the seat of the government of the United States, directed to the President of the Senate;—the President of the Senate shall, in the presence of the Senate and House of Representatives, open all the certificates and the votes shall then be counted;—The person having the greatest number of votes for President, shall be the President, if such number be a majority of the whole number of Electors appointed; and if no person have such majority, then from the persons having the highest numbers not exceeding three on the list of those voted for as President, the House of Representatives shall choose immediately, by ballot, the President. But in choosing the President, the votes shall be taken by states, the representation from each state having one vote; a quorum for this purpose shall consist of a member or members from two-thirds of the states, and a majority of all the states shall be necessary to a choice. And if the House of Representatives shall not choose a President whenever the right of choice shall devolve upon them ... then the Vice-President shall act as President, as in case of the death or other constitutional disability of the President. The person having the greatest number of votes as Vice-President, shall be the Vice-President, if such number be a majority of the whole number of Electors appointed, and if no person have a majority, then from the two highest numbers on the list, the Senate shall choose the Vice-President; a quorum for the purpose shall consist of two-thirds of the whole number of Senators, and a majority of the whole number shall be necessary to a choice. But no person constitutionally ineligible to the office of President shall be eligible to that of Vice-President of the United States.

[The Civil War Amendments, 1865–1870: Prohibition of Slavery (13); Guarantee of Equal Protection (14); Voting Rights Protections on the Basis of Race (15)]

Amendment XIII *[1865]*

Section 1. Neither slavery nor involuntary servitude, except as a punishment for crime whereof the party shall have been duly convicted, shall exist within the United States, or any place subject to their jurisdiction.

Section 2. Congress shall have power to enforce this article by appropriate legislation.

Amendment XIV *[1868]*

Section 1. All persons born or naturalized in the United States, and subject to the jurisdiction thereof, are citizens of the United States and of the State wherein they reside. No State shall make or enforce any law which shall abridge the privileges or immunities of citizens of the United States; nor shall any State deprive any person of life, liberty, or property, without due process of law; nor deny to any person within its jurisdiction the equal protection of the laws. . . .

Section 5. The Congress shall have the power to enforce, by appropriate legislation, the provisions of this article.

Amendment XV *[1870]*

Section 1. The right of citizens of the United States to vote shall not be denied or abridged by the United States or by any State on account of race, color, or previous condition of servitude.

Section 2. The Congress shall have the power to enforce this article by appropriate legislation.

[Direct Election of Senators]

Amendment XVII *[1913]*

The Senate of the United States shall be composed of two Senators from each State, elected by the people thereof, for six years; and each Senator shall have one vote. The electors in each State shall have the qualifications requisite for electors of the most numerous branch of the State legislatures.

When vacancies happen in the representation of any State in the Senate, the executive authority of such State shall issue writs of election to fill such vacancies: Provided, That the legislature of any State may empower the executive thereof to make temporary appointments until the people fill the vacancies by election as the legislature may direct. . . .

[Enfranchisement of Women]

Amendment XIX *[1920]*

The right of citizens of the United States to vote shall not be denied or abridged by the United States or by any State on account of sex.

Congress shall have power to enforce this article by appropriate legislation.

[Two-term Limit in the Presidency]

Amendment XXII [1951]

Section 1. No person shall be elected to the office of the President more than twice, and no person who has held the office of President, or acted as President, for more than two years of a term to which some other person was elected President shall be elected to the office of President more than once. . . .

[Vice Presidency Provisions]

Amendment XXV [1967]

Section 1. In case of the removal of the President from office or of his death or resignation, the Vice President shall become President.

Section 2. Whenever there is a vacancy in the office of the Vice President, the President shall nominate a Vice President who shall take office upon confirmation by a majority vote of both Houses of Congress.

Section 3. Whenever the President transmits to the President pro tempore of the Senate and the Speaker of the House of Representatives his written declaration that he is unable to discharge the powers and duties of his office, and until he transmits to them a written declaration to the contrary, such powers and duties shall be discharged by the Vice President as Acting President.

Section 4. Whenever the Vice President and a majority of either the principal officers of the executive departments or of such other body as Congress may by law provide, transmit to the President pro tempore of the Senate and the Speaker of the House of Representatives their written declaration that the President is unable to discharge the powers and duties of his office, the Vice President shall immediately assume the powers and duties of the office as Acting President.

Thereafter, when the President transmits to the President pro tempore of the Senate and the Speaker of the House of Representatives his written declaration that no inability exists, he shall resume the powers and duties of his office unless the Vice President and a majority of either the principal officers of the executive department or of such other body as Congress may by law provide, transmit within four days to the President pro tempore of the Senate and the Speaker of the House of Representatives their written declaration that the President is unable to discharge the powers and duties of his office. Thereupon Congress shall decide the issue, assembling within forty-eight hours for that purpose if not in session. If the Congress, within twenty-one days after receipt of the latter written declaration, or, if Congress is not in session, within twenty-one days after Congress is required to assemble, determines by two-thirds vote of both Houses that the President is unable to discharge the powers and duties of his office, the Vice President shall continue to discharge the same as Acting President; otherwise, the President shall resume the powers and duties of his office.

[Enfranchisement at Age 18]

Amendment XXVI *[1971]*

Section 1. The right of citizens of the United States, who are eighteen years of age or older, to vote shall not be denied or abridged by the United States or by any State on account of age.

Section 2. The Congress shall have power to enforce this article by appropriate legislation.

APPENDIX 2

The Presidential and Parliamentary Systems: A Comparison

Presidential System *Based on the U.S. Model*	Parliamentary System *Based on the British (Westminster) Model*
A single executive officer serves as head of state *and* head of government. The executive is elected by the people and claims their mandate for power.	There are two executives: a head of state (monarch or ceremonial president, usually unelected) and a head of government (i.e., prime minister).
All executive power is invested in a single person.	Executive power is shared by a cabinet led by the prime minister.
The executive and legislature are elected separately. Members cannot overlap and have different terms of office.	Executive power arises out of majority control of the legislature. All have the same term of office.
The legislature has two houses, both with roughly equal power.	The upper house of the legislature is much less powerful or even may have been abolished.
Individual legislators vote and act largely independently.	Individual legislators vote and act largely as their party leaders wish.
The executive and legislature act independently, with checks and balances, thus *dispersing power*.	The executive controls the legislature, thus *concentrating power*.
It is very slow and difficult for the legislature to remove the executive.	Legislature can remove the prime minister and cabinet at any time.
All elections are held on a rigid schedule for fixed terms of office.	Elections can be held at any time.

Presidential vs. Parliamentary Systems: Strengths and Weaknesses

Presidential	Parliamentary
Contains "checks and balances"	Prime minister is largely unchecked
Susceptible to "gridlock," especially under "divided government"	Total coordination between the executive and legislature
Rarely able to carry out sudden major changes	Can readily respond to changing needs rapidly
Can lead to centrist, compromised policies	Can create sharp shifts, some highly unpopular
Can be hard for voters to assign responsibility	Easy for voters to assign responsibility
In theory, prevents tyranny (but in practice may promote it)	In theory, can lead to tyranny (but in practice rarely does)

Key Features of Parliamentary Government

- After an election, the head of state formally invites the leader of the largest party to "form a government" as prime minister.
- The prime minister must demonstrate the support of the lower house of Parliament, such as through a confirmatory vote.
- If his or her party does not have an absolute majority of the seats, a coalition of parties can be formed. Coalitions can vary from about 2 to 10 parties. The more parties in a coalition, the more unstable will be its majority and thus its latitude to act.
- The prime minister chooses others from his or her party or coalition of parties to become cabinet ministers (e.g., defense, treasury, and agriculture). In a coalition, small parties will often get control of the single area of policy or single ministry of most importance to them (e.g., agriculture).
- Sometimes, two large parties that are normally opponents will form a "grand coalition" and cooperate for a time, particularly if the country faces a crisis. Sometimes, the largest party will be allowed to form a "minority government" without an absolute majority. It must then negotiate on an issue-by-issue basis with the other parties. Sometimes parties may support a "technocratic" nonpartisan prime minister on an interim basis, or, in an extreme, the head of state may call a new election to break a deadlock.

- The prime minister appoints, dismisses, and directs the cabinet but must listen to their input and rely on their expertise and support. Cabinet ministers can also be forced to resign by a majority vote of the legislature.
- Rank-and-file members of the legislature ("backbenchers") *must* vote as their leaders wish, or they can be politically punished. Thus, bills introduced by the government are generally assured of quick passage.
- Parties not in the majority form the "opposition" and can criticize and debate but have no actual power. The opposition forms a "shadow government" waiting to take over if they win the next election.
- The prime minister can be replaced in either of two ways:

  1. The majority party can elect a new leader, who becomes the new prime minister. The prime minister may step aside or be forced out. (This is more likely when a single party has a majority.)

  2. The majority can withdraw their support of the prime minister by a "vote of no confidence." The government "falls," and new elections must be held. (This is more likely in a coalition formed of multiple parties.)

- Elections must be called within a set period of time, five years of the previous election, but can be called at *any* time that the prime minister thinks is advantageous.

Glossary

Co-authored with Brandon L. H. Aultman

administration: In presidential systems, this refers to the tenure of any specific president (e.g., the Reagan administration) and in this sense is similar to how the word "government" is used in parliamentary systems. "The administration" is construed to include all the major actors of the executive branch, not just the president personally.

advisory opinion: A ruling issued by a court *before* a law or policy is enacted in order to determine its constitutionality.

amicus curiae: A brief filed in a legal procedure by an individual or institution that is not a direct party to the case but who has an interest in its outcome.

Australian ballot: A printed ballot that bears the names of all candidates and the texts of propositions and is distributed to the voter at the polls and marked in secret. The Australian ballot promotes confidentiality and thus potentially voter participation.

authoritarianism: A type of government regime in which leaders are not democratically elected or accountable and in which military, police, or other types of force are often used to suppress political opposition and maintain social control.

backbencher: Members of a legislature, particularly a parliament, who do not have leadership roles or do not head government ministries.

bicameralism: The division of a legislative branch into two chambers, usually called an upper and a lower house. In *symmetric* bicameralism, the two chambers have roughly equal authority; in *asymmetric* bicameralism, the lower house can override the upper house.

bill of rights: A statement or listing of protections by and from government, often as part of a written constitution.

branches of government: Under separation of powers, the subdivision of the functions of government into separate legislative, executive, and judicial institutions.

cabinet, parliamentary: The collection of ministers (led by a prime minister) that exercise collective executive power in a parliamentary system and are subject to confirmation and removal by the parliament.

cabinet, presidential: Executive actors appointed by and subordinate to an executive president and who head major government departments or ministries.

caucus: The grouping of members of the same party in a legislature for the purpose of establishing a working majority, electing leaders, and coordinating legislative strategies.

checks and balances: Powers given to one branch of government to prevent the abuse of power in another, such as the presidential veto or congressional impeachment powers.

civil liberties: Individual protections from the power of government, such as the freedom of expression or religion and the right to due process of law.

civil rights: Group protections by government against discriminatory practices, such as segregation or exclusion from employment or higher education.

coalition government: A parliamentary government composed of two or more parties, sharing in executive authority.

communism: A political ideology endorsing rule by a single party, centralized economic planning, and nationalization of industries, in practice usually through the use of political and military repression.

confederation: A state with a central government with extremely limited powers and little or no control over the constituent provinces or states, which are largely autonomous.

Congress: The collective term for the bicameral U.S. national legislature, comprised of a House of Representatives and a Senate; the term is also used for the legislative branch in some other separation-of-powers systems.

consociational democracy: A form of political arrangement in which certain major groupings (e.g., religious, ethnic, or linguistic) are guaranteed significant participation in the governing process and, sometimes, a veto on issues of crucial importance to them.

constituency: The population of the geographic district represented by an elected official or, more informally, groupings of a politician's supporters.

constituency service: The provision of special services to members of an elected official's constituency, usually through "casework" by the official's staff members.

constitution: The authoritative set of rules that organize a state, most typically compiled in a single written document that is considered binding in democratic systems.

Constitutional Convention: Referring to the formal meeting of U.S. delegates in the summer of 1787 who ultimately voted on the text of the U.S. Constitution, this term can be used to refer to similar meetings in the United States (as on the state level) or in other countries.

constitutional court: A high-level branch of the judiciary that is tasked with interpreting the meaning and application of a constitution and that typically does not hear other types of cases.

cooperative federalism: A type of U.S. federalism in which the functions and activities of the national and state governments are significantly intertwined, as opposed to dual federalism, in which they are entirely separate and distinct.

direct democracy: As opposed to representative democracy, an electoral procedure in which major decisions are made by citizens via a ballot or a large meeting. Referendums are a common if more limited mechanism for direct democracy used in many representative democracies.

districts: The geographic boundaries within which representatives to legislatures are elected; they are periodically subject to redistricting to achieve rough population parity over time.

double dissolution: In Australia, the practice of dissolving both chambers of the Parliament in order to resolve a deadlock between them.

Duverger's law: The observation advanced by sociologist Maurice Duverger that the number of parties in a political system is largely a function of its electoral process, with the use of proportional representation tending to create multiparty systems and the use of the plurality rule leading to two-party systems.

Electoral College: The unique and peculiar system in the United States in which presidents are formally chosen by electors from each state rather than directly as a result of the popular vote.

ethnoracial pentagon: A term used to refer to the five officially recognized major ethnic and racial categories in the United States: white, black, Hispanic, Asian American, and Native American.

exceptionalism: The concept that the United States, because of geographic isolation, social organization, and other factors, has followed a distinctive historical and institutional pattern. Often called "American exceptionalism."

executive: The portion of a government tasked with executing, enforcing, or implementing laws and regulations, usually through a large bureaucratic apparatus.

ex officio: Membership on member of one body by virtue of holding a particular office, such as committee memberships held by floor leaders in a legislature.

federalism: The division of sovereign functions between a strong central government and multiple states or provinces, with each level having distinctive as well as overlapping areas of power and responsibility.

gerrymandering: A pejorative term used for legislative redistricting into oddly shaped geographic boundaries in order to boost the prospects of particular parties or candidates.

government: In presidential systems, this term usually applies to the entirety of executive, legislative, and judicial branches. In parliamentary systems, the term applies only to the current majority in the lower house of Parliament that exercises executive power.

grand coalition: A parliamentary government in which multiple parties form a single, very broad coalition in the legislative body, usually because no one major party can establish a majority or because of the need for national unity at a time of war or other major challenges.

head of government: The head of the executive branch in the actual governance of a nation. In a parliamentary system, this is the prime minister; in a presidential system, this is the president.

head of state: The head of the executive branch in a symbolic or ceremonial capacity with little or no actual power. In a parliamentary system, this is generally a figurehead president or monarch; in a presidential system, this is the president.

impeachment: The charging of a government official with an offense meriting removal from office, generally carried out by the legislative body.

imperial presidency: A pejorative term used to critique excessive growth in the power of the U.S. president; first used by historian Arthur M. Schlesinger Jr.

incumbent: A politician in a particular elected office who is up for reelection.

instant runoff (also single-transferable vote): A method of tabulating an election in which voter preferences are listed in rank order, with losing candidates eliminated over successive rounds of tallying until a winner emerges.

interest group: An organized groups of individuals or organizations that makes policy-related appeals to the government.

judicial review: The power of the courts to declare legislation or the acts of an executive unconstitutional.

judiciary: The branch of government, composed of law courts, with the power to resolve legal conflicts and, in many countries, constitutional questions.

jurisprudence: The study of the law and its philosophical underpinnings.

legislature: A branch of government tasked with passing laws and, usually, appropriating public funds.

lobbying: Efforts by individuals or organizations to sway government officials to their position and/or to obtain benefits from government.

majority government: In a parliament, a government formed by a single party or coalition of parties.

maladministration: Incompetent or malfeasant administration of government.

malapportionment: An inappropriate or unfair proportional distribution of representatives to a legislative body.

minority government: In a parliament, a relatively unusual situation in which there is no majority party or coalition, but the largest party or coalition is permitted to govern on a temporary basis by the opposition parties.

mixed-member electoral system: A hybrid electoral process in which each voter casts two votes in a legislative election, one for a candidate in a plurality election and one for a party list.

monarchy: Rule by a king or queen, usually hereditary, and often in a purely figurehead capacity alongside an elected parliament. Constitutional monarchs are no longer able to exercise actual political power.

multimember district: Under rules of proportional representation, the election of multiple representatives to represent the same electoral district.

multiparty system: A party system with three, four, five, or more parties that all contend for power and win some legislative seats.

negative liberty: Freedom from government interference.

New Deal: The political program of President Franklin Delano Roosevelt that was put in place to help overcome the Great Depression and that greatly expanded the role of the federal government and created a limited social welfare system in the United States.

ombudsman (or ombudsperson): An official in an institution, included in a government, who hears complaints and works to investigate and resolve them.

opposition: In a parliament, members of parties that are not part of the governing coalition. The largest such party is sometimes called the "Official Opposition," and its head is the "Leader of the Opposition."

pardon power: A check on the judiciary through which an executive can grant clemency or commute punishment for a crime for an individual or class of individuals.

parliamentary threshold: The practice of excluding parties from legislative representation unless they win a minimum percentage of the vote, commonly 5 percent.

plurality system: An electoral process that awards a legislative seat or other political office to the individual with the largest number of votes, which may or may not be a majority when there are more than two candidates.

political party: A formally organized body that articulates public policy goals, contests elections, and forms caucuses within legislatures.

portfolio: The area of responsibilities of a minister in a parliamentary government, such as defense or finance.

positive liberty: The fulfillment human needs and potential through the support of government.

prefecture: A type of administrative subdivision in Japan.

president: In a presidential system, the elected head of state and head of government. In parliamentary republics, usually a figurehead with a ceremonial role but little actual political power.

presidential model: The separation-of-powers system of government, in which a single elected official is both head of state and head of government.

presidential succession: The formal rules for replacement of a president who is deceased or incapacitated or who resigns or is removed.

president pro tempore: A vague U.S. constitutional position used as a fill-in for the vice president when he or she is not present in the Senate. By convention, this is an honorific awarded to the longest-seated member of the majority party in the Senate.

prime minister: In parliamentary systems, the head of government and leader of the cabinet who is also generally the leader of the majority party or coalition in the Parliament.

procedural democracy: A definition of democracy with regard primarily to equal access to political participation.

proportional representation: The awarding of legislative seats in close proportion to the number of votes won in any given district, usually in a multimember district.

reapportionment: The periodic reallocation of seats in a legislature to reflect changes in population over time.

redistricting: The process of periodically changing the boundaries and composition of legislative districts, often following a census.

referendum: The making of public policy or other political decisions by a direct vote of the electorate.

representative democracy: In contrast to direct democracy, a system of government in which political and policy decisions are made by elected officials.

reserve powers: In parliaments, the discretion retained by a head of state to help form a parliamentary coalition or to choose ministers when an election has produced inconclusive results.

royal assent: The ceremonial approval required from a monarch before a bill can take effect in some parliamentary systems. Constitutional monarchs do not have the power to refuse royal assent in modern democracies.

semipresidential system: A hybrid system of government in which executive power is shared by a directly elected president and a prime minister with the support of the parliament, sometimes resulting in confused lines of power and responsibility.

separation of powers: The subdivision of government powers into distinct executive, legislative, and judicial functions, usually institutionally isolated from each other and elected or appointed through different processes.

Shadow Cabinet: In a parliament, the "cabinet in waiting" of the Opposition.

single-member-plurality system: An electoral system under which each election can have only one winner, the candidate who gains the most votes, which is usually an outright majority in a two-party system.

single transferable vote: *See* instant runoff election.

snap election: A quick vote called on short notice, such as several weeks, by a prime minister rather than an election occurring on a fixed, predictable schedule.

socialism: A political ideology emphasizing redistribution of wealth and an activist role for government.

substantive democracy: A definition of democracy with regard primarily to the equalization of socioeconomic status and access to basic human needs.

supreme court: Generally, the highest judicial body in a particular country or other jurisdiction.

two-party system: A political configuration in which only two major parties, relatively well matched in terms of electoral support, can effectively win elections, with minor parties relegated to virtually no effective political role. In a *two-party-plus system*, minor parties play a somewhat more active role.

umbrella coalition: In a two-party system, the tendency of each party to expand to encompass enough issues and voters to achieve electoral majorities.

veto: The ability of an executive to reject legislation, usually subject to a legislative override. More informally, the term refers to the ability to effectively stop a piece of legislation anywhere in the process, such as at the committee stage.

vote of no confidence: A motion to determine whether a prime minister or cabinet still has the support a majority in Parliament, without which it must resign and call a new election.

Westminster model: The parliamentary configuration first developed in the United Kingdom and since adopted, with some modifications, around the world.

Notes

INTRODUCTION

1. James Sundquist, *Constitutional Reform and Effective Government* (Washington, DC: Brookings Institution, 1992).

2. Daniel Lazare, *The Frozen Republic: How the Constitution Is Paralyzing Democracy* (New York: Harcourt Brace, 1996).

3. Sanford Levinson, *Our Undemocratic Constitution: Where the Constitution Goes Wrong (And How We the People Can Correct It)* (New York: Oxford University Press, 2006).

4. Larry Sabato, *A More Perfect Constitution: Why the Constitution Must Be Revised: Ideas to Inspire a New Generation* (New York: Walker Publishing, 2008).

CHAPTER 1

1. Paolo Belluci, "The Parliamentary Election in Italy, April 2006," *Electoral Studies* 27, no. 1 (March 2008): 185–90.

2. Maurice Duverger, "Factors in a Two-Party and Multiparty System," in *Party Politics and Pressure Groups* (New York: Crowell, 1972), 23–32.

CHAPTER 2

1. Peter James, *The German Electoral System* (Burlington, VT: Ashgate Publishing, 2003), see 18–33.

CHAPTER 3

1. Political Database of the Americas at Georgetown University, "Overview of Latin American Political Systems" (n.d.), http://pdba.georgetown.edu/Elecdata/systems.html (accessed October 25, 2009).

2. Rosanna Michelle Heath, "Presidential and Congressional Elections in Chile, December 2005 and January 2006," *Electoral Studies* 26, no. 2 (2007): 516–20.

3. Dinorah Azpuru, "The 2007 Presidential and Legislative Elections in Guatemala," *Electoral Studies* 27, no. 3 (2008): 562–66.

CHAPTER 4

1. Ernesto Cabrera, "Multiparty Politics in Argentina? Electoral Rules and Changing Patterns," *Electoral Studies* 15, no. 4 (1996): 477–95.

2. "Colorado as Ground Zero in Debate over Electoral College" (2004), http://www.csmonitor.com/2004/1018/p03s01-uspo.html (accessed October 25, 2009).

3. "National Briefing Mid-Atlantic, Maryland: Electoral Vote Change," *New York Times*, April 11, 2007.

CHAPTER 5

1. Office of Public Sector Information, UK Parliament, "Political Parties, Elections and Referendums Act 2000" (n.d.), http://www.opsi.gov.uk/Acts/acts2000/ukpga_20000041_en_1 (accessed on May 1, 2009).

2. Campaign Finance Institute, "House Campaign Expenditures, 1974–2006 (Net Dollars)" (n.d.), http://www.cfinst.org/data/pdf/VitalStats_t2.pdf (accessed August 19, 2009).

3. Section 93 of the Representation of the People Act of 1983 (n.d.), http://www.statutelaw.gov.uk/content.aspx?LegType=All+Primary&PageNumber=44&NavFrom=2&parentActiveTextDocId=2353486&ActiveTextDocId=2353614&filesize=14836 on May 1, 2009. See also http://www.ofcom.org.uk/tv/ifi/codes/bcode/elections (accessed October 14, 2009).

CHAPTER 6

1. Government of Belgium, "Understanding the Federal State," http://www.belgium.be/en/about_belgium/government (accessed October 25, 2009).

CHAPTER 7

1. Martin P. Wattenberg, *Where Have All the Voters Gone?* (Cambridge, MA: Harvard University Press, 2002).

2. Board of Elections in the City of New York, "Summary of Election Results" (n.d.), http://www.vote.nyc.ny.U.S./results.html (accessed October 25, 2009).

3. Sarah Birch, *Full Participation: A Comparative Study of Compulsory Voting* (Tokyo: United Nations University Press, 2009).

4. Birch, *Full Participation*.

5. British Broadcasting Company, "Saddam 'Wins 100% of Vote' " (2002), http://news.bbc.co.uk/2/hi/middle_east/2331951.stm (accessed August 24, 2009).

CHAPTER 8

1. Direct Democracy, "Switzerland's Referendums" (n.d.), http://direct -democracy.geschichte-schweiz.ch/switzerlands-system-referendums.html (accessed October 25, 2009).

2. Record of California Referenda, "1912–Present" (n.d.), http://www .sos.ca.gov/elections/referenda_history.pdf (accessed October 25, 2009).

CHAPTER 9

1. James L. Sundquist, *Constitutional Reform and Effective* Government (Washington, DC: Brookings Institution Press, 1992). See the rejection of "maladministration" as a reason for impeachment.

2. Seymour M. Hersh, *The Price of Power: Kissinger in the Nixon White House* (Orangeville, CA: Summit Books, 1983).

3. Sanford Levinson, *Our Undemocratic Constitution: Where the Constitution Goes Wrong (and How We the People Can Correct It)* (New York: Oxford University Press, 2006).

CHAPTER 10

1. Pedro Santoni, *Mexicans at Arms: Puro Federalists and the Politics of War 1845–1848* (Fort Worth: Texas Christian University Press, 1996).

CHAPTER 12

1. Gunnar Helgi Kristinssin, "Iceland," in *Semi-Presidentialism in Europe*, ed. Robert Elgie (New York: Oxford University Press, 1999), 86–103.

CHAPTER 13

1. Constitution of the Republic of Turkey, http://www.anayasa.gov.tr/
images/loaded/pdf_dosyalari/THE_CONSTITUTION_OF_THE
_REPUBLIC_OF_TURKEY.pdf (accessed October 25, 2009).

2. Consulate General of the Republic of Turkey, http://www.turkish
consulategeneral.us/abtturkey/govt/exec.shtml (accessed October 25, 2009).

CHAPTER 14

1. Eric Janse de Jonge, "The Netherlands," and Rudy B. Andeweg, "Parliamentary Democracy in the Netherlands," *Parliamentary Affairs* 57, no. 3
(2004): 568.

CHAPTER 15

1. Rajeev Dhavan and Rekha Saxena, "Republic of India," in *Legislative,
Executive, and Judicial Governance in Federal Countries*, ed. Katy Le Roy and
Cheryl Saunders (Montreal: McGill-Queens University Press, 2006).

CHAPTER 16

1. Toshimasha Moriwaki, "The Politics of Redistricting in Japan: A Con-
tradiction between Equal Population and Respect for Local Government
Boundaries," in *Redistricting in Comparative Perspective*, ed. Lisa Handley
and Bernard Grofman (Oxford: Oxford University Press, 2008).

2. Kelly Buck, "Iowa's Redistricting Process: An Example of the Right
Way to Draw Legislative Districts" (2004), http://www.centrists.org/pages/
2004/07/7_buck_trust.html (accessed September 20, 2009).

CHAPTER 17

1. Justice E. W. Thomas, "Centennial Lecture: The Relationship of
Parliament and the Courts: A Tentative Thought or Two for the New Mil-
lennium" (1999), http://www.austlii.edu.au/nz/journals/VUWLRev/2000/
3.html (accessed October 25, 2009).

2. Transparency International, "Surveys and Indices: 2007 Corruption
Perceptions Index" (n.d.), http://www.transparency.org/policy_research/
surveys_indices/cpi/2007 (accessed October 25, 2009).

CHAPTER 18

1. Hristo D. Dimitrov, "The Bulgarian Constitutional Court and Its Interpretive Jurisdiction," *Columbia Journal of Transnational Law* 37 (1999): 459.

CHAPTER 19

1. Steven Klasen, "Poverty, Inequality and Deprivation in South Africa: An Analysis of the 1993 Saldru Survey," *Social Indicators Research* 41: 51–94; available at http://ejscontent.ebsco.com/ContentServer.aspx?target=http%3A%2F%2Fwww%2Espringerlink%2Ecom%2Findex%2FJ11P35057H03331T%2Epdf (accessed October 25, 2009).

2. Franklin D. Roosevelt, "Presidential State of the Union" (1944), http://stateoftheunion.onetwothree.net/texts/19440111.html (accessed October 25, 2009).

3. Cass Sunstein, *The Second Bill of Rights: FDR's Unfinished Revolution and Why We Need It More Than Ever* (New York: Basic Books, 2004).

CHAPTER 20

1. The Constitution of Brazil (1988), http://www.v-brazil.com/government/laws/recent-amendments.html (accessed October 25, 2009).

CHAPTER 21

1. David Wurfel, *Filipino Politics: Development and Decay* (Ithaca, NY: Cornell University Press, 1988).

2. Larry J. Sabato, *A More Perfect Constitution: 23 Proposals to Revitalize Our Constitution and Make America a Fairer Country* (New York: Walker and Company, 2007).

Index

About the Author

RAYMOND A. SMITH, PHD, is adjunct assistant professor of political science at Columbia University and New York University. He is the author of *The American Anomaly: US Politics and Government in Comparative Perspective* and has served as editor of two political science book series: "Political Participation in America" and "New Ideas and Trends in American Politics."